A Historian's Progress

A HISTORIAN'S PROGRESS

by Roy F. Nichols

New York: ALFRED·A·KNOPF

1968

THIS IS A BORZOI BOOK

PUBLISHED BY ALFRED A. KNOPF, INC.

First Edition

 Distributed by Random House, Inc. Published simultaneously in Toronto, Canada, by Random House of Canada Limited.

Library of Congress Catalog Card Number: 68-12669

Manufactured in the United States of America

To the Memory of

Charles A. Beard and Edward P. Cheyney

who sought the reasons for things

FOREWORD

In a sense all men are historians for they all have memories and therein can live at moments of time other than the present and report to mankind about them. But notwithstanding this almost universal capacity for such service to society, it is obvious that relatively few make much use of it. Even a most casual consideration of man's history reveals that most of it is unrecorded and therefore lost. There is no way probably of compensating for such a loss, or even for explaining why so much that might be useful to society goes wasted, why so much substance from which wisdom might be forged goes unused, even unnoticed. Do historians not owe to society some effort to analyze themselves and their efforts? Alfred Knopf once asked me to write my testament and therein explain myself. I made various attempts but I did not bring it off until good fortune carried me away from my usual routine.

I retired from the University of Pennsylvania in June 1966, at the statutory age of seventy. Jeannette and I were honored by an invitation from the Henry E. Huntington Library to spend the summer there. I welcomed this opportunity to reorient myself, to get away from the interruptions of active university life, and to re-establish myself in the world of research and thought.

During these delightful months away from the telephone and university responsibilities, I rethought this book.

CONTENTS

A Historian's Progress

I

HOW IT ALL STARTED

ALTHOUGH I was only three at the time, I can remember my first introduction to history. On September 29, 1899, my father and mother took me to New York City to witness a spectacle. The war with Spain was over; the hero of Manila, the intrepid naval officer George Dewey, who had damned the torpedoes, had returned to the United States and was given a triumph. A Roman arch, like those of the Caesars in Rome, had been constructed at Union Square and a parade of armed might led by the commander was to pass under it amidst the resounding cheers of Americans there and all along the way. We came over that morning from our home in Newark, New Jersey, to add ourselves to the great welcoming crowd. Here I not only had my initial contact with history but I grappled with my first historical problem. As the parade marched by where we stood, one of my parents asked me: "Do you see the cannon?" Presumably an artillery unit was marching by, but I seemingly assumed that this cannon was one of the figures which decorated the arch. And look as intently as I could at that artistic jumble, I could not discover my objective. I lacked proper orientation, a not uncommon weakness of historians.

Later of course I learned the significance of what I had seen and puzzled over. These last years of the nineteenth century, when the war with Spain was fought, when the new heroes, Dewey and Theodore Roosevelt, took their places in history, when new responsibilities in the Caribbean and the Pacific were undertaken, were evidence that the nation had gained a new world outlook, foreign to its accustomed attitudes hitherto rather provincial. The historians would soon be writing a new chapter: "The United States Becomes a World Power."

I had been born in Newark, on March 3, 1896, and I had arrived safely before the fear set in that William Jennings Bryan might become President and ruin the country. What small perils we then feared! I was the son of Franklin Coriell and Annie Cairns Nichols. My behavior was to be determined by a tension of two forces transmitted by the genetic codes representing my inheritances from them. My father's forebears had been hard-working traditionalists who after the effort required to migrate to America remained almost stationary thereafter. Their initial impulse to cross the sea seems to have been religious, the product of seventeenth-century dissent which brought them with many like-minded to Connecticut. Four generations later, I believe through the accident of death which left him an orphan in boyhood, an ancestor came to live in Newark, New Jersey, where relatives dwelt, sometime about 1730, and there a straight line of descendants lived for nearly two centuries. Most of them were seemingly content with what appears to have been a routine existence. My paternal grandfather married into a family who had settled in a New Jersey farm community and had been even less inclined to enterprise. Though uninterested in any further migration these people possessed a reasonable intelligence, a capacity for participation in religious organization and, economically, were able to maintain a standard within the range of simple comfort, aided by certain manual skills.

My mother's family was more adventurous and more gifted in enterprise and the capacity to accumulate. They prospered, and set up positions in the suburban communities in New Jersey, to which they retired early after modest economic success in New York City. In these little Essex County towns they assumed places of limited prominence in church circles just as my father's had in Newark. There the two strains united; in neither had there ever been any education other than elementary nor any intellectual interest save in religion. My father's contribution was an undeviating consistency. In a sense I never left school, connected with some educational institution without a break from the age of five, living all my life so to speak on the Philadelphia division of the Pennsylvania Railroad, attending the Newark public schools, Rutgers, and Columbia and earning my living at the latter university and the University of Pennsylvania. From my mother and her forebears I inherited the enterprise to forge ahead and accomplish whatever I have in the educational world within the narrow confines of such a consistent residence, relieved by very extensive travel.

In September 1901, I began to go to school on the day McKinley was shot. The fact of significance, as far as I was concerned in developing an interest in history, was that I was learning to read. My mother enjoyed reading to me. I had learned the alphabet before I went to school and after a year in kindergarten began the process of reading prescribed in the first grade. A large chart was hung up before the class on which was printed the story "The Three Bears." I must then pick out the words which were on cards scrambled in a box on my desk, and piece the story together by matching the words of the chart. In later terms there followed a series of readers. One was bound in brilliant red and described the rather calm life of "The Little Red Hen." This was soon followed by *Twice Told Tales, Stories from Norse Mythology* containing accounts of the lives and adventures of the mythological figures Wotan, Thor, Loki, and other Norse gods. This may be described as my official introduction to history at school.

My mother's reading probably really awakened my historical interest more than my school experience. Among the books at home were two which influenced me most vividly; at least I still remember them. One was *Noble Lives and Brave Deeds* and the other *The History of the United States Told in One Syllable Words.* Each of these contained pictures designed to catch the childish eye. In one was a representation of Joan of Arc clad in armor with blood running from an arrow wound in her leg. The other depicted brown Indians, Redcoats of the Revolution, and blue-uniformed Union soldiers and the guns of the *Constitution* and the *Guerriere* spitting scarlet flame. These stories fascinated me and I learned to repeat them. I seem to have communicated some of my historical lore to my teachers; perhaps I was something of a showoff, at any rate I remember when some visitors were calling on the acting principal I was summoned to demonstrate my unusual erudition. And it was unusual, for to everybody's embarrassment I described the settlement at Jamestown, Virginia, as made by the New England Pilgrims. Presumably after that I was kept under wraps; at any rate I remember no similar efforts.

But the real base was books and they came early. My mother and father had married in 1880 but by 1895 they had been deprived of their two sons, and for my mother there was but one solace, there must be another child. So although she was nearly forty I was successfully brought into the world. Her earlier misfortunes made her careful, from some standpoints too careful, but she felt happier and safer if I were nearby and so she read to me constantly and encouraged me to read myself.

On many fair Saturday afternoons I was taken downtown shopping in certain department stores. One of these, Snyder's, had a book department and each Saturday I was given twenty cents to buy a book. On the counter devoted to children's books I found a series published by Henry Altemus described as "Arranged for Young Readers." And among *Robinson Crusoe, Gulliver's Travels, Alice in Wonderland, The Pilgrim's Progress, The Swiss Family Robinson, Tales from Shakespeare, Black Beauty, Grimm's Fairy Tales,* and *A Child's Garden of Verses* were Dickens' *Child's History of England, Grandfather's Chair, Battles of the War for Independence, Military Heroes of the United States, Heroes of the United States Navy, Lives of the Presidents of the United States, Battles of the War for the Union,* and *Young People's History of the War with Spain.* Week by week I acquired one of these and read them many times.

When I was nine I "took out" a card at the public library and every Saturday morning, if it wasn't raining, off I trudged right after breakfast. My taste then turned to boys' historical books by Everett T. Tomlinson and Edward S. Stratemeyer who wrote stories of the Revolution, the War of 1812, the war with Spain, and even the Mexican War, though for the Civil War I had to turn to Oliver Optic. Then I found on a store counter a shop-worn copy of Edward S. Ellis's *Altemus Young People's History of Germany,* which I purchased, and on the introductory pages I found that there were companion volumes for the United States, England, and France. These the store did not have, but some interested friends who for some reason allowed me to call on Sunday afternoons after Sunday school told me that there was an emporium farther away, called Mulligan's, which would order books from publishers, an art not practiced by department stores; and in due time the three companion volumes appeared from this mysterious source and these kind friends encouraged me to bring my treasures in on these same Sunday afternoons and read them to me and even suffered me to try my hand at showing my skill. We were beginning to read aloud in school and I enjoyed it. How much I owe to these two kindly ladies who let a little boy sharpen his historical interests week after week for two hours of a Sunday afternoon I simply cannot estimate. I guess they must have liked to have a child around.

When I entered the sixth grade I had my first formal introduction to history. I looked forward to it with gusto for I had been absorbing history for a good many of my eleven years and now I was to have it in school. Some twenty years before, a new guide for school children had appeared on the scene, David Henry Montgomery. This unsuccessful clergyman trained at Brown and Harvard Divinity, who had likewise failed in business, had at length at the age of fifty turned to schoolbook writing. Success with elementary books in English and French history had led him to write *The Leading*

Facts in American History, which Ginn and Company put on the market in 1890. This book had gone through various editions so successfully that Montgomery had placed Ginn on the map as well as himself, so he next essayed a smaller book, *An Elementary American History,* which was published in 1904.

This latter book was placed in my hands on a February day in 1907 and my study of history formally began. This text laid emphasis upon the colonial period and gave much space to our military involvements. While it had a good deal about economic and cultural developments the half of the book which dealt with matters after 1787 was organized by presidential administrations.

This process was amplified when, in the seventh year, I was given the larger Montgomery book, which had four hundred rather than three hundred pages but followed much the same outline. Its preface recorded the fact, which meant nothing to me then, even had I noticed it, that Professor J. Franklin Jameson of Brown had given the author "valuable assistance in the revision of the proof sheets." Dr. Jameson later was to figure a good deal in my experience with history. This book, though it did not have as many pictures as its smaller companion, was embellished with facsimiles of documents and the autographs and pictures of famous men, generally statesmen, and many more maps.

These books were designed to encourage the method of learning which I was taught, namely, to list events by colony, war, or presidential administration and learn them by heart. To ensure this more effectively I was required in the seventh year to compile a notebook in which these events were listed in such fashion. I can still repeat the list of generals who failed to capture Richmond, and many other organizational schemes. History was definitely something to be remembered and my memory was rigorously trained.

In the eighth year I was introduced to Harmon B. Niver's *A School History of England,* written by a blind teacher, an alumnus of my future alma mater, Rutgers. This book started with the striking statement, "The English race today occupies or controls a fourth of the land surface of the globe." It was designed to show our kinship and our indebtedness to our mother country and ended on another note so long part of our common knowledge: ". . . it is certain that British colonial government has been productive of the highest good to mankind and that English-speaking colonies everywhere are loyal and take a patriotic pride in owing allegiance to the empire on which the 'sun never sets.' " This text was arranged by reigns, with genealogical tables. The emphasis was on the growth of political institutions and the empire, but due attention was paid to its evolution "to the front rank of the world's manufacturing and commercial powers"; the growth of English culture was emphasized by occasional quotations from British poets. I continued my course in memory training, this time arranging my lists by reign.

My historical knowledge was both broadened and deepened when I transferred to high school. Here in my junior year I had William C. Morey's two books on Grecian and Roman history, while in my senior year I went back to American history for the third time. This text was written by James and Sanford and entitled *American History.* James Alton James was a professor at Northwestern and a disciple of Frederick Jackson Turner; a book, as its authors proclaimed in their preface, which subordinated military phases of American history "to the accounts of the victories of peace." Also probably due to Turner's influence they gave greater prominence than "usual in school texts to the advance of the frontier and to the growth and influence of the West." Of all this I was blissfully unaware and had no idea that I was exposed to the frontier interpretation. Perhaps I even failed to note that whereas I had first had a three hundred-page book, and then a four hundred-page work, my third textbook was five hundred pages long. There were just more facts to learn, though this book tried to get me out of the routine of political administrations and to substitute topics which encouraged concepts of expansion, development, and change. I have no recollection of abandoning my good memory for any thought, though I do recall some heated arguments in class over the growing labor movement and the right to strike. My father was in the retail hat business and had his ideas about the Danbury hatters whose wares he sold and whose woes he deplored. He, like his father before him, was a good Republican and I reflected his views in my discussions with my more liberal companions. But this phase of my experience was about to end.

In 1914 I graduated from high school and emerged from my basic education. I had acquired a large amount of historical information, mostly political and military, I had cultivated a good memory and an engrossing interest. I had no hesitancy about displaying my erudition. A large mass of fact and a great interest are perhaps as good an initial equipment for a historian as any, also perhaps it was an advantage to begin early though that meant that much had to be unlearned later. So I graduated from high school in January 1914, in a burst of historical enthusiasm as our commencement exercises included a production of scenes from Shakespeare's *Henry IV* and *Henry V* and my part was Henry V.

As there was an interval of seven months before entering college in September, I stayed in high school for a postgraduate term. Most of this was devoted to taking two courses in English history covering the whole of Edward P. Cheyney's *A Short History of England* (1904). As far as I can remember all I got was more facts and further assurance that my memory would earn me high marks. I left high school with my intention now fully established to teach history, though presumably at high school level. I had kept some notebooks in history which were almost exclusively factual chronological outlines, but I had written no essays or term papers of a historical nature.

A second fixed point developed between 1909 and 1915. These were the years of the centennial of Lincoln's birth in 1909 and the semicentennial of the Civil War of 1861–5. Various publications came my way relating to Lincoln, particularly the anniversary number of *The Century Magazine,* and then there was the Lincoln penny. A cent was still a coin that could buy something, particularly penny candy and ice cream. Furthermore the newspapers featured the Civil War. One paper had daily accounts of events fifty years ago and I cut these out and started a scrapbook. Also, the Mathew Brady war photos were exploited. Another newspaper printed daily coupons and these, when presented at the paper office with a small sum of money, procured a weekly installment which could be assembled in binders specially designed and then they eventually appeared in a book. But the crowning glory to me was the publication of the Brady photos in ten volumes sold on the installment plan. So I hoarded my allowance and bought monthly money orders at the post office, in the meantime poring over these masterpieces of the wet-plate artists. Imagine my enthusiasm when I found a picture with my uncle in it, together with others of his ship and the ship upon which another uncle served.

Then by an interesting turn of fate on one of my Saturday visits to the library I came across the three volumes of Gideon Welles's recently published *Diary* and spent some of the summer of 1913 on this salty work. As far as I can remember this was the first source material I ever "used" and I lived with Lincoln and his Cabinet on its pages and accepted Welles as gospel. I have found this latter confidence hard to shake. Not only was I interested in history but I had acquired a field of special interest never to be wholly abandoned, the Civil War.

This was the state of things when I went to college in 1914. I had had American history three times, in the sixth and seventh grade and in my last year in high school. I had had English history twice, in eighth grade and in postgraduate courses in high school between graduation in January, 1914, and entrance to college, and ancient history in my third high school year.

Events and influences entirely outside the classroom were shaping my major interest in history with a force which was to be compelling. My interests in politics and political history were so closely knit and so pervasive that there never was much chance that I could break away from this absorption. Anything I did appears to have had to be fitted into it and no influence ever even threatened to dislodge it, although I have since been able to view a wider horizon and chart broader paths of intellectual interest.

I came to political consciousness during the first administration of Theodore Roosevelt. It was then that I discovered that I was a Republican of the Straightest sect because all my family and most of our friends were. Democrats were prayed for but not spoken to any oftener than could be helped. At least that was the official attitude. My father, however, who was a past master at making friends, didn't really draw any lines. But I was somewhat puritanical in this respect and have never forgotten my dismay when he told me he was going to vote for the re-election of a Democratic mayor. This was particularly shocking because this mayor was connected with the "liquor interest." Following my mother's strict ideas, I was for local option and prohibition. I had taken the pledge in Sunday school, and besides I was easily shocked.

My interest in political campaigns began with that of 1904. I was emotionally committed to "Teddy." Large posters bearing the likeness of Roosevelt and Fairbanks and the Republican candidate for governor were pasted up in our front windows. I wore celluloid buttons proclaiming my loyalty to these candidates. I also acquired two portrait busts of Roosevelt and his running mate made out of soap. I almost made ikons of these images, though I really did not stoop to idolatry, despite the fact that I prayed for Republican success. As we lived in a Democratic ward of a city generally Democratic, my lack of success in the lower brackets tried my faith.

Politics thus early became an absorbing if not a consuming hobby. I collected campaign buttons and ballots and followed election news with avid interest. This interest I caught from my father and a cousin of my mother's. This latter relative visited us frequently. He was a political activist and it was said that in the neighboring town where he dwelt an associate of his tended to the voters in the saloons and my cousin to those in the churches. My father, who was active in the Royal Arcanum Lodge, met a great many people and had much opportunity to discuss politics. So both of these men were full of the subject, and I sat and listened through many a substantial meal, for they were both fond of eating. Came a time when I began to ask questions and even contribute my own views and enthusiasms. I liked to keep scrapbooks and to compile lists. So in course of time I had assembled records and pictures which I wrote up and pasted in, embracing political heads of state, governors, and U.S. Senators.

Each election day brought things to a climax. There were no radios or TV and early results could be obtained only by going downtown to one of the newspaper offices where returns were posted or displayed by lantern projection on large outdoor screens. For those who did not go out, the newspapers published "extras" which newsboys carried into the neighborhoods with their strident cries of "Extry, extry! Read all about the election!" To make election night the more exciting, it was the custom in our city to kindle a myriad bonfires on the Belgian-block streets fueled by boxes collected from hither and yon, generally from friendly grocers, with an occasional barrel; it was before the day of cartons.

Idealogically the nation was approaching the peak of the Progressive Era. In Essex County, New Jersey, Everett Colby, William Fellowes Morgan, Austen Colgate, and others were leading a crusade for the New Idea. This was the elimination of boss rule by the Progressive devices from direct primary to commission form of municipal government.

My voluminous but unplanned reading reinforced

my interest in this great enthusiasm. The newspapers played a large part. The Newark *Evening News* was the main journal which, with the old New York *Press,* now long defunct, made up the daily fare. The *Press* had a column on New Jersey politics written by Howard B. Tindell, a friend of my father's, and this I read avidly, particularly after my father took me to Trenton one day and we called on him in his office in the capitol. On Sunday there were the Newark *Sunday Call* and the New York *Herald;* in those days a boy was satisfied with only four pages of comics.

Then there were more books. My voluminous reading reinforced my interest in this great enthusiasm. I immersed myself at one period about 1910 in the writings of three "Progressives." The one that had the most influence on me was the New Hampshire novelist Winston Churchill. I had learned of him first from his historical novels, *Richard Carvel, The Crossing, The Crisis,* but my great enthusiasm came from two other of his alliterative C titles, *Coniston* and *Mr. Crewe's Career,* which were fascinating stories of New Hampshire politics told by the pen of a Progressive. This intimate glimpse of government by "personal influence" gripped my attention. Also at that time *La Follette's Autobiography* ran in the *American Magazine,* which was subscribed to for me, and the successive installments of that which I read so eagerly made me a La Follette man for life. Later on in 1924 I had the privilege of voting for him for President, and while at research in Washington in the 1920's Jeannette and I formed a very happy friendship with Fola La Follette and her husband, the playwright George Middleton.

The third of the Progressives was Lincoln Steffens. In 1913 while waiting for dreaded dental appointments I read installments of his *Shame of the Cities* in the waiting room, and when that summer we visited New England, under the guidance of one of our fellow "boarders" at Pigeon Cove I visited the City Hall at Salem, Massachusetts, and met the city clerk, one of the characters Steffens described in his account of that municipality. He was a very affable "public servant" who gave me an impression of the seal of the metropolis. I felt I was seeing the inside and could detect no shame. Some of these impressions were deepened by what I learned from reading W. E. Sackett's *Modern Battles of Trenton* and realized some of the unfortunate phases of New Jersey politics in the throes of railroad and race track lobby operations.

All this interest and activity and particularly the reading impressed upon me the stamp of the Progressive Era. There was evil abroad in the land, bosses, machine politicians, "stand-patters." Uncle Joe Cannon was the personification of the undesirable on the national scene. At home Jim Smith and Jim Nugent who ran the Democratic party in Essex County had sinister features, reminiscent of Thomas Nast's art. I lived up a very short hill from the Essex County Courthouse and frequently I could spy the very portly form and red face of Jake the Barber, who sat in a small shop opposite the temple of justice. He it was who was reputed to make the assignments and receive the orders. My father had once been selected to go to the Republican state convention. On the day set he went to the Pennsylvania Railroad station where he was handed a return ticket to Trenton. When he got to the convention it was made obvious to him how he should vote. So I, like so many, began to believe that the direct primary would be the answer.

However dedicated I might feel to political reform in

particular, I was only sympathetic when it appeared within a Republican frame of reference. I demonstrated this when a paradoxical situation developed. The boss-ridden Democrats controlled by Smith and Nugent in 1910 nominated the liberal political scientist, Woodrow Wilson, President of Princeton, to be their candidate for governor. Despite his liberalism I would have none of him; he was a Democrat. So I wore a button for Vivian M. Lewis whom the Republicans had nominated but who met an ignominious defeat.

The emotional climax came in the confused year of 1912, the year of the famous struggle between Taft and his former sponsor Theodore Roosevelt. My sympathies were all with Teddy and there was no more ardent Bull Moose than myself. The defeat of Roosevelt was a bitter disappointment. This carried over into 1916 when I was enthusiastic for Charles E. Hughes, one of the reform champions in cleaning up New York State in the first decade of the twentieth century. Again I would have none of Wilson. On election night many of my college associates who had gone downtown learned that Hughes had been elected, and paid their bets. When I awoke next morning the papers had withdrawn their announcement, the race was now declared to be close. During the day various of our fellowship went down to the office of the *Daily Home News* for bulletins between classes and finally we found Wilson re-elected. Despite the Progressive Era and my enthusiasm for reform I could not stifle my disappointment at Wilson's triumph over Hughes. Several years had to pass before I could admit any particular superiority in Wilson as man, scholar, or commander in chief.

In the meantime I was at college. It seemed to have always been assumed that I was to go to college and that the college should be Rutgers. I have no recollection of any doubts about either. A good many of the alumni of Barringer High School at Newark went there and two others of my particular class were so directed. I entered the college in September 1914, clearly headed toward a career of history teaching and therefore planning to take as much of the subject as was offered.

During my freshman year there was no formal instruction in history but each of the required courses in English, Latin, and Greek had historical elements. Part of the work in English was the history of English literature from Beowulf to Kipling and included required reading of such historical stimulants as Defoe's *Journal of the Great Plague,* Kingsley's *Westward Ho!* and Thackeray's *Henry Esmond.* The texts used in the Classics included Livy, Homer, Xenophon, and Herodotus.

All sophomores were required to take a year of history and I was back again in my element. It was at this point that I came into the classroom of a genius, John Hubbard Logan, Baptist clergyman and sometime Ph.D. candidate in a German university who had never published his thesis and had gotten no degree. He had no idea of method but he could arouse interest, and his queer mannerisms and pedagogical devices always kept me alert. Also he didn't think I was as good as I did and we became fast friends.

In the first term I had my first formal work in continental European history. In one term we "covered" Western Europe from the fall of Rome to the twentieth century via James Harvey Robinson and Charles A. Beard. Without any real comprehension of significance I had added two other "great names" to that of Edward P. Cheyney. Robinson and Beard's volumes of *Readings* gave me an introduction to the nature of historical sources though not much comprehension of how to use them. In the second term I was required to "take" American history for the fourth time. Now I was assigned John Spencer Bassett's *Short History of the United States,* a ponderous volume of over eight hundred pages. My knowledge of the facts of American history was becoming more exact and more voluminous. My great dependence as before was my memory. Again everything was carefully outlined in notebooks and exams were crammed for. Certain cram sessions were organized on the eve of quizzes and finals, and it was in these informal nocturnal gatherings that I got my first teaching experience because I happened to have "the stuff cold."

So far my history study had not included any written papers, save examinations of one sort or another, but in this my sophomore year I had my first opportunity. Each year the sophomores had the opportunity to compete for the Spader prize in history, an award of twenty dollars was offered for the best essay on an announced topic. This year the topic was "The Relations between the United States and South America, 1815–1915." I consulted a random bibliography, mostly of secondary material, and produced a factual narrative of the century's changes. It won the prize.

In the junior year there was another course with Logan on English constitutional history, with texts by A. B. White, A. L. Cross, and Adams and Stephens *Documents* which immersed me in charters and statutes, the rights of Englishmen, and caused me to keep a good notebook. At the same time I had a course, A History of Civilization, by the beloved and revered Dr. Austin Scott, using as a textbook Guizot's *History of Civilization in Europe* first brought out in 1842; my edition was published in 1911 with notes and commentary by Knight of Ohio State. Dr. Scott's method was to require a summary of each paragraph written in a notebook. Upon occasion I, with others, was required to go to the blackboard and write one of these summaries. Also I had to learn the Constitution by heart.

In the senior year came two specialized courses under Logan, one in American history 1830–77 and the other Europe since 1815. Bassett was my stand-by in the first although I purchased Turner's *Rise of the New West* in the American Nation Series. For the European history I had Charles Downer Hazen's *Europe Since 1815,* not realizing that I would be listening to his lectures two years hence.

It was at this point that I got my first chance to think about history. Rutgers required of each senior a graduation thesis in the field of his major. Mine was therefore to be in history. For the first time I had an idea, an idea that was not to be worked out entirely chronologically as a string of events. This was something I must think about—and in 1917–18 historical thought began just as I had turned twenty-one.

This thesis, entitled "Personal Influence in United States Politics," dealt primarily with the varying nature of "boss rule" in the successive periods in American history. It was based on reminiscences and secondary materials. It was quite in the spirit of the Progressive Era and concluded rather realistically that despite the various current reforms "influence . . . will have to be reckoned with for many decades still to come or until man is no longer influenced by wealth or ambition."

I graduated in May 1918, in what were the last months of the war. With so much uncertainty in the world and not being eligible for military service I continued at Rutgers for a postgraduate year. The college had no graduate school but it had a limited graduate program and work for the M.A. was available in history. I therefore presented myself to Professor Walter T. Marvin, secretary of the graduate program. He registered me and provided me with a course book similar to those long current in the German universities. Logan had left to take up war work with the Red Cross and history was to be taught by Irving S. Kull, a Ph.D. candidate of Dodd's at Chicago. He was to take over Logan's work and he inherited me.

I took my course book in to him and to Logan on one of his visits home and we put together a program. I was to attend Kull's class in recent American history, I was to take a course in Church history up in the seminary. Logan was emphatic that I did not have enough science, so first-year zoology was duly entered and I proceeded to follow a taxonomic outline from phyla to phyla, starting with an ameba and with a laboratory partner, Howard Wilcox, cutting up successive specimens from an earthworm to a cat. This was not orthodox but I profited.

My master's year included not only history and zoology but I had the great good fortune to have an experience in philosophy. As a junior I had taken the prescribed course in logic and psychology given by Walter Taylor Marvin, a disciple of Thorndike. From him I had learned SR and the famous exploits of the cat in the box. Now he gave me a course in the history of American thought. I used to meet him once a week in the philosophy library in Old Queens and report to him on assigned reading. In one of these sessions I came to see that there was no such thing as absolute truth and this was a striking-off of shackles from my thought. I was ready for pragmatism and relativism.

My main project in this first postgraduate year was a piece of research in the form of a master's essay. The field of Professor Kull's major interest was the Presbyterian Church and slavery and he assigned me the situation in New Jersey. The records of the New Jersey Presbyterians were filed at the Princeton Theological Seminary, some in manuscript and some in print. Professor Kull introduced me to the librarian, Mr. Shedden, and I spent a number of afternoons there poring over the Minutes of the Synod of New Jersey and various other New School and Old School records. I read a good many religious periodicals and pamphlets and the biographies of a number of Presbyterian clergymen. Eventually I wrote a factual narrative carefully footnoted and chronologically oriented and concluded "that on the question of slavery the Presbyterian Church of New Jersey was conservative, in a large measure even to the avoidance of the discussion of the issue, so that as a political factor in the fixing of the state policy its influence was nil. Whatever progress New Jersey made in the path of anti-slavery legislation or agitation was accomplished, not by the aid of but in face of the indifference of the Presbyterian Church."

This exercise was something I needed. Logan had not taught me any method nor any of the apparatus of research. Neither had I had any practice in going to another library for primary manuscript sources, of going away to explore. This Kull required for my master's work. I made notes on cards, I arranged my cards chronolgically, and took off the story they told. I brought back a conclusion, albeit a negative one, which smelled of the lamp. Also I now knew how to make footnotes and to arrange a bibliography. In June 1919, I received the M.A.

During the Rutgers years I had continued my custom of haphazard reading in quantity. Most of it was fiction and fiction of no great distinction, but there were several choices of a good deal of later significance which should be noted; C. J. H. Hayes's *Political and Social History of Modern Europe,* G. P. Gooch's *History and Historians of the Nineteenth Century,* Henry Adams's *Education* and *Mont St. Michel and Chartres,* and William A. Dunning's *Reconstruction, Political and Economic.* The choice of the latter was arrived at by magnificent indirection. At college I was an indefatigable movie fan and so went to one of the first showings of an early spectacle, *The Birth of a Nation,* during my sophomore year. This story of Reconstruction made a great impression on me and I immediately read Thomas Dixon's novel *The Clansman,* on which it was based. This took me to the history behind the novel, which I found in Dunning, little dreaming what that name was to mean to me. Nor could I anticipate the significance of Henry Adams.

From these, my five Rutgers years, I emerged with a comprehensive supply of memorized well-ordered fact. I knew something about sources and how history was compiled. I depended very greatly on outlines and chronology. My historical reading was first of all textbooks, then there was the reading for the Prize Essay, the bachelor's and the master's theses, but there was not a great deal of general reading required for courses and I had not really done any seminar work. In other words I had been learning rather than thinking. Reading had been largely for pleasure rather than for intellectual stimulation.

II

AN APPRENTICE ON MORNINGSIDE

THAT I SHOULD EARN a doctorate was just as much a foregone conclusion as that I should go to college. But as Rutgers had no Ph.D. program in those days except in a few of the sciences, a change of scene was necessary. Geographically the Raritan was halfway between Columbia and Princeton and I never really considered any other graduate school. I had been working recently in the Princeton libraries; on the other hand Logan had been a student at Columbia and if I went there William A. Dunning might be my teacher. Also as a boy I had come to know New York as a place for holiday treats at the theaters, the museums, and the parks, and this glamour played its part in the decision. Columbia it was to be.

My first step in the direction of Gotham was to make an application for a fellowship in the spring of 1919 and I sent in the necessary forms together with letters from Logan, Kull, and Scott. But Columbia, anticipating a lean postwar year with few students, suspended any appropriation for fellowship aid from its free funds and depended wholly on its endowed fellowships for 1919–20; few awards were made and none to me. However, I could manage without it and this action made no change in my plans.

I had no other uncertainties for it was a day of much simpler procedures. I did not have to apply for admission nor submit transcripts of grades or letters of recommendation—I did not have to wait in a state of suspense as to whether I would be accepted. All that was necessary was my appearance during registration armed with evidence that I had a bachelor's degree from Rutgers. I would then be supplied with registration forms, which I was to fill out and take to Professor Dunning's office. When he had signed my program I could pay my tuition and I was in. So all I did in advance was write to the history department for Professor Dunning's office hours during registration. The almost total absence of any documentation is today almost incomprehensible; to some registrars it would be appalling.

At length on a September day in 1919 I climbed the heights of Morningside, not up a steep cliffside trail but via the steps of the West Side subway. I was entering upon the scene of a most vital experience. Morningside in those days was a homogeneous university community with something of a village atmosphere. The carefully planned campus situated between the Hudson and Harlem featured the Low Library and Alma Mater in the center with the attendant red brick and limestone buildings extending up and down Broadway and Amsterdam Avenue from 114th Street to Teachers College six blocks to the north, flanked by Barnard College and Union Theological Seminary on the west. The university was likewise surrounded by apartment houses and all the miscellaneous shops and services required by a university community. The two parks, Riverside and Morningside, the Hudson River, and the wide vista stretching out over Harlem to the East River gave the university a setting of unique utility and beauty.

This was the university of Nicholas Murray Butler, of the Faculty of Political Science, of William A. Dunning, Edwin R. A. Seligman, Franklin H. Giddings, and until latterly James Harvey Robinson and Charles A. Beard. It was also the university of John Dewey, Edward L. Thorndike, Robert S. Woodworth, and Frederick J. E. Woodbridge, Dean of the Graduate Faculties. Various of these gentlemen appeared on the campus clad in frockcoats and carrying canes; silk hats had not long been left at home.

In 1919 it was a somewhat altered university. During the war not only had the ranks of its students been depleted by the calls of war service but there had been grievous faculty losses. The war years had been a period of turmoil and some schism. The intellectual world of the United States had had close ties with Germany. Much of the university idea which had transformed Columbia had been of German origin. Administration and faculty had maintained close contact with the German universities, particularly those who had spent Studenten Jahren there. Some could not accept the hatred of the Hun demanded by war emotion. There was division, ostracism, even attempted thought control. In the aftermath of this James Harvey Robinson and Charles A. Beard had left the university and had become founders of the New School of Social Research down in Chelsea. Also there had been deaths and retirements and the chairs of Osgood and Botsford were vacant. Now in the fall of 1919 the ranks of the students were again filling up, but those of the faculty were not being recruited so quickly.

The Columbia campus was a place of order and dignity with a minimum of "collegiate" atmosphere. Here minds were truly "in the making." The population was not predominately undergraduate and it was to the training of graduate students as creative scholars that a major effort of the university was dedicated. A graduate student as he walked eastward on 116th Street from the subway soon sensed that this great university had been designed to insure his intellectual nurture. It was his home, and he was a central figure in it.

After presenting my bachelor's certificate at the admissions office and securing my registration blanks in University Hall, I proceeded up to the top floor of Kent Hall to my first interview with my new guide, Professor William A. Dunning, in 608. I had studied the Bulletins of the Faculty of Political Science and had selected his seminar as my chief interest. In addition I had chosen lecture courses by Dixon Ryan Fox, Osgood's son-in-law, in American history, by Charles Downer Hazen, whose text I had used in European history and by H. L. Munro in the history of international relations. Dr. Dunning advised me to add another course and thus finish up my residence in this year. So I took a second seminar, William R. Shepherd's Latin American history. Later on in the second term I changed from Hazen and Munro to Carlton J. H. Hayes and Benjamin B. Kendrick.

After a few hours in class I made a decision. One of the first lectures I attended was delivered by Henry Munro in international relations, who gave a course labeled "History of Diplomacy," Mondays and Wednesdays at ten, in 615 Kent Hall. His first act was to write what he called a "prescription" of reading on the board. I industriously copied it and immediately after the lecture went downstairs to the law library to "take the prescription." I soon discovered that if I read what was listed for this one course I would do nothing else that term, so I gave up all pretense at reading for my lecture courses and devoted myself to the two seminars.

Professor Dunning's course was labeled "The United States in the Period of the Civil War," but all the topics assigned were in Reconstruction. He was a benevolent, witty, and admirably balanced scholar who with his white mustache and pointed beard seemed to be the perfect southern colonel although he was a New Jersey man who had been educated at Darmouth and Columbia. He had graduated in 1881 and in 1885 had taken one of the first Ph.D.'s under John W. Burgess in the newly organized graduate faculties.

So here my Ph.D. work began. There was no seminar room, ten of us, seven women and three men sat scattered in an ordinary classroom. Professor Dunning presided at the small table and the reporting student sat in a chair in front of the class. Dunning assigned topics on the first day and very shortly the reports began. There were two sessions a week of one hour each, Wednesdays and Fridays at eleven. During the year I was assigned three papers: "Did President Johnson Change His Reconstruction Policy During His First Six Weeks in Office?", "The Effort to Punish Jefferson Davis for His Part in the Rebellion," and "The Philadelphia Convention of 1866."

Professor William R. Shepherd gave his seminar in Hispanic America and its relations with the United States. He met his fourteen students in his office and his procedure was different: each student must present his paper in twenty minutes. When he assigned a paper he also supplied a bibliography of works, not only in English but in Spanish and Portuguese as well. I had taken a summer-school course in Spanish at Rutgers and had picked up Portuguese after a fashion by myself more or less out of curiosity. In this course I had four papers and a bibliographical exercise. The papers explored "Mexican Politics in the Time of Santa Anna," "The Origin and Meaning of the Monroe Doctrine, According to the Portuguese Americans," "Oil Politics in Honduras," and "The Tacna and Arica Question—the Neutral Standpoint." For this latter project three of us were assigned as a team.

The work on these papers and the preparations for my oral preliminaries insured maximum intellectual activity. The American history workroom for graduate students was 301 in the Low Library and there each of us had a drawer at a series of long tables adjoining the stacks. Then at the New York Public Library there was an American history room where we worked in those things which Columbia did not have. And for the Latin American study there was the Hispanic Society up at 155th Street. A fourth haunt was on the top floor of the Low Library, where an unusual source was shelved. At the time of the Civil War Thomas Seaman Townsend had begun an enormous scrapbook in great ledgers. The New York press was clipped daily and the war items were pasted in. Other pertinent matter dealing with the various phases of the war was also interleaved and the whole was indexed and then the index was indexed. It was indeed a formidable scholarly tool and one which challenged the student to plumb its mighty depths. But struggling with it yielded treasure.

The first of these seminar papers was put in the form of a question. Hitherto what writing I had done had been in the form of narration or the chronological pursuit of an idea. Now I was assigned a question about the behavior of an individual, Andrew Johnson. One of the first things I did was to resume my acquaintance with Gideon Welles's *Diary,* which furnished an intimate day-by-day account of the Johnson Administration from the assassination to the announcement of the President's Reconstruction policy. At the same time I began reading shelves, rather than depending on formal library catalogue analyses, and delving into the Townsend tomes. Also Professor Dunning showed me some notes he had taken on the Andrew Johnson papers in the Library of Congress. I was now working in the most fascinating source material and bringing the figures of the administration to life in my imagination. I reported that Johnson, despite his oft-reiterated announcement that treason was a crime and that traitors must be punished, had soon returned to his early feeling for states' rights, largely under the influence of Preston King and the Blairs. He had soon forsworn punishment and turned to speedy restoration of the seceded states. This was too simple an explanation for a complicated situation as Dr. Dunning pointed out to me when he read my written version.[1]

The two other papers read in this seminar were undertaken in a similar methodological spirit. I treated the failure to punish Jefferson Davis and the Philadelphia Convention of 1866 as exercises in the study of personal relations and motivation in politics. My most revealing

[1] As I was applying for a fellowship I wrote out the paper. Written papers were not handed in, in Dunning's seminars.

source continued to be Gideon Welles and the Townsend collection. Johnson and his Cabinet, his enemies and his allies were my main interest. The case of *United States vs. Jefferson Davis* became an example of bureaucratic inertia. The Philadelphia Convention was designed to start off a new political flight which never got off the ground. As a result of this year's work in "personal documents," I had translated my idea of personal influence into these three papers and I knew just how I wanted to go about my dissertation.

It was in Dunning's seminar that I formed certain lasting and vital relationships. I was one of three men; the other two were John Allen Krout, a native of Ohio from Heidelberg College at Tiffin and from the University of Michigan, and W. Randall Waterman of Rhode Island and Brown. We almost immediately began not only our graduate study but the exploration of New York and devoted many hours to visiting its historic landmarks. Waterman, upon achieving his doctorate, devoted his life to teaching at Dartmouth. Krout and I were to stay at Columbia, I for a brief time, he permanently. As my *Lebensraum* was always to be within ninety miles of Columbia we saw much of each other and enjoyed a constant interchange. For many years professional meetings brought me frequently to New York and that generally meant dinner together and friendship which grew richer as time marched on. Jeannette and Marion Krout shared in this and many of our dinners were delightful foursomes.

But the highlight of my personal relations was with one of the students of the other sex. Jeannette Paddock was returning for her second year of residence at Columbia. She was a Knox College graduate who, after a stint of teaching in Portland, Oregon, had come to

Columbia for a master's degree under James Harvey Robinson. Now in the fall of 1919 she had returned to finish her residence for the Ph.D. She enrolled in Dunning's seminar and we attracted each other almost from the moment of meeting. We became engaged during the course of the year, passed our preliminary examinations for the doctorate in the spring, and were married on May 27, 1920, in the chapel of Union Theological Seminary. We have been working together ever since, completely sharing our professional as well as our personal interests.

While entering into this varied exploration of new experiences I had begun to talk with Professor Dunning about a dissertation topic. I told him of my interest in personal influence in politics and that I wanted to work in this field, mentioning Hamilton and Jefferson particularly. He suggested that I take the Democrats on the eve of the Civil War. He said that though his students had generally been interested in Reconstruction or in the Republican party he had always hoped for some Democratic studies. Though I was about as rock-ribbed a Republican as there was I did not blink, and agreed. The main interest was to be the personal relationships of Democrats, North and South, from 1850 to 1860. I learned much later that his father had been a war Democrat, which probably accounted in part for this interest. The goal set was an understanding of the personal antagonisms among Democrats that were such important instruments in causing the breakup of the party in 1860, which in turn contributed so much to the election of Lincoln, secession, and war.

The diverting influence of passing my orals, getting married, and spending four months honeymooning in Europe meant that no real work on the dissertation began until the end of summer. After Dr. McGiffert performed our wedding ceremony in the beauty of the Union Theological Seminary chapel, we had planned to proceed at once to our European honeymoon, but the sailing we had engaged was postponed, so we retreated to the New Jersey countryside at Roseland for the time intervening and on June 2 set forth in the good ship *St. Paul* of the American Line. We took the grand tour from Cherbourg to Southampton via France, Italy, Switzerland, Germany, Holland, Belgium, England, and Scotland, enjoying four months of what a honeymoon should be. We set sail for home on the *Philadelphia* and there, strangely enough, my work on my dissertation was resumed.

I found in the ship's library two volumes in the American Statesmen Series, Shepard's *Van Buren,* and Roosevelt's *Benton.* When I got re-established at Columbia I went to work. My method was to give particular attention to the personal documents of those in politics, 1850–60, particularly Democrats. Biographies, reminiscences, letters, particularly those that were not published, caught my avid attention. I continued my reading of shelves in the Columbia Library and did what I could with the catalogues of the New York Public Library, although no one had access to the shelves. But it was obvious that what I wanted was the correspondence of the Democratic leaders. This was to be found in greatest abundance at the Library of Congress. Jeannette likewise found that the material for her dissertation on the history of Alaska's achieving home rule was also in Washington, so we decided to spend the spring semester of 1921 at the national capital.

We attended our first meeting of the American Historical Association at Christmas 1920 in Washington and found a room at the foot of the west façade of the Capitol. Our first Washington dwelling place was in an apartment house on Maryland Avenue, overlooking the Capitol, where Dr. and Mrs. Upham rented us a room and made us welcome for nearly six months. Beginning in February 1921, I began my work in the North Curtain reading room of the Library of Congress, which was the home of the manuscripts division. I started with the fragmentary scraps of Franklin Pierce's manuscripts, the voluminous correspondence of Martin Van Buren which included so much from Francis P. Blair, and moved on to that of William L. Marcy and Gideon Welles, to mention the most important. I cut typewriter paper in half and copied what I thought would be useful. Unfortunately I undertook to save paper and space and often copied what I wanted from several letters on both sides of these half sheets. It was not a good technique. After the closing of the manuscripts division there was a walk and supper and then the evening in the newspaper room reading Democratic organs, particularly the Washington *Union.* Here I used full sheets of typewriter paper and took notes on both sides of the sheet until they were full. I saved room, but I was later to waste time in finding what I needed in what I had noted.

My research was not to be confined to New York and Washington. I explored the Massachusetts Historical Society and the American Antiquarian Society, the New Hampshire Historical Society, and the Historical Society of Pennsylvania. Also I had the interesting experience of finding material in private hands. In talking over my project with Professor Hazen, it transpired that he had taught the granddaughter of General Benjamin F. Butler. He wrote her of my interest and she very graciously offered to help me. Jeannette and I called on her and her husband, Andrew Marshall, at their home in Jamaica Plain near Boston. With unusual generosity she brought down a clothes basket full of the general's correspondence which she let us take to our lodging for study. Also there had been a powerful newspaperman in New Hampshire, Edmund Burke. I learned that his daughter had material at Burkehaven on Lake Sunapee. We went up there and she allowed us to use it in her home and at a nearby boardinghouse on the lake.

As I conceived my problem then, it was to make an analysis of the Democratic party from 1850 to 1860 to show that the political behavior of the leaders of the American voters was "the fundamental and perhaps the most important cause of the War between the States of 1861–5." This War between the States was induced by the rivalries and emotions of the states' politicians. The predominant cause was not so much slavery as the personal ambitions and fears of that craft guild of politicians which the sections where slavery existed had brought into being and fostered until it destroyed itself. I would explore the party machinery which the political activists who had undertaken to operate the government had devised for the purpose. I would study particularly the psychology, the behavior of the genus politician.

After six months of research in Washington during 1921 I decided that the material for the years 1850–60 was too abundant to permit its use for a period of that length with the care which I desired. Therefore I made an outline and took it to Dr. Dunning in October 1921. I proposed to deal with the behavior of the Democratic politicos, 1850–4. This period between the Compromise of 1850 and the Kansas Nebraska Act was an interlude, a season of calm between two great battles. I felt it was a particularly good period in which to find how the politician functioned. Public opinion was generally apathetic and undisturbed by the unusual; political operators could behave normally. Their actions in such a period would be the best indices of their real nature. Professor Dunning agreed, so I proceeded to write fourteen chapters and entitled the study *The Democratic Machine, 1850–1854*. I concentrated on the operation of the political machinery of the Democratic party as it functioned in the rather spiritless election of 1852, tracing the personal behavior of the numerous candidates for the nomination.

In the summer of 1922, Professor Dunning died. He had undertaken to supervise our dissertations but had not been well enough to do anything but give us his encouragement. None of our work had been ready to read. That summer we had rented Professor Kendrick's summer place in Maine and I had taken all my notes there to wrote. I made a good deal of progress and had also done some more research in repositories in Maine, New Hampshire, and Massachusetts. When we returned to Columbia in the fall, Professor Nathaniel Wright Stephenson, on leave from the College of Charleston and at work in New York City with the Yale University Press Motion Picture project, gave Dunning's seminar and undertook to advise me on my dissertation. Early in the fall I finished my first draft and he gave it a very careful reading. He was an excellent stylist and he made numerous suggestions to me. He had a special talent for this and I learned from him much of what I know about style.

The conceptualization which I formulated of my historical responsibilities was my first effort at defining my interpretation of history. As I phrased it in 1923:

To know history is to know the psychology of peoples, to know the psychology of peoples we must know the psychology of individuals, those individuals in history that are most articulate are the politicians. This is an attempt at a study of the psychology of politicians in order that the psychology of the people of the United States may be better understood.[2]

The research student in discussing the problem of how history works has generally thought in terms of the reaction of groups to general external ideal or economic forces. But this problem may also be conceived of in terms of the actions of individuals guided by their own motives and desires unconscious of external forces. Much of this kind of study has been made, many volumes of biography and many pages of individual characterization in general works attest the interest in the great figures in history. A survey of these contributions however seems to leave the conviction that the personalities of history have received a one-sided treatment. They have been described as individuals who have been guided either by ideal or economic motives, who have been public servants either from a sense of duty, because of a desire to see the right flourish or in order to benefit themselves economically. But there is another class of motives which actuates men and which almost defies definition. A combination of heredity and environment makes the individual the individual. When this combination of heredity and environment has produced a person politically ambitious it has produced a separate type—not the ethical man nor the economic man but the politician. Most of the chief actors in American history have been politicians and as such they have been neglected. Now the politician's main desire in life is

[2] MSS memorandum.

not the triumph of principle, though he may so declare, nor the personal enrichment of himself though he may so act, but the wielding of political power.

Politicians have their "trade psychology"; they are in the business of carrying elections and running governmental enterprises, "selling" candidates and platforms. Like other entrepreneurs, their chief aim is success—success that means the wielding of power. The gaining and retaining of power and the satisfaction of vanity secured from occupying public place become their outstanding characteristics, and to obtain the satisfaction of these desires they bend their energies. Some are scrupulous, some are not; some are high-minded, many think they are; some strive for principles, some for graft, but the majority for the satisfaction of success. This political psychology has had its effect upon history. The politicians' place in our national development can be understood only in the light of a knowledge of these dominant traits. The history of the Democratic party during the interlude between the sectional struggles of 1850 and 1854 presents an excellent field for the study of the genus politician. In those days public opinion was generally apathetic and the politicians plied their trade with little interference.[3]

It is generally conceded today that the broad general forces which shape the history of the nation are climatic and economic. It may be also safely stated in

[3] Roy F. Nichols: *The Democratic Machine, 1850-1854* (New York, 1923), pp. 13-14. See also Nichols: "The Democratic Machine, 1850-1854," *Studies in History, Economics and Public Law.* ed. Faculty of Political Science of Columbia University, Vol. CXI, No. 1, p. 13. I have always read too fast to be a good proofreader, so it was necessary to insert an errata sheet in the version printed in *Studies.* This meant I had to condense pp. 13–14 into one page in that edition.

American history the causes of the struggles for independence, the conflict between North and South and now the fight between capital and labor which, generally speaking, have taken up our entire history are all fundamentally based on economic issues. To discuss these conflicts, their causes and effects, in general terms as the conflict of section against section and class against class does not however, lead to a profound understanding of the workings of history, unless particular attention is paid to the personnel of these groups and to the machinery used by these sections or classes in their struggle for control of government. This machinery has been the party system. This government of the United States almost from the adoption of the Constitution has been conducted by officials owing allegiance to one large party or another. The keystone of this system has been the party organization, or the machine.

Many historical writers in discussing the various parties in the history of the United States have only discussed the results of the movement of the machinery without studying its actual detailed workings. Those who have given it more attention have, however, confined themselves to attempts to generalize the peculiar methods of parties with here and there quoting an example to illustrate a general phenomenon. No very marked attempt has been made to take any period and study the consecutive workings of a nationwide party machine, taking it apart and analyzing the various little wheels and cogs and explaining their nature and the reasons and principles governing their movements. In order to explain the important place of party machinery as a vital force to be reckoned with in the true understanding of the history of the United States in any period, this study will aim to take apart and analyze the various parts of the machine, often minute and seemingly unimportant, and discover, if possible, the governing force of the machine. This analysis will in a manner show not only the composition of the machine and how it goes but more important why and if it accomplishes its purpose, will show how some events often take their turn merely because of friction among the parts of this machine.[4]

From this standpoint, namely the attitude of the politician through whom generally ethical and economic forces must work, we wish to approach the period of the Civil War.

This catastrophe has been studied as the work of powerful and purposeful leaders. Moral and economic prophets preached against a society's sin and on behalf of a section's interest and were able to arouse an indignant people to arms. But in all this the politician has been neglected. Then as always he was desirous of adding to his power, of gaining advancement and office and diverting attention from the "practical" side of his art. His hand was on the public pulse, he recognized the possibilities of stimulating popular prejudice to his own advantage. Political organization began to back propaganda, a political press and political orators did their work in manufacturing or adopting issues which pandered to a worked-up prejudice. There were always offices to be won, spoils to be enjoyed and above all power to be wielded—and the politician values power more than principle and economic gain. Politicians' methods contributed a great deal to the condition that brought on the Civil War.[5]

This frame of reference with the exception of the economic determinism was to continue to prove useful

[4] MSS memorandum written in 1922–3.
[5] Nichols: *Democratic Machine,* pp. 13-14.

as I proceeded with my research. In the meantime I concluded my initial study with a judgment:

> A more dangerous consequence of this system was becoming apparent. The continued policy of dodging issues and the continual fear of displeasing someone was destroying the moral calibre of the leaders of the Democracy. They had not that morale of security which would have come from the knowledge that they had the enthusiastic backing of a considerable body of public opinion. In its place was an inferiority complex produced by their lack of any inspiring ethical or moral guiding principle. Consequently their experiences as politicians bred in the politicians' school unfitted them for producing and laying before Congress in December, 1853, any program which would inspire the masses with the feeling that here were leaders, men of greater strength and foresight than their fellows. But worse than this, the leaders had lost the power of recognizing the force of a moral issue and when the Kansas-Nebraska Bill was introduced on the political stage after such a prelude, these so-called heads of the government failed to realize its consequences and were unable to understand or to cope with the rising tide of moral indignation.[6]

The year 1921–2 saw the completion of our two dissertations in sight. I was publishing mine in the Columbia University series of Studies in History, Economics, and Public Law, which was managed by the Faculty of Political Science. Jeannette's *History of Alaska* was of more general interest and Arthur H. Clark & Co. considered it a publishing venture under subsidy and offered her a contract. In that year, in order to earn the

[6] *Ibid.*, p. 226.

subsidy money, she accepted an acting professorship of history and the social sciences at Wesleyan College at Macon, Georgia. So in the fall of 1922 we bade each other good-bye as she undertook the ambitious task of teaching American history, European history, political science, economics, and sociology in this girls' college in the heart of the South. We had to make do with daily letters and two visits; we met in Atlanta at Thanksgiving and Jeannette came home at Christmas. At Commencement 1923 we were awarded our degrees, the first couple to receive them in the same department at Columbia on the same day.

Teaching had begun at Columbia even before the degree work was concluded. Jeannette had become an instructor in history in University Extension in the fall of 1919. During the Christmas vacation of 1920 an opportunity came for her to work on her dissertation in the Library of Congress. However, she was an instructor in Extension at Columbia in the introductory course in American history. For the three weeks remaining of the term it was arranged that I should teach the course so that she might stay in Washington and begin her research immediately after the opening of the new year. In January, therefore, I began to teach basic American history from David S. Muzzey's *American History* to the usual variety of students who attended extension classes.

The appointment was not immediately renewed because I, too, spent the second semester of 1920–1 in Washington working on my doctoral dissertation. But in 1921 I was given another one of these classes. More important, Professor Kendrick retained me in Columbia College to give two sections of History 9–10, which embraced American history from 1783 to 1920. So without a title in Columbia College I got my pay with the scrubwomen and maintenance staff. However, as my class in Extension entitled me to status as an "instructor in Extension," I was eligible for membership in the Faculty Club, then housed in one of the old Bloomingdale Asylum buildings at Broadway and 116th Street. It was not until the year following that Kendrick recommended that I be appointed an instructor in Columbia College to continue with two sections in History 9–10 and in addition to become a member of a group guiding a unique educational experiment. I would teach Contemporary Civilization. My first task in preparing myself was to master the art of teaching college American history from 1783 to 1920.

Meanwhile Jeannette undertook a new project. As I was to continue at Columbia on an annual appointment as instructor in history and we had had more than enough of separation, Jeannette accepted an opportunity in New York. While Nathaniel Wright Stephenson had been serving as visiting professor at Columbia he had become acquainted with us. Mrs. John D. Rockefeller, Jr., wished a biography written of her father, the late Senator Nelson W. Aldrich. She was attracted by Stephenson's biographical writing, particularly his work on Lincoln, and she invited him to make a similar interpretation of the Rhode Island leader. He agreed on the understanding that he need neither collect the material nor do the preliminary drafting, for at the time he was engrossed in producing a series of historical motion pictures based on the Yale Chronicles of America. Mrs. Rockefeller and Mr. Stephenson asked that Jeannette undertake to search out and prepare the material for the biography. They readily agreed to her stipulations that she have complete freedom in all phases of her work. She accepted the responsibility with some hesitation, because this was the Progressive Age, and she had a special concern not to become involved in a "commissioned" biography. Thereupon began the discovery and organization of the widely scattered material. During much of the next six years, Jeannette visited many parts of the country, visiting libraries, interviewing almost innumerable associates of Aldrich and their heirs and employees, making notes, organizing them, and also writing preliminary drafts.

Her most exciting and gratifying work was the ferreting out of hitherto undiscovered manuscript collections, to which she was the first person to gain access. She was able to expedite the deposit of a number of them in archival institutions. Mrs. Rockefeller endorsed these efforts, sharing Jeannette's delight when the delicate negotiations came to successful fruition. For example, she unhesitatingly approved conferences with the senior Senator LaFollette and other opponents of her father, despite disapproval by less historically minded members of the family. The relations between these two women representing different backgrounds and situations became one of mutual liking and respect; and during the larger part of the project, progress reporting concerned these two almost exclusively.

Occasionally there were reports to Stephenson from the field. In one instance he thought a Middle Western situation could not be solved and should be abandoned, but being on the ground she nevertheless pursued it and so successfully that he afterward pronounced it to be the most helpful collection of all she unearthed. Latterly, Mr. Stephenson became much interested and wrote the last three drafts of the biography, calling upon Jeannette for critiques of them. They reached different conclusions, as he conceived of Aldrich as primarily an artist in politics and she as the expert political master of the Senate. The work was duly published by Scribner's. It had been for her a strenuous postgraduate education. At its conclusion she began to work on enterprises of her own or of our joint creation.

In the meantime I had started my Columbia College teaching with a more elaborate outline than I had used in the Extension course. We had three textbooks for the two terms, Johnson and Dodd's volumes in the Riverside Series and Lingley's *Since the Civil War*. John Krout, whom I had met in Dunning's seminar, was also appointed as instructor and we were associated in History 9–10. Shortly we decided to make a syllabus and include in it a certain number of economic and social topics to enrich the basic political orientation. For we were in an atmosphere of *The New History* which Robinson had launched as the Intellectual History of Europe and which Dixon Ryan Fox, our mentor, and Arthur M. Schlesinger were developing in the History of American Life, projected in twelve volumes, four of which had already appeared. As we outlined it, American history began as an episode in the commercial revolution, with the colonies as several projects in this venturing. We consolidated the colonial period topically and emphasized environment, population analysis, growth of democracy, religious liberty, and cultural institutions. The revolution was first a striving for autonomy and then for independence. After establishing the republic at home and in the world's tolerance we followed the trail of nationalism and the emergence of an independent culture. The sectional struggle, the growing tensions arising from expansion and conflict produced Civil War and Reconstruction. The post-Reconstruction era was again divided topically into economic, political, thought and culture, and international relations. The twentieth century was presented as a period of social control and world war. This syllabus printed by Columbia was used in History 9–10.

The second part of my assignment as a Columbia instructor was one of my great adventures, namely, teaching sections of Contemporary Civilization, better known as "C. C." For my apprenticeship was not to be confined to doctoral study and conventional history teaching. A group of the Columbia College faculty at the conclusion of World War I had decided that the students needed a type of instruction which would send them into the world with a better grasp of the society in which they were living and the problems which they must face. They must be invited to study a synthesis of the society, culture, or civilization in which they lived and the principal problems, the "insistent" problems with which it was beset. Columbia had been the home of Dewey, Thorndike and Woodworth, James Harvey Robinson, and Charles A. Beard. A group of their disciples was carrying the responsibility for teaching the undergraduates in Columbia College and they had been ready for experiment.

Their purpose was implemented by a course to be required of all Columbia College freshmen in place of previous courses prescribed in history and philosophy. This course included three grand divisions. One dealt with how men behave and why. The second dealt with the evolution of these patterns in Western civilization. The third was an analysis of the insistent problems of the day in international relations; conservation of resources; industrial, political, and educational behavior. The design was to explain those elements of civilization, human values, and to encourage students to realize them by living the Life of Reason. The course met five days a week in sections of twenty-five. Those who taught the course under the leadership of John J. Coss of Philosophy and Harry J. Carman of History were a group numbering about fifteen drawn from the history, philosophy, economics, and government departments. They met once a week at lunch and worked from a syllabus which was constantly in a state of revision. It was the greatest educational experience in my life. It provided me with a broad "civilization" frame of reference and compelled me to think and teach in terms of broadest cultural significance.

I had not studied much European history save British history, except for a term in my sophomore year and a two-term course in my senior year. The texts had been Robinson and Hazen's *Europe Since 1815*. Then in my first Columbia year I had listened to Hazen for one term, but after that acquaintance with his nicely turned lectures, which he read, I went over to Carlton Hayes and his Gallic drama. Also, I had never taught any European history nor was I ever to teach it as such. In Contemporary Civilization, however, approximately a third of this course was entitled Survey of the Characteristics of the Present age, which consisted of two divisions, historical background of contemporary civilization, 1400–1870, and the recent history of the great nations, 1871 to the present, with only token reference to the United States. It was based very largely on Hayes's *Political and Social History of Modern Europe*, which I had used as my chief resource in preparing for my Ph.D. minor in European history.

This course was in a state of constant revision. I participated in two of these, the fourth and fifth, prepared in 1923–5. During my last year at Columbia, 1924–5,

I was freed from teaching American history so that I might devote my whole thought to Contemporary Civilization and was largely responsible for redrafting the history section. I incorporated more American history and emphasized the use of "Revolutions" as the division marks in the historical synthesis.

This experience broke the conventional mold of historical thinking and cast me anew in a behavioral form. Dewey, James, Thorndike, McDougall, Watson, Santayana, Robinson, and Beard all presided over this new birth. In fact, Beard had had a personal hand in it. In the winter of 1920–1 he had been our guest for dinner before a history club meeting at which he was to speak. He had written in our guest book, "Silence is best—says Henry Adams." Also at Jeannette's insistence I had gone down to see Beard at the New School to learn of the New Economics and had been advised to read Alfred Marshall and John Maynard Keynes. This latter we had already done.

This teaching program established me in a frame of reference, involving behavioral determination within a "civilization" conceptualization. This meant thinking of individuals and groups behaving in societies in a non-national schema. This was a foundation which I took for granted at the time and did not appreciate so much as an intellectual experience. Rather it was to me a committee project in which I learned much of the dynamics of small groups. I had never before had any such experience, particularly outside of classes. But this was a peer group engaged in a project which was to be of great advantage to me. For naturally by my experience I was shy and a lone worker.

Teaching Irwin Edman's *Human Traits and their Social Significance* and John Herman Randall, Jr.'s

Modern Mind in the Making was fitting my thinking into a frame of pragmatism as well as behaviorism. Surely new winds of doctrine were blowing and they were even nearer by in the history department. Not only was Carman a leader in the Civilization approach but Dixon Ryan Fox was pioneering in the new Social History move. Kendrick was the first at Columbia to teach recent American history, discovering the twentieth century.

This too was a day of idealism, a new liberalism. The liberal weeklies, *The Nation, The New Republic,* and *The Freeman* were much read in the spirit of Herbert Croly's *Promise of American Life,* and the *American Mercury* spoke for Mencken, Nathan, and, some seemed to think, for God. Also in the narrower realm of history there was beginning the great controversy over who was responsible for the recent war, the *Kriegschuldfrage.* One of the main protagonists of a reassignment of blame was Harry Elmer Barnes, a Columbia Ph.D. who began to reveal allied ulterior motivation and to attempt to lift some of the burden of guilt from Germany's shoulders. He took special issue with Professor Charles Downer Hazen, friend of France, and acrimonious dispute flowed out from tongue and pen, in the halls, classrooms, cafeterias, and the Faculty Club.

Besides the seminars and lecture courses, there were gatherings in the library and the cafeterias, amidst the weird decorations in University Hall and in the Flying Fame on Amsterdam Avenue. Also there was tea in the Women's Lounge in Philosophy Hall and meetings of the various departmental clubs in and out of Kent Hall, notably the history group. In these various gathering places there was much discussion, not only of courses and preliminary examinations, but also of current books. Benedetto Croce's *History: Its Theory and Practice* was one of the favorites, though then not mine. My principal historical philosopher was Henry Adams. I had read his *Education* at Rutgers, so when I came to Columbia and found all agog about this book I brushed up my interest.

Professor Dunning had written a review article of it entitled "Henry Adams on Things in General" which several of us secured as reprints from the *Political Science Quarterly*. Adams's pessimism and the more reassuring theories of Croce were matters of frequent debate. At the time I made note of a characteristic passage from Henry Adams and dedicated myself to overcoming it: "Meanwhile he watched mankind march on, like a trained pack horse on the Snake River, tumbling from one morass into another, and at short intervals, for no reason but temper, falling to butchery, like Cain."

Another of the influences of these seminar years on Morningside was Benjamin B. Kendrick. He was in charge of the American history teaching in Columbia College and he was pioneering in recent American history. For at that time it was hardly respectable to be interested in anything after 1876, presumably on the ground that nothing could be effectively described and interpreted until at least fifty years after the event, for not until then would the evidence be in. But Kendrick would accept no such limitations. He was giving a very thoughtful course in recent American history in the graduate school and was active in the conceptualization of the Contemporary Civilization Course.

Another of his interests was the organization of informal discussion groups. In 1922, for instance, Harold E. Stearns together with Van Wyck Brooks, George Jean Nathan, Walton Hamilton, Lewis Mumford, H. L.

Mencken, and various other active minds shared a concern. They felt that "the most moving and pathetic fact in the social life of America" was "emotional and aesthetic starvation." As they believed that American civilization was "still in the embryonic stage, with rich and with disastrous possibilities of growth," they wanted to drive "home with telling force" an understanding of this situation "to the consciousness of the ordinary man." So they produced thirty essays on the various phases of American life which were published under the title *Civilization in the United States. An Inquiry by Thirty Americans.* Some wag shortly denominated them as "Thirty Tired Radicals." Kendrick invited a number of us to meet with him weekly and discuss these essays, one by one, each under the leadership of one of the group. I undertook to guide the discussion of Walton Hamilton's essay on "Economic Opinion." Here we had an opportunity to consider the "new economics" of the Progressive Era which turned away from the Manchester school of iron laws to the heady doctrine that if "problems can be intelligently handled as they emerge," the "good life for all" might be within the realm of realization. This was the doctrine of editors of the liberal weeklies, *The Freeman, The Nation, The New Republic,* which we found so congenial.

We read *The Nation* on our honeymoon and Keynes's *Economic Consequences of the Peace* which Dr. McGiffert (who was sailing with Mrs. McGiffert and their daughter Katherine, on the S.S. *St. Paul*) lent us. Also it was a presidential year. In Paris we learned that the Republicans had nominated Harding and Coolidge, and in Florence that Cox and Roosevelt were to be their opponents. From *The Nation* we learned about the revolt against these choices, the formation of the Farmer

Labor party and the nomination of a ticket which we determined to support. On the voyage home we were part of a lively university group and there we talked a good deal of politics. We took a straw vote on this one-class boat which produced 34 Farmer Labor tallies out of 242, the majority were for Harding (129). Our enthusiasm continued after we landed. We attended a street rally which Columbia permitted us to hold on the campus, and one Saturday night a carload of us toured part of Manhattan making speeches. Needless to say, we made no impression on the Harding landslide of that year. Progressivism for the time being was in eclipse.

These Columbia years were indeed rich in variety and new experience. We soon realized that we had the cultural wealth of the great metropolis at our command. Short rides on the subway expresses, the "elevated," and the picturesque promenades on the Fifth Avenue buses along either Riverside Drive or Central Park brought us to the New York Public Library, the great variety of the Broadway stage, the Metropolitan Opera, Carnegie Hall, the Metropolitan Museum of Art, the Museum of Natural History, the zoos, the Aquarium. The variety was infinite and so rich. In sharp contrast in the world of sports, New York was the home of the Giants and the Yankees, while the Dodgers were across the East River; and there was Madison Square Garden. In the fall there were football spectacles at the Polo Grounds.

New York was also the place where the Horatio Alger heroes made good. Wall Street was down at the tip of the island, and interestingly enough Columbia's business offices and the treasurer, in some respects superior to President Butler, had his headquarters in Wall Street. New York too was the great port, the gateway to Europe, and every June throngs from the university embarked for inspiration and relaxation in the famed centers of the older, parent cultures. Gotham was likewise the great newspaper center. The *Times,* the *Tribune,* the *Post* were flourishing and some new tabloids were beginning to appear. Here likewise were the great publishing houses, Macmillan, Harper's, Century, and an enterprising young man, Alfred A. Knopf, had entered the lists as an innovator.

New York was the place too of religious ferment. Fundamentalists and Modernists were in combat. A great cathedral had been in the building since 1892, a commanding feature of Morningside. Union Theological Seminary with its neat campus and jewel-like chapel was the home of Arthur C. McGiffert, Hugh Black, and Harry Emerson Fosdick. John Haynes Holmes was establishing his Community Church, soon to be joined in his pulpit by John Herman Randall. New York had a distinguished clergy and the graduate student were he so minded could make a different choice of a preacher each Sunday with no need for duplication during any academic year term.

A very definite phase of our graduate experience was to travel. This was particularly important for me, as I had never been anywhere outside of the East. The spring of 1922, as soon as the university closed, I was to cross the Alleghenies and have my first sight of the West; also I was to be introduced to relatives. We started off from Grand Central on the Wolverine, for we were to make our first stop at Kalamazoo to be driven to Schoolcraft, Michigan, to see a dearly beloved great aunt. The train stopped a few minutes at an overlook of Niagara Falls, so I saw my first great natural wonder. After a most delightful visit at Schoolcraft where Jeannette's great-grandfather had taken out a section of land on Gourdneck Prairie in 1850, we proceeded to Chicago. Here all at once I met five brothers and sisters, three sisters and brothers-in-law, and five nieces and nephews. For one with no relatives, save two cousins, this was a very unusual and pleasant experience. Then on Memorial Day we drove down to another homestead in Kankakee County at Momence, Illinois, and met some dozen more. Despite the interference of the Memorial Day parade, holiday traffic, and a puncture we made our train in Chicago and returned eastward on the Pennsylvania with a view of Horseshoe Curve and a stopover at Harrisburg to visit the munificent and magnificent capitol of the Commonwealth.

The year 1924 brought a new high point in travel. One of our dear friends at Columbia was a fellow graduate student, A. Howard Meneely, of the University of Washington, later to be president of Wheaton College in Massachusetts. He realized my provincial limitations and arranged for me to be invited to teach in the summer session at the University of Washington. In those days transcontinental railroads were eager for passenger business and when the arrangements for our sojourn in Seattle were consummated, the railroads soon found it out. An agent visited me and we bought a huge round-trip ticket. For a fare and a third we acquired a ticket which allowed us to go to Seattle via Los Angeles and return by the Canadian Pacific with numerous stopovers. We started out again on the Wolverine, stopped off in Schoolcraft and Chicago for brief visits—and then westward ho! We set out on the Rock Island and then came to me a great experience: we crossed the Mississippi at Rock Island and, as I viewed its broad expanse, I had a flash of historical understanding which I have never forgotten. I was now in the Great West. We stopped at Des Moines, Iowa, to see Jeannette's sister and another capitol, on to Denver and another state capitol, then through the Royal Gorge and my first sight of the Rockies. Incidentally, I got altitude sickness and arrived at Salt Lake City in rather bad shape. Here were more hospitable relatives and a third state capitol. Then the desert, the heat, and eventually Los Angeles. It seemed that almost all of Jeannette's relatives had gone there or to Long Beach, Venice, San Gabriel, and other missions and their hospitality was delightful. We worked up the great state via Yosemite and came around to San Francisco by Sacramento and a fourth state capitol.

Here was San Francisco Bay and Jeannette's brother. He boarded the train before it reached Oakland and introduced us to the great city via the ferry, alas no more. To approach the Bay City at sunset was another of the many almost overwhelming experiences of that glorious summer. We had several days at what I was told must never be called Frisco with a ride to the Cliff House, my first sight of the Pacific, a trip down the peninsula to my first visit at Stanford where I was then and later to find so much. But we had to go on, for summer session in Seattle was almost at hand. So we boarded a through train at Third Street and, passing Shasta, two days later were at Seattle, with our only glimpse of Portland through the car window after dark.

The summer at Seattle was delightful. The grand master of things historic, Edmond S. Meany, welcomed us. The students were alert, the climate ideal, no heat, no rain, perpetual sun and blue sky. The only drawback of nature was a constant haze made more impenetrable by the smoke of forest fires and we only saw mighty Rainier but twice, even though we went up to Paradise Valley only to spend a weekend in rain with no visibility. My teaching duties enabled us to take numerous trips. One unforgettable weekend was spent in Portland where I learned of the beauty of the Columbia, Multnomah Falls, and Mt. Hood. A trip down the great river to Astoria brought a new wave of history which nearly ended in heart failure as we ran to stop the night train to Seattle, all poised to start down the track as we ran in front of the engine to keep it from starting. Fortunately for us our efforts were persuasive. Also we became acquainted with silver dollars and occasional gold pieces. But it all had to end.

And then our return trip. We were going Canadian Pacific. We sailed from Seattle to Vancouver with a stopover at Victoria, that most English of American cities. From Vancouver we turned our faces eastward. We were going to break our journey at various points to enjoy the full scenic beauty of the Rockies and to have a little vacation. The first night we spent at Kamloops at the foot of the Rockies and early next morning the glory began. This was before the days of dome coaches but there were open air railroad gondolas with rows of seats. We sat in one of these most of the time as we got deeper and deeper into the heart of the great mountains. We spent a night at Glacier where the Canadian Pacific had a hotel. Here we clambered to and over the Glacier and had a ride to a beaver dam. Then on to Hector, B.C., where the railroad maintained a camp and where we had a bungalow for a week at Lake Wapta. This was full of hiking and exploring with some congenial young Canadians. Then on to Banff and Lake Louise. At Banff we essayed horseback riding. I had a horse who only knew trail work and even on Banff's main street he or she insisted on walking behind Jeannette's mount and nothing I did would bring the horse up beside hers.

With regret we came down out of the mountain via Medicine Hat and were soon on the monotonous plains. Two stopovers at St. Paul and Minneapolis and then Madison to visit two more state capitols and the universities of Minnesota and Wisconsin. Then Arlington Heights—but our journey was not over. We were going down to Springfield for Lincoln's home town and another state capitol, and finally I was to visit Jeannette's Alma Mater, Knox College. There we spent two delightful days visiting those who had taught her, notably Dr. and Mrs. Drew and her history mentor, John Leonard Conger. We visited Old Main, Whiting Hall, saw Jean's room, Miss Stayt the dean of women, Dean Simonds, and numerous others. We little thought then that later we would return for honorary degrees—but this was far in the future. I got back to New York for what was to be my last year at Columbia.

Thus from 1920 to 1924 I had entered for the first time the great United States. In 1920 I knew it only from the pages of books. In these five years I had traveled its great breadth, seen much of the beauty, grasped but faintly its size, seen many of its historic spots and become conditioned to constant journeying for research, recreation and a broadening of the mind. It was in the most real sense a part of my preparation for my understanding of my profession.

While I was working on my dissertation beginning my teaching and traveling I was already thinking about further writing and publication. I had three seminar reports which might become articles and also I had a mass of notes for the years between 1854 and 1860 which had been put aside when I redefined the chronological limits of my thesis. There was one group from the Gideon Welles papers dealing with the financing of the First Republican National Campaign in 1856 which I found particularly interesting. I had first tackled the question of political campaign funds in studying the financing of the Democratic presidential race in 1852 but had been able to find very little. So this correspondence among the Republican National Committee four years later which offered a good deal of detail in facts and figures led me to write it up. The complete story was not in these papers and so I sought further manuscript material, particularly the papers of the chairman of the committee, Governor Edwin D. Morgan of New York. We sometimes attended the Brick Presbyterian Church on Fifth Avenue and I had noticed a stained-glass window to his memory. So I asked the pastor, Rev. Dr. William P. Merrill, if there were any of that family still in the church who might have the governor's papers or know where they were. I could discover none. Therefore in writing up what I had I decided to put the matter in the form of a question. Here is what we know, where can we find the whole story? This I sent to the *American Historical Review,* submitted for publication in the department "Notes and Suggestions." This was accepted. A number of years later the Morgan papers were deposited in Albany and I was able to study them.

I had typed up my seminar paper on Andrew Johnson's first six weeks to submit with my application for a fellowship in 1920 and now I undertook to rewrite it as a possible article. Professor Fox gave it a critical reading with a number of suggestions, but in the end I decided not to submit it. Quite otherwise was the account of the efforts to punish Jefferson Davis. During the winter of 1922–3 President Butler authorized the appointment of three new professors to fill up the ranks so sadly depleted by the deaths of Botsford, Dunning, and Osgood. Osgood's successor was Evarts B. Greene, who came on from Illinois to take the leadership in American history. One of his projects was the organizing of a conference in American history which should meet monthly and to which the historians in the metropolitan area would be invited. He acted as chairman and appointed me secretary. Various members of the conference were invited to read papers. In due course I was asked to present the Jefferson Davis piece. Also, Greene spoke to Jameson about it and the program committee of the American Historical Association heard of it in the course of their planning. The Association was to meet in Richmond in December, 1924, and one of the sessions was to be devoted to the Confederacy. Professor St. George L. Sioussat of the University of Pennsylvania was chairman of the committee and invited me to read this paper. I had already met him at the Historical Society of Pennsylvania while working there on my thesis. I had sent him and Dean Herman V. Ames copies of my book and they had invited me to come to Philadelphia in the spring of 1924 to discuss joining the department of the university of Pennsylvania. I had gone over to dinner but nothing had come of it at that time. Now Professor Sioussat invited me to read the paper. I accepted and prepared a twenty minute version which I read in due course in the historic capital city of the Confederacy at the Jefferson Hotel. At Greene's encouragement I rewrote this paper with the proper annotation and sent it to Dr. Jameson for the *American Historical Review*. This too was accepted.

But these were articles and more important was the

question of what should be the next book. This was an age of interest in biography. Scholarly biographies, popular biographies, and debunking biographies came into the bookstores in profusion. I was closely associated with Nathaniel Wright Stephenson, who took over Dunning's work at his death, who had published his *Lincoln* in the spring of 1922. I had been thrilled by it and had my first chance at reviewing when at his suggestion the New York *Tribune* asked me to review it for their Sunday literary section. I was in midstream of biographical waters; I would write one. After considering Salmon P. Chase, I got a new idea. My attention had been fixed on President Franklin Pierce by the intensive study I had made of his election. Likewise I had done a good deal of research on his administration when my thesis project had a more comprehensive definition. I soon decided that I would join Hawthorne and become a biographer of the fourteenth President.

This meant a new approach to research. Working on the Democratic machine, I had been reading the papers of a variety of active politicians seeking to fathom their individual motivations and behavior patterns, their personal relations and the results thereof, their behavior in small groups and in the mass, the drama of conventions, influenced by the New Hampshire Winston Churchill. And I did this without any conscious relationship to other disciplines. In graduate school I had on occasion gone in to listen to Giddings and Ogburn of the sociology department and, curiously enough, I had remembered one of Giddings' lectures on leadership in which he had discussed the proposition that in any group there were always two classes, one that fished and the other that cut bait. Also I had listened in on McBain when he was talking about the relation of social psychology to the problems of democracy and citing Wallas's *The Great Society,* McDougall's *The Group Mind,* and Trotter's *Instincts of the Herd in Peace and War* and anticipating some phases of the New Deal.

Now I would concentrate on the behavior of one politico. Here I was again to be influenced by Winston Churchill and his novels on New Hampshire politics. For New Hampshire was Pierce's state and I was going back there to use the sources and to learn the environment.

But this was to be from another base, at another time. The years of my apprenticeship were about over and the time was approaching for me to start on my own.

Living in Gotham had been a stimulating education, for here was every type of intellectual activity. It was the center of the nation's cultural life. There, a dweller of any perception knew he was living where things happened, where the leaders in his world dwelt and labored. In a real sense he could not only see their visions and dream their dreams, but feel that he had some small part in the great surge of intellectual creation. Great was it then to be alive, but to be young was very heaven.

III

INDEPENDENCE

IN 1925 we received an invitation that enabled us to leave Columbia and set up for ourselves. A call from the University of Pennsylvania brought us to live in Philadelphia, at the other end of the Philadelphia division of the Pennsylvania Railroad. We had no previous acquaintances in that city, as I had visited it but once before and but for two weeks while working on my dissertation at the Historical Society of Pennsylvania. Though I had not gone out to the university, I met Professor St. George L. Sioussat, who had recently been called there from Brown to succeed McMaster. He worked at the Historical Society frequently and he hospitably invited me to lunch. In 1924 I went over to meet the history department, I believe at Dr. Sioussat's suggestion, and in 1925 accepted tender of an assistant professorship. We took the shift rather casually and during the summer made no move to secure a place to live. I taught in the 1925 Columbia summer session and at its close we renewed our explorations, traveling a month in Nova Scotia and New Brunswick. When we got home September 15 we had everything to do and in two weeks we did it. We spent a day in Philadelphia, where by canvassing the streets in the near vicinity of the university we found an apartment for ourselves and another within a block for my mother, then we went back to New York, packed up our things and moved. Not until this had been accomplished did I visit the university and find out where the history department was and where I was to be quartered.

The department I was joining was unique in its composition. All but one colleague and myself, six in number, were full professors. Four of them, Edward P. Cheyney, Herman V. Ames, Arthur C. Howland, and William E. Lingelbach, had been associated together for about twenty years. Cheyney had been at the university for some forty years and he and John Bach McMaster had built the department, with McMaster retiring in 1920. About the same time Albert E. McKinley had been invited from Temple to develop work in teacher training for the department. As Dr. Cheyney had recently been very ill, an assistant professor, Witt Bowden, a recent Ph.D. in the department, was invited to share the English history load as I was invited to share the load in American economic history, a course swollen by the postwar influx of students.

My colleagues gave us a warm welcome and let me have almost complete freedom. I was treated as an equal partner despite my youth and inexperience. My suggestions were given sympathetic attention and often accepted. Immediately I felt that I was a part of the team and as much responsibility as I wanted was mine.

I was promptly introduced to the Lenape Club and my acquaintance grew. There was no faculty club, but a small group of kindred spirits had thrown three small dwellings on McAlpin Street together and had set up a luncheon club where a steward and his wife served the daily midday meal at two long tables. Here I fellowshipped with congenial spirits like Don Young, James T. Young, Karl Miller, Sam Fernberger, Bob Brotemarkle, Francis Philbrick, Les Klimm, Cyril James, E. M. Patterson, Tom Cope, my colleagues in the history department, and many others. Then after lunch the lounge provided place for conversation, reading, cards, and chess and I could watch the perpetual cribbage contest between Fernberger and Brotemarkle as well as the weird varieties of chess. As these were the days of prohibition there was no bar. The club was a cross section of the faculty. As all schools were represented in its membership, no one of them dominated, although there were more from the College and Wharton School, but that was natural as there were more of them.

At first my teaching experience was traumatic. Hitherto I had worked as part of a team, teaching courses which had been planned collectively, always meeting the students in small sections. My method of teaching was to lead discussions based on texts and syllabi. Now I must lecture to large groups ranging from seventy-five to a hundred and seventy-five. I had three pairs of lectures to prepare each week, one pair of which I gave twice. One set for the girls in the School of Education could be drawn largely from the material I had gotten together for History 9–10 at Columbia. A second on the Civil War era in American history, 1850–65, represented my special interest, then and thereafter; it was my intellectual stimulant and I "got it up" with relish. The third was a horse of another color.

The principal reason for the invitation to Pennsyl vania had been the post-World War I expansion of the student body. It had been particularly great in a course in American economic history, known as History 8, elected largely by students from the Wharton School of Finance and Commerce. Professor Albert E. McKinley was in charge of it but it had outgrown any lecture hall available on the campus and it had to be divided. So I was assigned the overflow, which amounted this first year to a hundred and seventy-five.

Dr. McKinley lectured on the history of a series of economic functions, agriculture, finance, commerce, industry, labor, and the like, and assignments were added for use in the weekly quiz sections from Ernest L. Bogart's *Economic History of the United States* and Bogart and Thompson's *Readings in the Economic History of the United States.* I followed the program carefully and endeavored to interest the students and myself, but I was a political historian out of water.

I looked back nostalgically to my "Civilization" frame of reference at Columbia and I soon undertook to introduce that idea at Penn. I worked with my colleague, Witt Bowden, and succeeded in persuading the faculty to approve a course in the history of civilization to be required of all who did not present European history at entrance. At this particular time Lynn Thorndike launched his *History of Civilization,* which could be used as a text, and Bowden and I prepared a syllabus for it which was published by the same firm. I never taught the course; Bowden and a new assistant professor of European history, Arthur P. Watts, called for the purpose, were assigned that responsibility.

It was at this point that Charles and Mary Beard brought out their *Rise of American Civilization.* As Beard was the foremost American economic historian of the day, I had no difficulty in substituting this masterpiece for Bogart in History 8, and as I assumed responsibility for all the lecturing, I united the civilization concept with Beard's economic interpretation in place of the descriptions of economic functioning which Dr. McKinley and I had been using. At this time Julian P. Boyd came up from Duke to be one of our corps of teaching fellows. He and I prepared a syllabus following a simple general outline:

Organizing a New Society
Becoming Independent
Experimenting 1819–50
Nationalizing 1850–79
Realizing Economic Potentialities 1879–98
World Power 1898–

It was his idea that the subheadings should not be topics but a series of questions designed "to stimulate a speculative and critical attitude toward history which is the very antithesis of the memorizing process."

The reorientation involved in the preparation of these various courses did not give me much time for research but it was not completely neglected. Samuel F. Bemis, then of George Washington University, was editing a series of volumes called *The American Secretaries of State.* He invited me to write a sketch of Jeremiah S. Black. So during the Christmas recess in 1925–6 I went back to Washington to work in the State Department archives. Then as soon as the spring term was over I returned to my work on Franklin Pierce, spending a good part of the summer in his native New Hampshire. I had been there before when, working on my dissertation, I had sought Pierce material for the campaign of 1852. I had stayed at the Eagle Hotel, the Pelican House of Churchill's imagining, where Jethro Bass held forth in the Throne Room. Now that I was including Pierce's whole career, there was much more to be done. This time I did not stay at the Eagle but in Mrs. Kimball's boardinghouse on Warren Street not far from the Historical Society and the Capitol.

The Historical Society was a beautiful marble building, built by Amos Tuck, who was a benefactor of New Hampshire's cultural institutions, notably the society and Dartmouth, and who lived in Paris. This institution was directed by Major Otis G. Hammond and maintained immaculately. He was most cooperative and friendly. He introduced me to a number of people who reminisced to me. He took me down to Pierce's family home and birthplace in Hillsboro where his introduction to Pierce's grandnieces, the Misses Susan and Mary Pierce, proved very helpful. They not only showed me the home, books, furniture, pictures, but a number of items of personalia belonging to the President and his wife. They had a mass of miscellaneous papers which they permitted me to take to Concord and use in the Historical Society. Then too there was the major's staff, Miss Freeman, Miss Fulford, Mrs. Martin, and Miss Sanborn, who helped me find and use the society's rich store of material.

I started in immediately on a large group of letters that Pierce had written to his sister, Fanny McNeil, and in which he had artlessly revealed much of his character. I also read newspapers, explored the shelves, and talked to the major and certain of his friends about New Hampshire politics. After hours I walked much in Concord streets, reconstructing the capital of Pierce's day. I learned the state capitol almost by heart and I browsed in the state library and the little local library. I attended the churches, visited the cemetery, and in general tried to place Pierce in his habitat. Almost everyone was cooperative and the people in the Historical Society soon became my friends and did everything possible to aid my explorations.

In only two instances was the experience disappointing. Pierce had two law partners, Josiah Minot and John H. George. The former was survived by a daughter who refused to see me; later I found out that her father's papers had been destroyed, so I probably lost nothing there. The latter was represented by a son who received me at his house but assured me that little had survived. When the son died, Major Hammond found in his attic a great mass of correspondence, including the campaign correspondence of 1852 which George's father had filed as Pierce's campaign manager. Fortunately I had not yet concluded my work and back I went to Concord for another profitable sojourn in this friendly atmosphere.

By 1929 the biography of Pierce began to show signs of being finished. At the same time the research on Aldrich was done and it was then that Mrs. Rockefeller prescribed and provided a winter holiday for Jeannette. At Christmastime Jeannette invited me to be her guest on a trip to Cuba. I had been hesitant about flying but after a stormy boat trip from Key West to Havana I was glad to agree to fly back, Pan-American. Thus our flying days began. What an awe-inspiring experience it was. We took all kinds of precautions. I didn't eat anything on the day of our trip so that there would be nothing to cause nausea. We stuffed our ears and chewed gum vigorously. Nothing happened but a smooth gliding over the sea and the Florida Keys, during which, at the suggestion of the pilot, we sent a radiogram home: "Flying high. Everything lovely." Thereupon I had to return to university classes while Jeannette settled down in Miami Beach to relax and swim. As I had finished the draft of Franklin Pierce, she read it by the sea and gave me the benefit of expert criticism, incidentally removing some seven hundred "considerables," a word that had become an obsession with me. It was a labor of love which I much appreciated, but which certainly limited the extent of her relaxation; nevertheless she obviously was happy in doing it. Before she returned north I rejoined her and we completed exploring Florida by bus and visiting Savannah, Charleston, and Columbia, South Carolina.

Not until 1931 did she bring to a climax her acquaintance with Pierce. Then when the book was going through the University of Pennsylvania Press, I unexpectedly turned up some new material. Jeannette suggested that she could see it through while I showed my mother much of the United States. Mother was not getting any younger and had traveled very little. So she and I had planned a rail trip to the Pacific Coast via the Canadian Pacific and then down the coast to Los Angeles and back through Salt Lake City and the Yellowstone, Chicago, and Niagara Falls. With the cooperation of the University of Pennsylvania Press, Jeannette managed to inject a brief but delightful motor trip along New England's back roads as far north as Barre, Vermont, before returning to complete the proof revision. Altogether it was a strenuous summer.

So the Pierce book was published; in its pages I had taken stock of what I had done. I had not undertaken this biography in order to defend an unpopular figure from his detractors. I endeavored to make this a personal history rather than a general "life and times" biography. I profited as much as I could from the prevailing modes of biographical writing that sought to explain the behavior and motivation of the man with such attention to the findings of psychology and psychiatry as I could muster. But beyond this I was convinced that he was the victim of the peculiar time in which he lived and of the important social changes that marked it.

Pierce, I believed, could not be judged fairly without considering the temper of the times and his own interpretation of them. The four years of Pierce's administration were only a fragment of a longer period marked by important social changes. The United States was beginning to shift from a rural to an urban society; cities and towns, rather than farm and plantation communities, were becoming the centers of American life. Industrialization had established factories and was bringing workers by the hundreds from the country into the towns. The increasing immigration from Europe swelled the population of the coast cities. The building of railroads, the settlement and growth of the West, the increase of trade in the newer regions—all these promoted the establishment and rapid growth of towns. The great multiplication of business enterprises of all kinds and the steady accumulation of capital in the hands of a growing number of wealthy men caused the rich to concentrate in the cities where they gained their wealth. Such tendencies produced an urban environment which was the seat of a rising power. There dwelt men of enterprise and imagination who saw the desirability of quick development which would make more money, provide more comfort, and encourage a higher standard of living.

The progress of the great social change, however, was not uniform throughout the country; the rise of cities and towns occurred largely in the North and West. The South, on the other hand, remained definitely rural because of the investment of its capital in cotton production and because an inflexible social system had developed, quite feudal in some of its aspects, which was stable, conservative, and not easily changed. Two definite societies had emerged, the slow-moving South and the rapidly expanding North. Naturally they could not think alike.

Even in respect to those traditions and ideals which were prized alike by all parts of the country, sectionalism became more pronounced. The nation was thought of as a democracy, an example to those living under monarchy. It had already experienced a surprising growth and development that was prophetic of even greater advance. Americans were proud of their country, its growth, its wealth, and its progressive and enlightened spirit. Their very pride and the common desire to advance brought differences of opinion as to method and rate of progress in such matters as territorial acquisition, business expansion, and social reform.

Pierce's chief difficulty was shared by practically all the political leaders of his day; he did not understand the complex nature of the conflict between the social forces but thought it much simpler than it really was. He did not realize the depth of sectional prejudice, especially the antisouthern feeling in his own New England. He had always dismissed the antislavery movement as an attempt of the opponents of the Democratic party to use and stimulate a prejudice for their own ends. As a consequence neither he nor the other leaders of his party could foresee the popular fury over the repeal of the Missouri Compromise or the inevitable bleeding of Kansas as a result of the application of the cherished principle of popular sovereignty. Pierce believed that democracy was a panacea and that turning the disputed question of slavery in the territories over to the people themselves, far from favoring the South, was an act of the purest patriotism of which any Democratic nationalist could be capable.

Pierce's ideals were the ideals of the pastoral age when life was simple and society less complex. He failed to realize the growing strength and persistence of the new urban power, keenly competitive and acquisitive. The victories over the bank and his battle with the railroads, the defeat of the protective tariff, the Compromise of 1850, all lulled him to a false sense of the strength of a laissez-faire government. Corporations, trade associations, lobbies, organized propaganda—all these devices were in their infancy and their powers were not yet fully recognized. He rested securely in the ideals of the eighteenth-century political and economic thinkers, without realizing that their ideals were no longer sacred, and that powers were rising that knew but little of the struggle for independence which had bred an understanding of these principles.

Urbanization and industrialization are blind, irresistible forces, and no man or set of men can stop them; they are characteristic of the modern age. Pierce, not fully realizing what the new forces were but apprehensive of danger, attempted with all the ability and strength of which he was capable to avoid some of their evils by preaching the historic doctrines of the early days of the republic and by pursuing policies which Buchanan and Lincoln were to attempt to carry on until the latter realized the uselessness of the effort in April 1861. Thus, as American institutions were changing, Pierce was but one of many political leaders who tried and failed to fit the ideals of American democracy to the conditions of an urbanized American society. The Civil War did not really make the needed adjustment; American leaders have been struggling with the puzzle ever since and the problem is still to be solved. Such was my interpretation in 1931 when the book was published.

The year previously I had been promoted as the result of some interest shown in me elsewhere. When this occurred Dr. Ames went to see the provost. Dr. Penniman asked him to write a note in longhand recommending promotion. Then he conferred with Mr. Gates the chairman of the finance committee of the trustees, and by late afternoon I was a full professor. When I think of the paraphernalia of curricula vitarum, outside letters, personnel panels, and provost staff conferences which prevail today, I realize that I grew up in a day of simpler things.

By 1933 we had come to another decision about our way of life. Since we had come to Philadelphia we had been living in apartments, almost literally under the eaves of the university, but now we were thinking of a house in the suburbs. The winter of 1933–4 was very snowy, which complicated our search somewhat but did not dim our enthusiasm. After looking carefully around we narrowed our interest to the college towns of Bryn Mawr, Haverford, and Swarthmore, so that we would be near good libraries at home as well as at the university. We made an offer for a house in Haverford which was not accepted and then we found a wooded lot in Swarthmore upon which we could build.

We bought it under snow. It was a deep lot with eighteen trees, most of which we found we could save. We planned the house ourselves, with Jeannette serving as architect, and contracted with an excellent builder to construct it according to our ideas of an early Georgian house of stone. We sometimes facetiously said we planned a library and built the house around it. With two fireplaces, lots of windows, and five of what the British call "facilities," we had the ultimate in convenience. The stakes were set May 4, 1934, when we personally turned the first spadeful of earth. I hied me to Duke summer school for more "wherewithal," while Jeannette architected. We moved in the first of September. It proved to be a very comfortable and convenient abode through eighteen happy years, in every sense our own. When I became a dean in 1952 we had to move in close to the university.

Teaching and syllabus writing had in the meantime been moving us steadily in the direction of writing a textbook. There were various suggestions from publishers, one of which we accepted when Professor Dana C. Munro, editor of a series for what was then the Century, offered Jeannette and me a contract. Our idea was a one-volume text that would be a synthesis of political, social, and economic history, in other words a cultural history. The plan would be to arrange the history in a series of epochs: European background, colonial, revolutionary, and the like, dividing each of these into its social, economic, and political phases. We wanted particularly to take the material which the authors of the History of American Life series were providing and work it into a new synthesis. We compressed the colonial period into three chapters: the migration, the building of colonies, and the creation of a culture and a sense of autonomy.

We conceived of the work of securing independence as extending from 1763 until 1819 and dividing this section into four parts. The first two had to do with the Revolutionary War and the creation of the republic down to the demonstration of its stability in the election of 1800, and the last two with the threats from European war and internal economic instability. The third period, 1819–65, dealt with the western expansion of population and the move to concentrate in eastern industrial cities and towns. The theme stressed was that these movements of population pulling in opposite directions created a tension which became so taut that it finally snapped and parted. Instead of dividing American history in half at the conclusion of the Civil War, we placed the halfway point at the end of Reconstruction, thus leaving more room for the twentieth century.

The second half of the book featured the growth of big business, urbanization, the farmers' disadvantages, large-scale politics, and our expanding imperial outlook in the world. The problems of this large-scale organization introduced the Progressive age and the responsibilities of world power. World War I and the riot of heedless business expansion brought the crash of 1929 and inaugurated the New Deal which was raising social control to new heights of power at the date of publication.

This volume, published May 1, 1939, was entitled *The Growth of American Democracy,* and we announced our philosophy in its preface.

> The experiment of creating and maintaining a unique republic has been the predominating interest of the people of the United States. Their creation has evolved in an isolated area, discovered and peopled by a much older civilization, under circumstances which left the pioneers and their descendants relatively free and unhampered by direct foreign influence. The character of this American society has been variously described by succeeding generations, but the increasing tendency has been to denominate it a Democracy. In fact today there is no phrase more frequently

spoken or more carelessly defined, than the term "American Democracy." The classic statements most generally revered by Americans have described the experiment as unique because it was dedicated to the equality of men.

This concept of democracy has never included the idea that all men should be maintained at an equal level. Rather, it implies that each shall be given an equal opportunity to reach the level to which his abilities entitle him, unhampered by the control or hindrance of any form of human behavior by a privileged group. Politically, all are supposed to be equal before the law and may vote and hold office. Economically, all should have the right to earn a decent living, to accumulate savings if they so desire, and to raise the level of their standard of living if they are capable. Socially and culturally, all should enjoy liberty of behavior and the pursuit of their ambitions and their interests so long as a reasonable degree of social responsibility governs this liberty. The history of this democracy must embrace therefore a synthesis of American endeavor to establish the ideal socially, economically, and politically.

The course of this experiment has been conditioned by a conflict between two trends produced by the peculiar circumstances of its setting. These trends are the struggle for wealth and power, so generously stimulated by the great resources of the hemisphere, and the desire for a larger measure of freedom and happiness for the individual than has ever been afforded by older civilizations. These conflicting trends have developed simultaneously and often cooperatively. For many years they seemed compatible and correlating. But of late there has been questioning. Can the liberties possible in an age of unused resources and unsettled acres be maintained in a society hemmed in by urban living and dominated by mechanical processes?

> Can America maintain her individuality across a plane-spanned ocean? The success or failure of American Democracy may well be determined by the ability of this versatile society to continue to harmonize changing conditions to fit the cherished spirit of equality.

The coming of the Second World War and the call for a larger, two-volume work led us to expand our text. It was now to be called *The Republic of the United States.* We enlarged it by adding a good deal of material before the Civil War and including the story of the coming of the Second World War and its early phases. The space allotted to the years prior to 1865 increased from thirty to forty per cent of the pages. We emphasized the federal nature of American society and the fact that it was made up of a group of societies which expanded from thirteen to forty-eight. We stressed the significance of the constant process of community building. We introduced this by tracing the establishment of the French and Spanish colonies which became part of the United States as well as the British.

After independence we traced the extension of this process beyond the Alleghenies. This analysis would not only give those living in Florida, along the Gulf, in the Southwest, and along the Pacific shore a clearer sense of their origin but it would remove some of the emphasis on a purely national development and focus attention on the fact that for the first three centuries of our development the idea of community building was one of the main preoccupations of the growing society. It also permitted emphasis on the federal character of the republic and its regional organization, an emphasis which was appealing to me with continually growing attraction. I was learning to appreciate more the problem of the process of cultural evolution and the significance of the fact that as our society had a political image there should be a necessary preoccupation with that image and the process of its formation. The tendency to push aside the political must be resisted.

As the war advanced, the United States government organized a series of American history courses for army and navy trainees who were assigned to the various universities and colleges. They were all required to take American history, so there was a demand for texts. This time the requirement was for a short book. Therefore we cut and rewrote our work and a third version was published under the title of *A Short History of American Democracy* which also included more of the story of the Second World War. Jeannette also prepared a segment which she had written to be published as *Twentieth Century America.* These publications were our teaching adjuncts whenever we worked with undergraduates. We had created a structure of professional activity.

The completion of the textbooks as joint enterprises was followed by a division of interest. We had another joint project, a biography of John Sherman, but to each of us there was a work of major proportions. Jeannette was developing an increasing interest in economics and economic history. The discovery of a mass of data in the papers of Senator William E. Chandler of New Hampshire pointed the way to a study of the use by the United States government of its control of the nature and quality of money as a means of directing its foreign relations. In the years after the Civil War, in the course of re-establishing national credit by regulating the definition of the dollar in terms of world currencies, it began the use of monetary diplomacy. In following this interest she wrote a series of studies bringing the subject down into the present troubled era when the United States attempted, by developing financial aid administered through diplomatic channels, to promote its interests, and particularly to strengthen economies and polities like our own, in the face of hostile communist imperialism. This study carried her into many repositories of data, and while I was traveling about among the archives and depositories in search of my particular interest she was following hers. She reported on some of her findings in papers delivered at historical conventions and in published articles.

Despite the fact that the projects were not so closely knit as when we were working on our joint studies, the kinship of scholarship and mutual historical interest meant that the association was as mutually interesting as ever. We discussed our individual findings and the formulation of problems. We read aloud our writing for critical comment. We were oftentimes in the same archives. We traveled on missions of the same character. We attended innumerable historical conventions; we had the preponderance of our friends among historians. Of course there was some diversity. We both were constant attendants at meetings of the American Historical Association and served it in various responsible assignments. Jeannette, however, was also constant in her attendance at the Mississippi Valley Historical Association, now the Organization of American Historians, at first because she had been born a citizen of the Valley and the Great West. She was a member of its council, its editorial board, and various committees. I specialized in meetings of the various Pennsylvania historical organizations rather than the western associations. She and I were both interested in the Middle States Council for the Social Studies and for a number of years we spent our Thanksgiving recess at their meetings at Atlantic City and wherever the spring sessions were held. In 1942–4 she served as vice president and president, giving the organization a new birth of activity in several very vigorous sessions.

In the meantime I had embarked on another field of investigation. I had not been long at Pennsylvania when Dr. Sioussat pointed out to me that both he and Dr. Ames were more or less committed to political history and I would perhaps advance more rapidly if I undertook to develop an interest not then represented in the department, namely, Latin American history, which I had studied under Shepherd. I agreed to organize work in this field.

The first step was to offer an advanced lecture course for undergraduates based on my work with Shepherd and covering the whole field in textbook fashion. I was not willing to follow this approach with graduate students so I undertook a seminar there. I felt it was essential to choose topics that would enable the students to work in the sources, so, as there were printed records of colonial Spanish American municipalities, I set up several papers in this field for the small seminar that registered. I also needed a research field for myself, for to me research and teaching were inseparable. So I selected the development of diplomatic relations with the Latin American regions. I determined to start at the beginning, namely, with sending commercial agents and consuls to Spanish American ports during the Revolution.

This choice meant research in Washington. The Library of Congress had transcripts and photocopies from the Spanish archives and the diplomatic correspondence of the Continental Congress. The archives of the State

Department were likewise essential. I had already had a brief experience there when I undertook to prepare the sketch of Jeremiah S. Black. It was then that I had become acquainted with Mrs. Natalia Summers, who presided in Room 10 on the ground floor of the old State Department building. This delightful lady, a member of the old Russian Czarist noblesse, had married an American diplomat and when widowed had been placed in charge of the diplomatic archives. She was a lady of great charm and capability who had mastered not only the archival art but had also made herself mistress of much of the contents of the great volumes of dispatches and instructions, in and out letters and reports. I was a frequent visitor and found Mrs. Summers a superb guide who made her domain a most pleasant place in which to work. Besides she was usually able to point out material in out-of-the-way filings that research students might well have overlooked.

I began on the first consular representatives in the West Indies, especially in Cuba. I also investigated our relations with the revolutionaries, particularly in Mexico, where I discovered the redoubtable William Shaler. At the same time I had gotten some material, in my investigation of the diplomacy of Pierce and Buchanan, about the influence of the American farmers' need for fertilizer on our diplomatic relations with Latin America. These interests resulted in papers at the American Historical Association, at George Washington University, and the Second General Assembly of the Pan American Institute of Geography and History, which initially were published separately. These pieces were narrative history with particular reference to the personalities and the wide range of interests involved. One of the agents studied, William Shaler, was active not only in the

Latin American region but in the Far East briefly and in North Africa extensively. The guano interest included a miniature empire among the islands of both hemispheres. But this was but an interlude. In 1936 a specialist in Latin American history, Professor Arthur P. Whitaker, joined the university faculty and I turned to other interests.

Despite my deflection into Latin American history I had no intention of leaving the study of the Democratic party in the 1850's. When I taught in the summer session at Duke in 1934 I worked there and at Chapel Hill, particularly in the C. C. Clay papers at Duke. In 1936 when I taught at Harvard summer session I examined the papers of Charles Sumner, and at home there was always the wealth of the Historical Society of Pennsylvania, particularly the papers of James Buchanan, which I had hurriedly examined in 1921 and which I was giving a more careful reading now that I was nearby. Then there were frequent visits to the Library of Congress. My work at the university was so arranged that I could get away first on Thursday night and then later on Wednesday night to spend the rest of the week at the great library. In 1938 I had my first sabbatical and this took us to Athens, Georgia, where dwelt Miss Mary Lamar Erwin, granddaughter of Howell Cobb, to whom we were introduced by my friend Merton Coulter of the University of Georgia. She had her grandfather's papers in her home and we hoped she would let us examine them. We were none too certain what her response would be. In the course of feeling our way through conversation, she referred with much pride to her collection of old-time gowns. Jeannette expressed a desire to see the dresses. Miss Erwin forthwith led Jeannette up the stairs, turned on the middle landing and called down to the two men below, "Here are the keys to the outhouse full of papers. You can go out to see them while I show Mrs. Nichols the gowns." Squirrels and rain had preceded ourselves, but in time the papers went into the expert care of the University of Georgia.

What I was working on had no very careful definition. I was proceeding from the close of the administration of Pierce to the breakup of the Democratic party in 1860, completing the field I had chosen for my dissertation, but I had not decided upon any name for it. As it was all happening in the Buchanan administration I generally replied, when asked, that I was working on Buchanan. However, I had no intention of writing his biography, for this would have meant an intensive study of Pennsylvania politics from 1815 on, a reading of his long record in Congress, both House and Senate, and an analysis of our diplomacy while he was minister to Russia and to Great Britain and Secretary of State. I was confining myself to the history of the Democratic party from 1856 to 1861 and seeking the answer to the question of why it broke up, namely, the answer to the question I had asked in 1919.

Search for material took me into all parts of the nation. The University of Chicago secured the Douglas papers, so I spent a month there, finishing the study of them I had begun in North Carolina at the invitation of George Fort Milton. The complexities of Bleeding Kansas led me to spend another month at Topeka. I taught a summer at the University of Oregon and visited the library of the University of Washington. I had a few days in Utah and a few more in the Huntington Library, the Stanford Library, and the University of California. And so it went. When I was finished I had worked in twenty-six states.

Much of my time since 1920 has been spent in research libraries and I cannot say too much in their praise. The Historical Society of Pennsylvania was almost a second home to me for many years. New Hampshire proved an ideal environment in which to work and I learned much about what the staffs of historical societies and libraries can do, if they are professionally and temperamentally expert, to contribute to the success of those who consult their files. Traveling from state to state over the years I am glad to be able to say that my experiences have been uniformly pleasant and have contributed much to the quality of my work. I have had contact with librarians and custodians from Maine to California and from Florida to the State of Washington and I know whereof I speak. I have on rare occasions found a lack of intimate knowledge of the material in their charge but never any unwillingness to be helpful. In some instances, as in the Library of Congress, the National Archives, the Historical Society of Pennsylvania, and the New Hampshire Historical Society, the cooperation went far beyond the line of duty. While mentioning these four, at least a score more come to mind which I am almost ashamed not to cite.

Most important were the resources in Washington. During these years it was possible to spend an increasing amount of time on research there. We had had our first view of Washington in 1920. Arriving at the Union Station, we looked out to see the Capitol dome looming ahead, but in the foreground there was then a mass of temporary construction built to house government workers during the late war. We were to live to see this finally torn down together with a mass of unsightly dwellings cluttering the area and to see the landscaping and redesigning that made it possible to arrive at the nation's capital city without being so ashamed. Then too, we were to live to see another world war and another mass of "temporary" constuction, though fortunately not in that area. But this was all in the future.

Our first trip had been a very memorable one but all that need concern us here is the introduction to the Library of Congress. On that visit we first saw and worked in the great reading room, the catalogue, and the manuscript division. This latter facility was up in the so-called north curtain on the second floor. Here in the northwest corner was a lofty pavilion with a circular desk, divided into study spaces separated from one another by glass, making compartments large enough to hold a book rest and to give writing space for taking notes. There were some score of these. Here the manuscripts were brought, either mounted in books or contained in boxes, and study began. From this pavilion the north curtain extended eastward containing two stories of cases in which the material was stored. In the rather wide spaces between the locked stacks were desks for scholars with longer-term projects.

This division was presided over by Charles Moore, its acting chief, but the genius whom the students saw was John C. Fitzpatrick, the assistant chief, a native of Washington, whose forebears had been in government service for nearly a century. He was always natty and spruce, keen and witty. He had a phenomenal knowledge of the material he managed, though he had not then become the editor and "proprietor" of George Washington. He became our very good friend and helped us in countless ways during the years we literally spent in his company.

We also spent some hours in the great reading room. I went to the card catalogue and copied out many references from the cards under the Democratic party. This great room, like so much of the library, was elaborately decorated with many quotations. My eye lit on two which seemed particularly appropriate, and I have never forgotten them:

> As one lamp lights another, nor grows less,
> So nobleness enkindleth nobleness
>
> —LOWELL
>
> One God, one law, one element,
> And one far off divine event,
> To which the whole creation moves
>
> —TENNYSON

On this visit we had seen the Capitol, the Congress, the Washington Monument, the exterior of the White House in which President Wilson lay a wreck of himself, Mt. Vernon, and many other historic spots from a sight-seeing bus. Also we went to service at St. John's Church and attended a performance of Percy Mackaye's ballad play, *Washington,* at the old Belasco.

Over the years there were many other historic spots to visit. The various places associated with Lincoln, particularly the great Lincoln Memorial, Henry Adams and the St. Gaudens statue at Rock Creek Cemetery, Arlington and Lee, Rock Creek Park and its zoo; the White House as we visited it rarely in the Coolidge, Hoover, Kennedy, and Johnson regimes; Dr. Pierce and the First Unitarian Church; the New York Avenue Presbyterian Church with the Lincoln Pew, and the preachers, Dr. Sizoo and Peter Marshall; the Washington Cathedral where Wilson didn't belong; the art galleries, Corcoran, Frear, and finally The National; the Smithsonian Institution; the Old and New Cosmos clubs; American Historical Association meetings at the

Willard, the Mayflower, the Shoreham, and the Sheraton Park; Haines Point; the cherry blossoms, the Jefferson Memorial, the Potomac, the seafood restaurants at the wharves, O'Donnell's; the Supreme Court, the House and Senate office buildings—with their restaurants and cafeterias. Recollection just runs away with me—but it can all be summed up in this fashion; Washington made research the most fascinating pursuit possible, something to look forward to, to be eager for. And as we were both equally absorbed and attracted, it contributed so much to our life together.

From here on out Washington was to be as much of a home to us as either New York or Philadelphia. From 1920 until I became dean in 1952 and less regularly thereafter, we were constantly at work at the library. Then as professional meetings and responsibilities multiplied there were countless meetings of the Social Science Research Council, the American Historical Association, the Council of Graduate Schools, and the Association of Graduate Schools of the A.A.U. which called for frequent visits over forty-five years and promise to continue as long as I do.

It is probably impossible for me to describe what Washington has contributed to me intellectually and emotionally. Certainly had not such a profusion of material been available here in the Library of Congress, the State Department, and the National Archives, so convenient for use and managed by so many efficient and friendly people, I should never have come so often, stayed so long, or accomplished so much. So many of those managing these resources became our warm friends. Also over the years we met so many of our fellow workers in the historical vineyard who became our friends. These were not only people of our own age and station but leaders in the profession like Dr. J. Franklin Jameson and men of leisure and resources like Dr. H. Barrett Learned. The fact that there was such a convenient, such a rich, and such a congenial place made work so attractive. At Washington we made many friends among the visiting scholars like ourselves and those in the library of Congress, State Department, and Archives who did so much to help us. We would lunch in good weather on park benches, at other times in various cafeterias in and out of the Library of Congress, starting off our gustatory careers at Bryan's, opposite the House Office Building, where even pretentious Senators might be found. I early became a member of the Cosmos Club where, during my Social Science Research Council years, I lunched and dined and did much business. Jeannette and I found the American Association of University Women clubhouse on Farragut Square convenient for dining and entertaining, as well as the Cosmos.

In Washington we had many friends among the historical researchers—Curti, Coulter, Connor, Buck, Beale, Paullen, Sears, Tansill, Bemis, Mearns, Fitzpatrick, Stock, Margaret Stewart, Grace Griffin, to mention but a few. This may seem just a miscellaneous catalogue of names but they meant a good deal to us and suggest an association of congenial spirits. It is not possible to describe what part such a coterie played in the lives, thoughts, and insights of a couple engrossed as we were in professional pursuits, confined as we confined ourselves to concentrated effort. We worked and traveled back and forth actually seven days a week between Pennsylvania and Washington, with suburban living and the needs of my mother to complicate matters. At home, Sunday morning was devoted to rest, at the expense of religious observance, though in Washington we were so inspired by Dr. Ulysses G. B. Pierce's preaching that we attended the Unitarian Church frequently. As I read over my diaries in these later days of retirement I wonder how we did it. Some indefinable strength and spirit, some urge to achieve was constantly at work. And most important, we both liked to do it. Our work was our hobby and our relaxation and we could do it together.

Our association was particularly close because we found our recreation like our labor in concentrated relationship. After a day of close application we would put aside our work and then would come the theater or movies, in season the opera and orchestra. For several years I taught history at the Curtis Institute of Music and among the perquisites were tickets to the opera company in which Mrs. Edward Bok, sponsor and supporter of this institute, was interested. Also in season the Metropolitan Opera came over on Tuesday evenings and we had tickets for these performances, coming down over the years from the top gallery to the parquet. With two operas and perhaps a movie in some weeks, together with my teaching and our research, trips back and forth between Washington, and, after our move, to Swarthmore with two hours each day on train or bus we found little time for social life, and although we entertained on occasion and "went out" when invited, we spent relatively little time "socially."

For many years in the 1930's and 1940's we kept a room a block from the Library of Congress. Had we not had this privilege of a double life our intellectual activity would have been much restricted. Furthermore, living so much in Washington, spending so many "after hours" in the galleries of the Senate and House made what I was generally writing about seem so real.

With the same material I could not have done what I did in Philadelphia. Day after day as I sat reading the letters of the politicos I could shift my eyes but slightly and there was the Capitol Dome. There was the republic in symbol and a sense of reality and comprehension would come to me which I am sure I could never have experienced merely from reading. I became a part of Washington—there was a mystic union. I had similar undefinable identifications with Rutgers and the University of Pennsylvania and for a much shorter time with Columbia. How these identifications determine an intellectual activity I cannot say, but effect it I know they do.

As our research took us away from our home a good deal we early adopted the custom of writing to each other daily when we were apart. These letters meant a constant formulation of our thinking and an equally constant exchange of expressions of interest and affection which custom was never to stale. These thousands of letters have contributed to this joint personality of ours in a fashion that I am afraid we are unable to analyze and evaluate. An association which was to achieve at least an approach to half a century of uninterrupted intimate relationship around a common historical interest has produced "a career" which belongs to us both and which cannot really be thought of in two parts. Whatever may be the labels of elements in it, it is "ours" and thus has a unity which must be grasped if it is to be understood. This description placed early in the book applies through most of it. Other clues can be found in our published writings and our files, though probably the most revealing evidence of all has been lost in the intricate give and take of nearly a half century of constant association.

IV

THE SEARCH FOR MEANING

MY STUDY of history was to be a continuous revelation of its philosophical implications, of its intellectual potential, of the increasing demands that it has made upon my capacity for thought and analysis. At first it was merely interesting reading, for then it was all in books. Anything I wanted to know could be "looked up." As an embryo historian I merely read something labeled history, and recorded, remembered, and retold it. Then came a time when I began to realize that it was something more than this, more than reading, learning, teaching, research, and the communication of new findings. There eventually came a curiosity about what historical knowledge might mean and then I began to be conscious of an intellectual challenge. Could I find meaning in chains of events? I had two concepts which I sought to combine into a theory of meaning. One of these was my interest in political behavior and the other was the cultural concept of civilization. The first I had picked up at home and from my schoolbooks, the second was very definitely the result of my Columbia teaching.

My first effort at formulating a frame of reference from these materials, of thinking about what history is, came from my experience with the "biography" fashion of the 1920's. At that particular time the enthusiasm for this form of literature was being reflected in certain educational developments. One or two departments of biography were created in colleges and a few "biography" courses were developed in departments of English and history, despite some objection from those who maintained that biography was not a subject. A few of the less charitable even were suggesting that such teaching was a device to get ahead on the academic ladder by applying the seductiveness of novelty.

As this enthusiasm was in the air in the 1920's and as I was beginning a biography myself, it was not too strange that my first attempt at a written formulation of an understanding of the meaning of history should be influenced by this interest. As an instructor in the Columbia summer session of 1925 I gave one of a series of public lectures offered by the staff.[1] I spoke to the question "Can Biography be Taught?" making particular use of a teaching experiment which I had undertaken at the University of Washington during the summer session in 1924. I had thought that the students might better understand the process of the western expansion of our population by a study of cases of actual migration. So I prepared a questionnaire and asked each to fill it out and then write a paper based on the experience of the relative or relatives who had come to America and

[1] August 7, 1925. This was published under the title "Biography the 'Case' Method in History," *Historical Outlook,* XVII (October 1926), 270–2.

thence to the Pacific Coast, or on the experience of some other transcontinental migrant.

This personalized analysis I hoped would promote a clearer and more accurate understanding of the process of social change and development in terms of something immediately concerning each student, his family experience. For the blind forces of environment and the relentlessness of economic determinism which I then thought provided the easiest and perhaps the most fundamental explanation were so general that I feared that those interested might be in danger of losing sight of process and of forgetting the individual and his part in social change. After all, historical forces must work upon and through human beings.

Two years later I reverted to the theme of biography as an instrument of history teaching. I then affirmed my belief in the intellectual character of history and took issue with Henry Adams's implication that history was the resort of the lazy-minded. I maintained that history was not merely concerned with facts but with cause and effect. Historians were too prone to speak of vague and general forces or striking interpretations built around startling words, such as revolution, and finally to concoct theories of progress or degradation. I insisted that we were not responsible for assigning praise or blame but for providing wider knowledge. I urged my colleagues to study motivation and, making use of the findings of biologists and psychologists, to attempt to discover more satisfying answers to the question "Why?"

Thus my first general thinking defining history was behavioral. I would not cast myself in an institutional mold, I was not too much concerned with function, nor did I speculate on cosmic forces determining the affairs of men. I was interested in people and their behavior as individuals, in groups or in the mass.

My progress in generalizing about history was encouraged by one of the great men whom it has been my good fortune to know, Edward P. Cheyney. As I entered the life of the University of Pennsylvania I was not slow to discover the quality of this very wise scholar. He was a man of no pretense, essentially humble, serene in a wisdom which he never paraded. He had lived a life of the intellect, practical, sane, kindly, honest, and courageous. If he had any major fault it was perhaps that he was too tolerant, too confident in laisser-faire and in the capacity of men to profit by the liberty which he always defended. He was the genuine liberal; some in conservative Philadelphia thought him a radical, but few failed to respect him. You were never with him before you were shortly engaged in useful conversation, often about your own ideas and intellectual interests. He had a sympathetic gentle way of drawing you out, and making you sure that he was really interested in what you were thinking and doing. All acknowledged that he was one of the greatest and wisest figures in the university. This acknowledgment came simply and naturally.

Shortly before I became acquainted with him, he had been president of the American Historical Association and had delivered an outstanding presidential address which had been greeted by an ovation unprecedented. He had entitled it "Law in History" and had presented a thesis of order and progress in human affairs which was stimulating and encouraging. It emerged out of the optimism of the Progressive Era.

In various conversations I had with Dr. Cheyney, often at lunch, we shared an interest in such generalizations. It was a day in which a number of discoveries were being made regarding the nature and architecture of the universe, the macrocosmos and the microcosmos, such concepts as the indestructibility of matter, indeterminancy, relativity, and the immaterial nature of matter. There were certain popularizers of this basic knowledge who were widely read by the intelligent public. Two of these were J. H. Jeans and A. S. Eddington.[2] Then Henry Adams and Benedetto Croce had been joined by an obscure figure from Eastern Europe, Egon Friedell, whose *Cultural History of the Modern Age* (New York, 1932), with its generalizations based on scientific discovery, were opening many eyes.

The intellectual influences that had been most significant in shaping my thought in Columbia had been behavioral. Now at Pennsylvania they were the current speculations and demonstrations in basic concepts in the physical sciences. To these were added others in biology. Friedell was interested in the influence of such trauma as plagues and epidemics and he made much of the Black Death of the fourteenth century. Also there was a group of biologists in the medical school, notably Detlev Bronk of the Johnson Foundation in Biophysics. He and his colleagues were interested in applying the principles of dynamics developing in physics to the life sciences. They were in close contact with the University of Cambridge, with Adrian and his colleagues.

In the history department closely associated with Dr. Cheyney was his student and friend, William E. Lingelbach. He was a man of great energy and wide interests, particularly active in all sorts of organizational en-

[2] J. H. Jeans: *The Universe Around Us* (Cambridge, Mass., 1930) and *The New Background of Science* (Cambridge, Mass., 1934); A. S. Eddington: *The Nature of the Physical World* (Cambridge, Mass., 1928).

deavor. In 1926 he had become president of the Association of History Teachers of the Middle States and Maryland in which the Columbia department had likewise been active, particularly Carman and Hayes. Also Professor Albert E. McKinley at the university, who had set up and was publishing *The History Teachers Magazine,* recently become *The Historical Outlook,* was an active figure in this group. While at Columbia, at the invitation of Harry Carman I had joined this association. When I arrived at Philadelphia I found that Dr. Lingelbach, who was most interested in it, was shortly to become its president. In the spring of 1927 its meetings were to be at the university and at Drexel and in the fall of that year at Atlantic City, where it met annually in affiliation with the Middle States Association of Colleges and Secondary Schools. Lingelbach put me on the local arrangements committee for the Philadelphia meeting and I had the pleasure of welcoming Dr. Shepherd, who was one of the featured speakers. Then in the fall Carman invited me to speak my piece on biography at the Atlantic City meeting. I also began reviewing books for the *Historical Outlook* and it published two papers of mine. In 1931 I was elected vice president of the Association of History Teachers and in the following year became its chief officer. That meant that a presidential address would be in order for the spring of 1933.

As it was the thirtieth anniversary of the association I undertook to stage a special dinner at Philadelphia in May 1933. I invited the former presidents to come back and a large number did, including Charles A. Beard, who also spoke at lunch next day. I undertook to give my presidential address that morning and used it as an opportunity to raise my theoretical sights. I made use of the fruits of my discussions with Dr. Cheyney, my reading of Jeans, Eddington, and Friedell, and the matter then current in the press about the ideas of the physicists which seemed to be destroying long-held Newtonian principles. I undertook to make some applications of these ideas which I thought would be helpful to history teachers in revising their frames of reference.

My point was that the analogy of the Newtonian concept of physical law was too simple to guide historians. The idea of a static universe running on unvaryingly like a clock was being superseded by a world into which Darwin, Kelvin, and Einstein had introduced such dynamic concepts as evolution, dissipation of energy, relativity, and the like. The old universe of matter was giving way to one in which the basic element was force. Instead of law there was statistical probability. Man's knowledge seemed "no longer based upon the observational knowledge of the senses but upon his ability to calculate by the use of symbols."

Referring to current scientific activity I pointed out that the laws of science had become "probabilities built upon statistics which show that as far as we can tell the fields of force do as we predict." Man had in a sense made his own world; he had taken aggregations of force and provided them with names, such as dish, light, blue, music, cow, or what not. He had studied their habits and had prepared his statistics which enabled him to predict in general what they were going to do. When they did not, the scientist had to make new statistical tables and new predictions.

Briefly summed up, seeing was no longer believing—in fact, nothing we could see could in proper science be believed. Mankind gained insight into reality by using symbols which must be changed from time to time as the human mind grew in its power to invent new ones.

These scientific discoveries together with accompanying technological and social changes were bringing teachers into a state of crisis produced by the startling consequences of these new ideas.

The prevailing concepts of science which I thought might influence the teaching and writing of history I predicted would operate in four areas of intellectual interest. A new technique was becoming available in research, one emphasizing the metaphysical. For as science was entering the realm of the transcendental so must the historian. He was finding that historical epochs were more than the sum total of the physical, visible facts. There were data beyond the facts which the historian must seek. Facts, like electrons, are in motion, therefore it is essential not only to know their mass but their motion as well, to use a species of historical fourth dimension. In history as in the universe there were a great macrocosmos and a great microcosmos which men may not readily comprehend by means of their senses but which they can approach by the use of symbols of thought, by mathematics. As scientists have presented mathematical proof that matter is an abstraction and that space is curved and finite, so historians who grasp the possibility that there is much more in history than can ever be found in any record or described in any of the terms of experience, may seek to develop similar modes for discovering the metaphysical data of history. This might even be some sort of a historical higher mathematics that could help society to look farther into the future and predict more accurately.

I told the teachers that not only were research methods and conceptual framing in the process of adjusting but teaching techniques were likewise responding to the new age. Reflecting twentieth-century changes of environment and interpretation, education was being socialized, there was more project work, and methods devised on the basis of the increased knowledge of behavioral psychology. Students needed to be conditioned to change and more perceptive instinctive social attitudes needed to be encouraged. I advised that history be presented as a method of approach to social problems rather than as content material divorced from life. History teaching should fit into the processes of making social consciousness instinctive and designed to make habits of useful social attitudes.

This intellectual crisis also called for a new synthesis of history which the teachers of history should utilize in creating curricular outlines. The new principle should be akin to relativity; it should have as its core a theory of relative values. The complexity of life could be taught only by sorting out some of its threads, analyzing and comparing them. The confused assortment, political, economic, social, and cultural elements should be brought together in a new and more meaningful fusion. I advocated discontinuity and presentism and suggested that history be taught backward, that a course be started with an analysis of present conditions followed by a number of teaching units designed as throwbacks to trace the evolution of the stipulated present conditions. I also denigrated national history and other labeled history such as political or economic history.

I urged that more social and cultural history be included in the new synthesis and became prophetic. "If the tendency to reduce the hours of labor persists, . . . then people must be taught to use leisure." Historians should "turn toward avocational guidance" and emphasize "knowledge of art and letters." Also, as scientists were using terms that suggested religious mysticism, the historian should realize that the problem of teaching religion in the schools should be "faced rather than avoided."

I warned my colleagues that not the least of the characteristics of this period of intellectual crisis was the attitude then current that history was accorded too much space in the school curricula and that their colleagues in the social sciences were demanding more hours and courses. I urged that our resources be pooled and that history and social science teachers work together for a new curricular arrangement with a historical outline. Historians must be able to answer demands for new synthesis. This, of course, was a reflection of my experience with Contemporary Civilization.

Thus in research technique, in methods of teaching, in revised and expanded synthesis, and in the historians' conception of their own position in the world of scholarship there were insistent calls for readjustments made by the intellectual changes all around. What should be the answer?

I was soon to have an opportunity to attempt an answer. It so happened that 1934 was to mark the fiftieth anniversary of the founding of the American Historical Association. Its council decided to take due notice of the event and appointed Professor Samuel F. Bemis, then of George Washington University, to be chairman of the program committee. He and I had first worked together when he asked me to write one of the sketches in his *American Secretaries of State*. He now sought some advice from me in planning the program. He was interested in featuring certain sessions dealing with broad philosophical conceptions of history. We had some conversation and correspondence on this planning. Also Professor Cheyney had brought my Middle States address to his attention and he had written me pleasantly about it. We discussed the possibility of interesting such men as John Dewey, Carl Becker, T. V. Smith, James H. Breasted, and Croce in a session devoted to history and philosophy. Another session designated "Dynamics and History" was planned and I was invited to discuss "The Dynamic Interpretation of History." George Sarton presided over this session and Harry Carman and Victor Clark agreed to read papers on "Technology and History" and "Machines and Employment in History."

Since preparing my Middle States anniversary remarks I had continued reading in current popular science. *The New York Times*[3] had been running occasional articles on the current discussions and findings in physics, on relativity, on uncertainty, on the immaterial nature of matter, on curved space and the non-Euclidian geometry, on the nature of force. Also I had some of the reports from the new biophysics group in the Johnson Foundation at the university. I talked with a number of my colleagues, particularly Detlev Bronk and his associates in the Johnson group and with some of our physicists.

In the course of this reading and discussion I had returned to my long-standing interest in Henry Adams. I was particularly concerned with his interpretation of the second law of thermodynamics which held forth the possibility that we were faced with the dissipation of man's intellectual energy. He had even gone so far as to

[3] Headlines announced: "Jeans Holds Mind the Only Reality. Says New Physics Reopens Door to Free Will and Lives of Emotion and Endeavor" (September 6, 1932); "Millikan Modifies Creation Theory. He Tells Physicists . . . Cosmic Rays Show Death of Matter as Well as Birth" (October 3, 1932).

apply Gibbs's rule of phase and predict that the low point of this dissipation was about to be reached and that therefore man was approaching the limit of his mental capacity. I took an opportunity of talking with Dr. J. Franklin Jameson and he gave me a copy of an interesting letter that Adams had written him. When I had gotten my ideas together I decided to seek a consultation with the highest authority.

During the summer of 1930 we had spent five weeks in Germany and had returned home on the *St. Louis* of the Hamburg American Line. On this voyage we had met a group of German scientists, associates of Einstein, connected with the Kaiser Wilhelm Institut für physikalische Chemie und Electro Chemie in Berlin-Dahlem. Among them were Max von Laue and Rudolf W. Ladenburg. In the intervening time Professor Ladenburg had been called to Princeton University and was therefore near his friend Einstein at the Institute for Advanced Study. Now I sought an interview with Einstein. I wrote Ladenburg, who very graciously undertook to make this possible. In a very short time I had an interview scheduled.

I went over to Princeton on a sparkling December day. The beauty of the campus bathed in sunshine was wonderfully apparent as I cut through the Quadrangles to Dr. Einstein's office. He received me with a quiet graciousness which became his unpretending person, in a cold room, clad informally in slacks, a leather jacket fastened to the neck, sandals, and no socks. I soon realized that he could anticipate each question before I had half finished asking it. Never before or since have I been so conscious of a mind in the lightning process of perception. I explained to him that I was a historian, like Henry Adams, intrigued by the possibility of a dynamic interpretation of history. What was the validity of Adams's concern with the second law of thermodynamics and the rule of phase? Was man's intellectual force dissipating at a calculable rate and if so, should the historian report the fact and attempt to calculate the rate of deterioration?

My questions were of this order:

Is there any form of dynamic law or theory which a scientist would recognize that would be particularly applicable to history? Can laws of human conduct be expressed in mathematical terms? Is science abandoning determinism? Is indeterminism applicable elsewhere than in the microcosmos? Has radioactivity led us to supersensual chaos into which man cannot go?

What is the status of the concept that matter dissipates into radiation and radiation re-forms into matter? Of the theory of an expanding and contracting universe? Has relativity corrected the concept of a theory of the disintegrating force of radioactivity? Or is the universe still conceived of as a closed system? What has been the influence of relativity on the second law of thermodynamics?

Are there new laws designed to show that the newly defined forces are law-abiding? If there be such laws can they be called laws of progress or degradation? Or has law been succeeded by the statistics of probability? Have physics and biology moved closer together? Is experiment at war with observation? Has science become metaphysical?

Can the future of human behavior be determined by the application of scientific laws?

Has indeterminacy made it any longer possible to develop any theory of historical certainty? Must we look ahead to a dreary expanse of declining achievement end-ing either in energy largely dissipated and civilization and even life destroyed?

Dr. Einstein disposed very quickly of the second law of thermodynamics. It applies only to a closed system, and the universe cannot be described as a closed system. He emphasized the fact that physics does not deal with human behavior or with organic systems. The concepts of physics are described in a language of their own and deal with pheonomena divorced from human behavoir. These are too *elementar,* dealing with the elements of the universe, not the limited range of human behavior. These concepts of physics have been very much distorted by the human imagination. Human causality, the causes of human action, are based upon human desires, upon acts committed by other human beings. These in turn can be influenced by physical phenomena, such as changes of climate or other ecological conditions. Physics has to do with these determinants rather than directly with human behavior. Adaptation was not a term used in physics. In fact, the scientists' sense of precision is shocked by the loose use made of their terms by those in the realm of philosophy.

Historians can use analogies but not laws. Principles pertaining to inorganic systems cannot be applied to organic systems. The second law of thermodynamics cannot be applied to history; scientists and historians are not talking of the same thing. Physical concepts must not be shaped by human desires. Henry Adams was luxuriating in *Geisteswissenschaft.* Furthermore Einstein had no use for Spengler because he was so poor a mathematician. Egon Friedell he described as an Austrian actor who wrote as a hobby under great difficulties. He considered him intelligent even if his ideas were sometimes farfetched.

I came away from the interview with a sense that man might create as much, or possibly more, intellectual energy than he could dissipate. Never again need I be tightly bound by the analogies of mechanics in the realm of thought. Men's minds have a dynamics conditioned by their own nature. For the historian there is no convenient "*F* equals *MA*." He should be dealing with the subtler process which is initiated by the application of the force of thought to human behavior.

In the paper that I read[4] I concluded therefore that "Physics and history, in fact, are concerned with questions which are so far removed from each other in fundamentals as not to be reducible to the same language. Even the term "dynamic" does not mean what we commonly mean—to the physicist it is not a force or power: it is merely a change of motion. Scientists object to having read into science, purposes dictated by man's desires and not warranted by the formulae. History deals with human conduct, the behavior of one species of organic matter, the human organism; physics is concerned with inorganic systems, the very elements of the universe. Man, the subject of history, inhabits one small speck in a vast myriad of systems; physics sweeps through space, dealing with quantities so small and so large as to be quite remote from anything in the experience of man—except to those few gifted with mathematical perception. History deals with the events of human behavior for six thousand years, physics with cosmic cycles—with thousands of millions of years. Forces which operate in such inconceivably long periods of time (even were it to ulti-

[4] "The Dynamic Interpretation of History," delivered at the Annual Meeting of the American Historical Association, December 27, 1934, at Washington and published in the *New England Quarterly,* VIII (1935), 163–178.

mate destruction) could have but little effect upon man's history in any length of time open to the consideration of the historian.

"Then what of Adams's theory?" Force undoubtedly affects thought, and forces have been predominant generally in the sequence of Adams's phases, but that there is a definite calculable connection, such as is expressed in the phase rule of chemistry, or that there is an increase of entropy pointing to the end of thought or the destruction of the human species in any definite epoch is not now to be believed. Instead of loss of energy the thought of the last thirty years shows such vigor as to render possible a high degree of optimism. The synthetic power of Einstein and his associates had changed our horizon.

On the other hand, if physics and chemistry did not hold forth the answers, could they be found in the biological sciences? Here I maintained that we might well consider ideas used by biologists and psychologists. They were developing dynamic concepts. In certain ventures then new in cytology, biophysics, and biochemistry, they were seeking to comprehend the structure of the organism and its behavior. Major attention was given to the cell, which seemed to have within it the secret of life, of growth and decay. Intensive study of its behavior might answer many questions regarding the processes of more complicated structures.

I expressed the hope that a knowledge of biological forces might make it possible to construct a dynamic theory based upon concepts more immediately concerning human behavior than those at work in the macrocosmos. New biological and psychological knowledge might conceivably produce the formulae and the generalizations which Henry Adams challenged historians to discover, a formulation which might be neither a law of progress nor the law of degradation which had so impressed Adams. The possibility which I suggested might be the formulation of a law of laws of human adaptation.

The principle of adaptation I have found to be peculiarly useful in interpreting human history. "Man seems to be the organism best fitted not only to adapt himself to his environment but to adapt his environment to himself. Adaptation is one of the primary concerns of life and can be made the unifying principle of historical evolution. If the laws of adaptation can be worked out scientifically, on a dynamic basis, that is, the laws of interaction of measurable forces, then we shall have the theory which Henry Adams considered necessary. History would no longer stand as a "Chinese Play, without end and without lesson."[5]

I took this opportunity to urge a broadening of graduate programs for those working in history so that they might include work in basic social science and biology. But I added that this course work could not be prescribed from much of the existent highly specialized programs in these fields but would have to be specially constructed. Properly designed collateral work of this sort I believed would not only give the historian a more realistic approach to his main task but make him alive intellectually to the significance of these various scientific revolutions as they burst into human consciousness. Possibly the immediate dynamics effecting human behavior, and the direction and acceleration of thought, might be found not as Adams suggested in the physical sciences but in the biological and social realms.

[5] Henry Adams to J. Franklin Jameson, Washington, November 17, 1896. Jameson MSS, Library of Congress.

Thus the meaning of history to me by 1934 had become the dynamics of human behavior. Why did people behave and what were the results of this behavior? I was constantly seeking to apply it in the area of politics. The historian should be concerned not with the laws of matter and motion but with the processes of adaptation.

V

TEAM PLAY

THE WAY IN WHICH new interests are introduced into the stream of our activities can be bizarre. As soon as I came to Philadelphia, one of my favorite work spots was to be the Historical Society of Pennsylvania. I shortly noted that at one end of the main reading room, then on the first floor, was a pre-empted table where on many a morning a short, rather dour-looking man of middle years would spread a large sheet of brown paper and then proceed to his work. It was a metal-top table and the paper seemed superfluous, but this was one of many personal idiosyncrasies which marked this ferretlike scholar.

A graduate of Swarthmore College, his career had begun brilliantly and he had become a leading Quaker historian. He was collecting and busily engaged in editing the definitive edition of the works of William Penn. His work seemingly had prospered and he proudly pointed out the manuscript volumes containing the fruits of his labor, safely housed in steel bookcases. However, he had developed other interests, including a natural concern for Pennsylvania history. Governor Pinchot had appointed him a member of the state historical commission and in January 1928 he had been elected president of the Pennsylvania Federation of Historical Societies, when representatives of various such societies in the commonwealth met at their annual gathering in Harrisburg to promote the cause by a day of reports highlighted on occasion by a presidential address.

Albert Cook Myers was gregarious and made it a point to speak to most of those who came to work at the society. So in due course we fell into conversation. He had once been a graduate student at the university but had never finished his work for the Ph.D. He seemed to gain some compensation for his failure to complete his degree program by disparaging the department that had once thought of him as a very promising "man with a future." Now he took delight in reminding me that my colleagues were lacking in proper interest in Pennsylvania history. In a certain sense he was right; they were nationalistic in their outlook and interests. In his somewhat exasperating way he in effect dared me to take some interest in the long and famous history of the commonwealth. One day in the spring of 1928 he told me that he was calling a special meeting of the federation at Valley Forge in May and he invited me to attend. I did and thereby gained a new and different historical interest.

The immediate result of this May meeting was that I was appointed chairman of a federation committee on the needs of Pennsylvania history. Julian P. Boyd, who had gone up to Wilkes-Barre to take charge of an ambitious editorial project, was associated with me. He and I now planned to circulate questionnaires around the commonwealth to discover what Pennsylvania history needed. A large committee was appointed of which

Boyd was the secretary and I the chairman. Two questionnaires were drawn up; one of them was sent to teachers of history and the other to local historians, members of historical and patriotic societies, and to a sampling of those with general interest. We circulated these extensively. In November Boyd and I went up to Towanda where the Historical Commission of the Commonwealth was holding a meeting to advise them of our project. They gave us their blessing and requested a copy of the report.

In due course a generous number of the questionnaires were returned and their contents compiled by Boyd, who presented the results to the meeting of the federation held in January 1929, and the report was printed in the proceedings. Also the committee was continued and a copy of the report transmitted to the Historical Commission. Several of us, mostly connected with the universities and colleges of the commonwealth, now sought to persuade the Pennsylvania Federation of Historical Societies to alter its structure somewhat so that the teachers of history might be encouraged to play a more active role in it. The federation was, as its name implied, a group of representatives of seventy-nine societies of various sorts. There were no individual members, nor were there any representatives of educational institutions. We proposed some amendments to the federation's constitution but they would not agree to any change.

We on our part would not be denied. A group of us from State College, Pitt, Penn, and some of the other colleges started a new effort. At the time of the Sesquicentennial of the Declaration of Independence in 1926 a move had been made to establish a Pennsylvania historical association, which had had a meeting or two and died. We now revived that idea. The federation had no place for individuals. The respected Historical Society of Pennsylvania was located in Philadelphia and never met elsewhere; neither were any of its officers or directors from outside Philadelphia. We wanted an association that would hold meetings in various parts of the commonwealth and stir up interest on a state-wide basis. Our cause was much aided because Professor John W. Oliver of the University of Pittsburgh had secured support for a western Pennsylvania historical survey and Dr. Solon J. Buck of the Minnesota Historical Society had come on to manage it. A number of us had been conferring at the Christmas meetings of the A.H.A., and when we found our efforts with the federation were largely ineffectual we undertook a new departure.

During these efforts at promoting Pennsylvania history I was asked by the committee on research in colleges of the American Historical Association to participate in a session at the association's annual meeting at Indianapolis in 1928. I read a paper in which I advocated the use of local history as a convenient and efficient way to get historians who were not in a position to work on a larger scale to do much-needed research in local history from sources nearby. I described our efforts in Pennsylvania and invited similar activity in other states, urging the committee to prepare and circulate a plan for research in state history and act as advisers to those seeking to promote it in order to get those who were not working to consider entering the local vineyards. I urged the committee to compile a list of specific projects which it could promote.

I maintained that if the committee had some general plan which it could circulate and then invite various individuals to cooperate in it and work up portions of it from materials easily available and collaboration with others, then this plan would give the stimulus of suggestion and competition. One of the chief reasons for lack of productivity on the part of college teachers was the fact that in many cases there was enforced isolation, no real contact with the rest of the historical world, and individuals had built up a series of local contacts which were generally not connected with historical research. If lines of communication could be opened up locally, if projects for local history could be stimulated, interest would be renewed. If the value of local historical work could be better recognized, more people would want to work in these fields, for then there would be greater incentive. Writing so often depends upon the conviction on the part of the writer that his subject is worthwhile. If local history were advertised and exploited at its true worth under the auspices of the association, and if the location and nature of the materials were catalogued, the determination to do research would be combined with a new sense of value and possibility of local work which would not only stimulate more productivity but would also awaken a new zeal for the collection and preservation of material, a new interest in the work of local organizations, and more cooperation between professors and historical societies. Any quickening of interest of this nature would be communicated to undergraduates, who in turn might become more interested in history.

I tried to avoid giving the impression that these proposals for a research guide, for a comprehensive plan for American history, for university or local historical institutions, were impractical from the standpoint of a committee of five with many other duties. I admitted that charting the field of research, mobilizing agencies to assist in the committee's project, and then getting the unproductive to produce were, indeed, difficult tasks, but I reminded my audience that this was a day of projects. It appeared to be a fact that more money was being made available each year by various foundations and committees to carry out definite projects. Consequently, the most valuable form of endeavor which the committee could pursue would be to plan some project or projects based upon a study of the research situation in colleges, to make a report to the association in definite terms, setting forth specific things that would aid in solving the important problem for which as a committee they were created.

The yeast finally worked and Asa E. Martin and Wayland F. Dunaway of Penn State set the ball rolling. They invited a group of us to meet at Penn State in April 1932. After a very frank discussion of the situation this group decided to call a state convention of historians to consider whether or not to create a state-wide historical association. The federation and the state commission cooperated and in September an enthusiastic and numerous group met at Penn State. They voted unanimously to organize. A constitution was proposed, temporary officers were chosen, and the first meeting was called for Lehigh University in April, 1933. Lawrence H. Gipson was to be the host.

The venture prospered from the start. Growth was steady and uninterrupted. I was its first vice-president and its second president, and for many years I was busy at its annual meetings which were held as nearly as possible on William Penn's birthday in October. This cause furnished me with an interest which has persisted. I have advocated local history as a means of promoting effort designed to collect and preserve the history of the commonwealth with the main objective to get a scholarly history of Pennsylvania written.

These organizational activities in the local Pennsylvania region were to expand to encompass interests in a larger field. The sense of participating in professional organizations continued to develop. Not only was there the activity in the Middle States History Teachers Association but we had been attending meetings of the American Historical Association since 1920. I read papers at the sessions of 1924 and 1928, and in 1926 I became chairman of the membership committee. In the spring of 1931 I was invited to undertake a task of broader and deeper significance for the profession.

Two interdisciplinary groups, the Social Science Research Council and the American Council of Learned Societies, had recently been formed and they were interested in promoting concepts in the social sciences and the humanities that were interdisciplinary, broader than those which the individual disciplines were accustomed to entertain. They were particularly interested in promoting research of wider significance. These two organizations included representatives of the American Historical Association on their boards of directors and they had recently granted money to the association to enable it to encourage such research. The council of the association appointed a committee on the planning of research and they in turn set up five small conferences to meet and make recommendations. There were to be one each in ancient, medieval, and modern history and two in American history. I was invited to attend one of the latter.

The conference agenda included a series of topics designed to elicit views and recommendations regarding neglected fields of research, better materials, personnel, methods and organization to promote research, publication needs, and financial assistance.

As my preparation for this conference I undertook to study the lists of *Dissertations in Progress* for a number of years and tabulate the various fields in American history to see what the distribution among them might be. This study emphasized the fact that social and cultural and even economic history were less frequently represented than the more traditional political, constitutional, and diplomatic areas. This listing I took to our rendezvous, which was at the Teachers College Country Club in Ossining, New York. There I found the chairman, Arthur M. Schlesinger, and Dexter Perkins and we were joined by Dixon Ryan Fox, R. D. W. Connor, Merle Curti, Ralph Gabriel, and Samuel F. Bemis. With all of them I had been or was to become closely associated.

The report of this conference based its recommendations on a concept of endeavoring to recapture the many-sidedness of life and the need of profiting by the insights and new information developed by "more specialized branches of learning concerned with the study of human behavior." This conceptualization was one that I have found basic to much of my own thinking and working.

The report went on to enumerate twenty neglected fields with a decided "behavioral" flavor. Limited space confined us to a very few examples under each of the fields listed, but a wide variety of other illustrations we thought would readily occur to historical scholars. Approaches to the subject matter might be made in many ways. Biographical studies would reveal social conditions and tendencies in every one of the fields; even studies of undistinguished figures would often illustrate these forces at work. Intensive investigations of societal changes in localities should be made, contributing in the aggregate to an understanding of regional and national civilization; local history might wisely be an active interest of historical scholarship. Likewise general pictures of social conditions in given short periods, valuable as ends in themselves, would reveal new opportunities for research and interpretation.

Though the suggestions outlined placed chief emphasis upon nonpolitical history, it was the judgment of the conference that studies of this type would establish new points of view for a significant reappraisal of American political history. Something was being done, and much more could be done, to vitalize knowledge of political development by examining it, not as the predominant element in our history but as one phase of a many-sided social evolution. Political history had not evolved independently of the American environment.

As a further means of stimulating research along the above lines, as well as of avoiding undesirable duplication, we recommended the publication of an inventory of research and editorial enterprises (similar to the list of doctoral dissertations in progress) actively being carried forward by mature writers. Such a list would be particularly useful if undertaken in cooperation with foreign scholars and ought not, of course, be confined to the field of American history. We urged the Council of the American Historical Association to undertake the publication of such an inventory, preferably at regular intervals. It has been said that this list has had a marked effect on dissertation writing since its publication in 1931. We laid stress on archival organization with adequately trained staffs, the control of data, founding of archives and museums, collection of motion-picture film, the microfilming of sources, regional organization of libraries of reproductions, and the publication of guides. The conference stressed possible improvement of research by establishing situations attractive to more highly competent personnel, better fellowships, appropriate leaves of absence for research purposes, adjusted teaching loads. It recommended the adjustment of Ph.D. training programs to make them more flexible and productive of more highly literate—even literary—dissertations. Its recommendations included some designed to promote better research organization, closer relationships among history departments, historical societies, state commissions, and the like, and stressed the need of better publication facilities.[1]

This conference and the four others, their reports, and the overall report of the master committee laid out a program which was extremely practical, so much so that a great deal of it has been carried out in the more than thirty years since it was published. It provided a platform on which I have always stood and a program I have labored to implement. I was soon to have a new role to play in promoting these objectives as more evidence appeared that chance plays a curious part in setting patterns of behavior.

When age finally decreed Dr. Cheyney's retirement, Dr. Conyers Read was chosen to be his successor. At this particular moment the American Historical Association was in the throes of reorganization and had decided to establish an executive secretary. Read was appointed to

[1] *Historical Scholarship in America,* a Report by the Committee of the American Historical Association on the Planning of Research (New York: Ray Long and Richard R. Smith, 1932).

the post and set up headquarters in Philadelphia devoting part time to the university and part time to the association.

During the year 1934 Read's official attention was turned to the Social Science Research Council. This organization, made up of representatives of the professional associations representing the social sciences among which history had been included, somewhat belatedly had been created in 1924 and was supported by funds primarily from the Rockefeller and Carnegie foundations. Each professional social science association sent three representatives to serve on the council. One of the activities of the council was the administration of considerable sums of money for fellowships and grants-in-aid. The general purpose of the council was to encourage broader and more effective understanding of the problems of society by pooling the resources of anthropology, economics, political science, psychology, sociology, and statistics, as well as history, in creating a comprehensive science of society. The council stressed interdisciplinary concepts and cooperation. This was a new association for historians who had lived much to themselves, and had the reputation at least for sticking pretty much to a political and diplomatic synthesis with much concern for government and little for society. Therefore in advertising certain attractive fellowships and awarding grants-in-aid, the committees in charge frequently ruled out many applicants in history on the ground that their interests were not in social science but were narrow, technically historical rather than interdisciplinary, social-science-oriented. This presumed denial to historians, full-fledged members of the council, of what some considered their share of grants became a matter of concern to some members of the American Historical Association, and Read received a letter protesting against what was described as "descrimination." He was called upon as executive secretary to take measures to secure proper consideration of historians' interests.

Read undertook to meet this responsibility. He conferred with one of the association's delegates, Arthur M. Schlesinger, Sr., and showed him a draft of a letter he was writing the Social Science Research Council. Schlesinger felt that this communication should be revised, so he was invited to attend the meeting of the council of the American Historical Association at its Christmas session in Washington. After a full discussion Read and Schlesinger were asked to write to Robert T. Crane, the executive officer of the S.S.R.C., to the effect that the council of the association had been reassured and though "it does not altogether approve of the present emphasis in the general program of the S.S.R.C., it has no disposition to press the matter further" at that time. At the 1934 annual meeting I was elected to fill a vacancy in the association's delegation on the Social Science Research Council. Thus I began what was to prove to be a twenty-two-year service.

In the spring of 1935 I joined Guy Stanton Ford and Arthur M. Schlesinger as the historians' representatives on the council. During most of the next quarter century my acquaintance was constantly widened and my professional associations and outlook constantly expanded by this association. The headquarters of the council were at 230 Park Avenue, New York City. Each year in the spring there was a two-day meeting there and in the fall the council met for the better part of a week at some resort hotel, usually at Skytop in the Poconos. At these meetings the historians were given an opportunity to hear and discuss concepts, techniques, projects with which they normally would have felt minor concern. They likewise became more aware than ever that their social-science colleagues were not particularly interested in or even conscious of history and were not apt to think in terms of time. Their specialty was contemporary analysis rather than social evolution. The circumstances of my appointment gave me a sense of mission, for there was a proper field of mutual interest which needed development.

Shortly after my association with the council began there appeared an opportunity to further the cause of local history. Certain of the other social sciences were active in community studies, particularly in sociology and anthropology, so here was a common interest which historians shared. I began to urge that the council support work in local history because so much of the science of society could be best studied in the communities, where most people did their behaving. Consequently a special conference was called in September 1937 by the council and it recommended that a guide to the study of local history be compiled. The result was the publication after some delay in 1944 of Donald D. Parker's *Local History, How to Gather It, Write It, and Publish It,* edited for the council's purposes by Bertha E. Josephson.

A second activity which the delegates from the A.H.A. on the S.S.R.C. were able to develop came as a result of a great advance in the historians' world. This was the final success of efforts initiated many years earlier and pushed vigorously by J. Franklin Jameson to establish a national archives at Washington. In 1934 this long-pursued effort resulted in the construction of the great building. After a considerable amount of political maneuvering Professor R. D. W. Connor of North Carolina, our long-time friend, was made archivist and the great work of bringing the masses of national records into a central repository got under way. It was a great boon. I had spent much time on occasion in searching some of these scattered items in hot attics and in cold garages and now to have everything brought together in one great air-conditioned marble temple of record was magnificent.

At this time I was invited by the Society of American Archivists to speak at luncheon at the December 1939 meeting of the American Historical Association. I took this opportunity to suggest that with this new organization and its resources that the historian was an Alice in a new Wonderland. I outlined various controls of the new material and prophesied that if proper archival procedures were developed and if historians and their brethren in the other social sciences would make efficient use of them, the archives would be a Wonderland indeed and Alice would have great new opportunities for discovery and perhaps might stop wasting time chasing White Rabbits.

I stressed the problems presented by masses of material. Particular reference was made to the problem of quantity in relation to source material. This would be particularly striking to Alice as she read the "Guide to the Material in the National Archives." For there she learned that records connected with United States Food Administration, 1917–30, measure 22,000 feet; those of Veterans Administration, 1861–1929, 59,000 feet; those pertaining to NRA, 4,200 feet; and measurements likewise lengthy were found for a variety of other classes of materials. Anyone stopping to consider the number of feet in a mile would begin to understand the problem.

This question of quantity, I pointed out, had proved perplexing in various ways. In the first place, the archival problem of storing such a multitude of documents in one place in such a way as to be readily accessible upon call provided a series of headaches difficult for the uninitiated to understand. The solution of the storage problem was admirable. Alice went to the National Archives, wrote down what she wanted on a slip and then it was brought to her in short order, unfolded, cleaned, and ready for use. Or, if she might not be able to come to the archives, she could write for and receive copies at cost. But this left two vital questions squarely before her in this Wonderland. She must know what she wanted, and, if her problems were at all comprehensive, she must have the time to examine the quantities of material at her disposal.

Too often, however, a searcher in the archives does not know exactly what he wants. If he wishes the pension papers of his grandfather, that's easy. But if he is interested in the topic "American Ethics as Illustrated by Pension Applications," he is confronted by the simple statement "Veterans Administration, 59,000 feet," or approximately eleven miles.

Many of the historical profession, at least at that time, did not appear to be well equipped to deal with such masses of material. Most had had careful training in a meticulous technique which called for the study of elaborate manuals and the examination of individual documents and sources in the light of their precepts. Each document, according to the rules, should be considered by the student and its value and truthfulness weighed judicially. Then, its pertinent contents should be recorded on a card or piece of paper of the proper size and color. Most students, as conscientious as Alice, had tried in a measure to live up to the implications of this scientific technique. But life was becoming more complex, more was happening, much more is being recorded, and then, alas, historians have done their work along certain lines only too well.

For years, they had been preaching the need of the preservation of documents, the recording of evidence, the collection of every scrap as sure to have use for someone, particularly among the social historians. They have been taken at their word. Historical societies, libraries, state archives, and this great national organization have risen at their behest and now they are literally hoist by their own petard. How could they use the result, how could they sit quietly, even in an air-conditioned room, and carefully examine and evaluate documents by the mile? Yet if one were to write the history of the New Deal in the manner that Channing and the colonial historians used for our early history, some university professor or free-lance historian has got to find the time to tread these last long miles and his seminar training won't help him much.

New techniques, I reminded the archivists and their friends, were needed to solve the problem of handling mass. Seminar directors may find a partial solution of this difficulty by developing methods of cooperative research, for seminar groups are being and will be more carefully chosen, and their work more carefully planned and articulated. It might be that in history, as in science, there would be publication of joint products as dissertations. This need not necessarily mean joint authorship of professor and student, but it would be worthwhile to consider the possibility of several degrees for one piece of work. It was at least conceivable that a well-articulated seminar might produce a book, the joint product of several students, edited perhaps by the director, for which the various students might receive Ph.D.'s.

Furthermore, I pointed out the need of a new group in the university world, namely, research assistants. The time might come when university authorities could be educated to realize that to each major professorship should be attached a research assistant, not a neophyte, but a trained worker at a livable salary who could be trusted to do much of the spade work. Unfortunately, then as since, so heavy are the demands of teaching and administration upon university budgets that such ideas, when suggested, are looked upon as luxuries, ideally desirable but impractical save where contract research is concerned.

However, Alice should be hopeful of aid from the archives in solving this problem. Any archival establishment, national or otherwise, if it plans to do more than serve as a guardian of records, might well study the possibility of pre-digesting material for the use of scholars. This is not a new problem and there are shelf loads of descriptive lists and calendars; in the National Archives itself there are many such, products of the staff and of thousands of WPA workers. Also the various division heads and their assistants know a great deal about the records they handle and are always available for advice. Divisions of cataloguing and classification are wrestling with this matter with good results, but the job was and still is literally stupendous.

If the archives, particularly in records of most recent times, were to perform their true functions for scholarship, they could well undertake to do what the universities seemingly have not been able to do, namely, build up a staff to study the various classes of material with a view to acting as research assistants as well as consultants when scholars come to the archives. One may at least study the possibility of a procedure whereby scholars of maturity and experience using the archives be assigned the services of a research expert to work along with the visitor, selecting and preparing from the mass a variety of data. This has been done in a very limited way on occasion by those in charge of the stacks, but it is a function that could be worked out more systematically.

This staff also might work upon research plans. Lists of subjects and suggestions as to the type of material might be compiled such as were planned some time ago in the field of diplomatic history. The archives could become a national seminar with a blueprint of national research. Private endowment, the national government, or the archives in cooperation with some university or universities might create a group of archival fellowships, the beneficiaries of which would be invited or permitted to work singly or in cooperation on some segment of this general plan. A good way to start this off would be the publishing of an occasional series of pamphlets entitled "Research in the Archives," for particular sectors. In such ways might the archives aid the historian in wrestling with the problem of quantity.

But it must be remembered that Alice was more than a venturer in Wonderland. She added to her experiences and broadened her point of view by a later journey "Through the Looking-Glass." In this experience she was like historians who join their brethren in the other social sciences and share their interests and problems. The reorientation which they are called upon to make is often like passing through a glass into a world of altered perspective. The National Archives, I suggested, could do much to adjust this perspective to a clearer view of the processes of social evolution and thereby serve Alice in her later capacity of social scientist.

As one of the interests of the S.S.R.C. had been mobilizing, preserving, and controlling materials for research in collaboration with the A.C.L.S., the archives operation fitted in neatly. This interest had been carried on under the energetic leadership of Robert C. Binkley, but after his untimely death the work had been arrested. Now, however, that the archives staff had been organized and the ever increasing material began to be brought under control, the time seemed ripe to move for wider knowledge of what was now available.

A committee was set up by the S.S.R.C. named the Committee on the Control of Social Data, of which I became chairman; it was commissioned to take up where Robert Binkley had left off. One of the first tasks of the new committee was to secure a report on such data for social science use which might be found in the archives. We had the hearty cooperation of the archivist and he gave every facility to a group sent by us to make the survey. W. Rex Crawford, sociologist, headed the team which included an anthropologist, Sarah Jones Tucker, and an economist, Lowell M. Pumphrey. They spent a month among the newly organized files. They duly reported their findings and those relating to sociology and anthropology were published in the appropriate learned journals.

So far, though my preoccupation with politics was continuous, I had never been in what might be called public life. However, my interest in Pennsylvania history and my connection with the Pennsylvania Federation of Historical Societies and the Pennsylvania Historical Association had upon occasion taken me up to Harrisburg where the federation met annually. Also my increasingly close association with the Historical Society of Pennsylvania and the Genealogical Society of Pennsylvania brought me new and particularly interesting friends. One of the wisest and most knowledgeable women I have ever known was Miss May Atheton Leach, who was the most distinguished genealogist in Pennsylvania. Her knowledge of Pennsylvania families, inherited in part from her kinsman, Colonel J. Granville Leach, was seemingly unlimited. She was also a gifted writer and editor who after Colonel Leach's death was the guiding spirit in the Genealogical Society and editor of its publication. She was very kind to me and was very helpful in the founding of the Pennsylvania Historical Association. She appeared annually at the federation meetings in Harrisburg and had a wide acquaintance with politicians. Another kinsman, Frank Willing Leach, had been private secretary to Senator Matthew S. Quay, and through him she had many political connections. I helped Miss Leach in certain of her enterprises and we became good friends. In 1941 I was elected to the board of the Historical Society—I always thought at her instance, and later on I became a member of the board of the Genealogical Society and its president.

A second associate whose acquaintance I made as a result of my interest in Pennsylvania history was a Harrisburg newspaperman and member of the state Republican organization, A. Boyd Hamilton. He for a time was secretary of the state senate and usually was on the staff of the Republican state committee. He was very active in the federation, and when we started the move which eventually produced the Historical Association, we first tried to work through him to change the federation so that the educational institutions might play a definite role in it. He headed us off, so we enlisted him in the new organization and made him its first president, with me as vice president, and on occasion prompter. He was an extremely skillful politician, with a real interest in history. We worked well together. When his term expired as president, I succeeded him. We made it a policy to work closely with the federation and in due time I became president of that organization.

There was another agency in Pennsylvania interested in its history, the official historical agent of the commonwealth. This was the Pennsylvania Historical Commission, a body of five people appointed by the governor for a four-year term. Hamilton had been a member and chairman of this commission and then Miss Leach had been one of the group. However, even her great strength and energy failed and in her eighties her health caused her to resign the post. Her mantle fell upon me. I was president of the federation and logic pointed in my direction. So in 1940 Governor James appointed me. The commission spent a day each month at the Capitol. Its reponsibilities were varied. A number of historic buildings and historical sites were under its charge. There was a growing program of historical publications, both scholarly and popular, and there was an extensive and expanding plan for setting up wayside markers to point out places and events of historical significance. One of the phases of our work was archaeological, concerned primarily with the aboriginal inhabitants. We had on the staff a young and enterprising historian from Penn State, S. K. Stevens, whom we soon made state historian. Eventually he became executive director of a reorganized state agency known as the State Historical and Museum Commission. During the four years I served on the old commission, we had worked upon the possibility of securing a state archives building. And eventually when he was executive director it came to pass. Today it stands a great memorial to William Penn, opposite to the state capitol. At the time of its dedication in 1965 I wrote a history of the Pennsylvania Commission and made one of the dedicatory addresses. Much water had gone over the dam since I accepted Myers's invitation in 1928 to the meeting at Valley Forge.

By such assignments beginning in the 1930's I became much involved in cooperative scholarly and promotional operations through membership and official responsibility in an increasing variety of professional organizations. These activities widened my acquaintance, broadened my outlook, and furnished me with a more comprehensive collection of intellectual instruments.

VI

AMONG THE BEHAVIORAL SCIENTISTS

DURING THE SCORE and more years of my membership in the Social Science Research Council the "behavioral sciences" came into their own, and my association with my colleagues in these fields gave me a clearer insight into the significance of history as a mental discipline. Knowledge of history was certainly a phase of behavioral science and my behavioral conceptualization was guiding me into a broader humanism.

When I joined the Social Science Research Council I found Charles A. Beard among my associates and we took up where we had left off when he participated in the thirtieth anniversary of the Middle States Association of History and Social Science Teachers. The American Historical Association was shortly to celebrate the 150th anniversary of the creation of the United States Constitution and I was a member of its program committee to arrange the annual meeting to be held in Philadelphia in December, 1937. The committee hit upon the idea of having one of the sessions in Independence Hall, and of inviting Beard to give the principal address. A group of us drove up to his farm, in New Milford, Connecticut, and delivered the invitation in person. To everyone's great satisfaction he accepted. Eventually he spoke to a group that filled the chamber to capacity and to a larger audience seated in Congress Hall to which his speech was carried on a public-address system. His address modifying his earlier "An Economic Interpretation of the Constitution" was notable.

When Beard spent the winter of 1940–1 at Johns Hopkins as scholar in residence, he conducted a seminar and on occasion others were asked to join him. The chairman of the history department, Kent Roberts Greenfield, invited me to come down in March to deliver one of the Schouler lectures and to discuss a paper to be given in Beard's seminar. This lecture enabled me to proceed further in my thought about history.

My continuing interest in the types of scholarly activity implicit in a broader behaviorism and humanism had borne in upon me the realization that history was not a very precise intellectual instrument and that historians were not playing a very effective role in the world of thought formulation in general or in the emerging behavioral science of society. I therefore shared my concern with my audience and presented them with a series of questions.

When the historian thinks:

(a) does he clearly define and maintain a balance among his varied functions?

(b) has he a well-established ethics which guides him in the contest between his scientific principles and the demands of society?

(c) has he wrestled sufficiently with the stultifying influence of the pervasive practice of historical labeling?

(d) does he fully comprehend the devious influence of our subjective minds and seek the proper methods of corrective thinking?

In the lecture and the discussions I dwelt upon the fact that in point of time historians had only recently begun to think about the nature and the method of history. Not until the nineteenth century had modern history been recognized as a subject for study in the universities or as an educational discipline. Only in the relatively few years since had historians become self-conscious about their "method" and ways of thought. The recent transition from a storyteller to a scientific scholar had caused philosophic confusion which could be described in the psychiatric terms appropriate for diagnosing divided personality.

Historians often were indeed divided against themselves, some were willing to venture hypotheses, others determined to stick only to so-called facts, keeping *themselves* out of the picture. A third group strove to be both Macaulays and Rankes, to be both literary and scientific at the same time without reaching the heights of either and thus involving themselves in confusion. Unfortunately some of their graduate students had found this uncertainty contagious. This confusion had become a handicap to scholars confronted with the demands made upon them as keepers of the traditions of society to become the arbiters of current standards of ethics and ideals.

Another handicap to effective thinking was a second fundamental dichotomy in the historian's interest. As he transferred his attention from the narrative to the scientific in history, he had laid much stress on its objective quality. Scientific methodology he preferred to believe would produce absolute truth, objective history.

But recently there had been provocative controversy which emphasized the truly subjective character of historical thinking and the impossibility of objective history except in a very relative sense.

This realization of the subjective, the importance of the frame of reference which each individual brings to his task, had emphasized the importance of the quality of mind of the historian. The kind of interpretation of past events depended not so much upon research as upon the way in which the historian interpreted present events, viewed the world around him, and judged the character and motive of those with whom he might come in contact. What he knew of the fundamentals of human conduct, of psychology, of biology had become important, for his subjective situation would condition his consideration of human behavior in other ages. The Puritan had difficulty in understanding the nuances of the Restoration. Religious partisans are not generally successful historians of the Reformation. In other words, one is no better historian than he is a citizen of the world.

Consequently, I entertained the hope that more attention be paid in graduate training to the implications of these subjective influences. Life itself can be incoherent; so may the course of human events. To understand them we strain our impressions of them through the reorganizing process of our receptors. The historian interprets what he perceives according to the way in which his nervous system and his imagination function. The high-strung do not write the history the phlegmatic prepare. Therefore the historian should try to classify himself as to type so that he may better assign himself a handicap and correct his findings by a knowledge of his own quality. The historian must more fully comprehend the devious influence of his subjective mind and seek the proper methods of corrective thinking.

These considerations press upon historians the need of more attention to their philosophical responsibilities. It had become too patent that the quality of historical thinking was suspect by the more thoughtful workers in other disciplines who charged that historians have not contributed what they should to the understanding of the past behavior of men. Historians were accused of not studying or writing about the phases of human experience which other social scientists wanted explained. They neither asked nor answered the right questions.

In answering the question of how the intellectual challenges to the historian might be met, I made certain suggestions. One great difficulty had been the fact that historians had not troubled to keep abreast of contemporary currents of thought. They had seemed unaware of the philosophical trends in each generation and their work had not been affected by them until they had long been accepted in the scientific world. Therefore, the historian should constantly enrich and vary his intellectual exercise. Too often he was preoccupied in exploring and solving small problems. By minute observation of small things he sought to learn the realities of the great. Unfortunately the result often fell far short of the goal. The search for the facts and the preoccupation with the minutiae seemed in too many cases to have become the sole end in view. Descriptive monographs rather than suggestive theses had been too often the sum total of accomplishment.

The little theorizing that had emerged, however, was the product of some vigorous thought and was pointing the way for further extensions into that realm. Even the best of it, however, had the weakness of following too closely scientific analogies, but the laws and postulates of science rarely take into account the center of the historian's constant preoccupation, namely, the fact that each man is not merely the product of physical reproductive process with his behavior shaped by his genes, rather what he does is largely determined by his cultural inheritance transmitted to him from without throughout his life. Such a difficulty I somewhat fancifully represented in mathematical symbols. The historian was apt to take a given situation, such as a contemporary condition which might be represented as x, and speak of its past in terms of x minus the intervening years. Thus the origin of the x condition in its process of evolution through some n years is considered as x minus the accretion of n years or $x\text{-}n$, using arithmetical regression, as it were. However, a better representation would be to take a contemporary situation and describe its origin as the nth root of x wherein n represents a geometrical progression of developments produced by the process of an accumulating cultural heritage transmitted through successive generations.

In other words, historians are prone to make their thought processes too simple. They put too great a premium upon patience and persistence in accumulating data with the comfortable idea that if such an accumulation be properly and neatly arranged, it will somehow tell its own story and the historian therefore may content himself with displaying rather than explaining his labor. Consequently, a greater sense of responsibility for intellectual activity needs to be infused into training. There is need of mental gymnastics, a dialectic which considers abstractions, tendencies, and future eventualities, as well as facts and past happenings. Historical students should be drilled in the application of behavioral knowledge to their findings. Such a dialectic I suggested should be sought.

I concluded that the historian had a very definite and difficult place among the technicians working in the maze of human problems which are the central interest of the behavioral sciences. The historian could supply the fourth dimension to these sciences, for it is the only one of the social disciplines, with the possible exception of anthropology, that has any comprehensive time sense or that feels real responsibility for delving into the problem of the process, so long drawn out, of institutional development. Most of the social sciences are quite necessarily three-dimensional, analytical disciplines. They are largely concerned with present and future conditions, and when they delve into the past it is to study only restricted types of institutions. The historian, on the other hand, is interested in the evolution of institutions of whatever kind, with no restrictions as to type. Unfortunately, despite this interest and responsibility, historians quite frequently have been too unaware of the problems of their fellow social scientists and so ignorant of their vocabulary as to make dialogue difficult. Conversely, the latter sometimes have failed to find what they have wanted in the historian's work because he on his part speaks a different language. Historians, with a long ancestry of literary and theological forebears, often have found new associations confusing. Some, at least, therefore need a broader outlook on society.

The remedy for clarifying the historians' philosophical confusion I suggested was a clear understanding by them that they were primarily concerned with the relatively new science of society. They would profit by a more definite alliance with those who are studying human behavior not only in the usually denominated social sciences, but to some extent in biology, psychology, biochemistry, and biophysics as well. These latter disciplines may seem at first glance to have relatively little to contribute but they are interested in fundamental research in human dynamics in a fashion which may well enable them to contribute the key to those seeking to formulate theories of origin and evolution.

A further step in my theorizing was connected with the Ossining meeting, with my visit to Johns Hopkins, and with my acquaintance with Beard. In working out a closer relation between the historians and the other social scientists on the S.S.R.C., I undertook to make a report to the Council on the state of historical research in American history. I secured a research assistant who compiled a list of the historical publications in the last five years which I classified by fields in American history. I wrote a report interpreting the listing and including also a list of historians who seemed to exhibit an interest in social science. In this statement I emphasized my concept that history was more than a method; it was concerned with difficult problems of analysis and needed a dialectic of its own and a technique of synthesis which it had never developed to the satisfaction of its fellow social philosophers. A better frame of reference for the use of historians, which would enable them to seek and secure the significant causal data and give the analyses and explanations of the evolution of human behavior, was a crying need. More attention should be given to this frame of reference which should be formulated in universal terms applicable to any group or series of groups.

To illustrate this problem of the frame of reference, I formulated the following model:

History of a Cultural Group

A. Mobilization and Distribution of the Population
- Physiography
- Initial Migration
- Immigration, Emigration, and Redistribution

B. Organization of Institutions
- Subsistence
  - Production
  - Distribution
- Reproduction
  - Family
  - Health
- Communication and Expression
  - Press
  - Literature
  - Arts
- Adjustment
  - Protection and Restraint
    - Government
    - Crime
    - Morals and Morale
  - Recreation
    - Use of Leisure
    - Sport and Entertainment
  - Improvement
    - Religion
    - Philosophy
    - Science
    - Education

C. Group Relationships
- Racial
- Intercommunity and interclass
- International

Diplomacy
War

I developed this frame of reference for the purpose of suggesting types of studies needed, fields that should be explored, not to serve as an outline for the writing of the history of any community. Each community, like every individual, has a unique history directed not only by the normal processes but by the cataclysmic influences affecting it as well. Therefore the life history of each social cell or group of cells must describe the process of community evolution in terms of the singular conditioning factors such as the inspirations, frictions, and cataclysms, and the development should be worked out in terms of the necessary readjustments and adaptations. A secondary problem was fitting the various topics in the above outline into some realistic pattern of functional development which avoided as much as possible artificial or mechanical arrangement. To illustrate, I suggested a study of the real relation of such diverse interests as leisure, science, family relationship, and diplomacy. How could these various forms of behavior be worked into a valid synthesis? To do this, I stressed the idea that historians needed the social-science training that would give them adequate knowledge of the current theories of social causation.

As I was finishing this report, my Schouler lecture, somewhat revised, was published and I sent Dr. Beard a reprint. In acknowledging it he wrote, "Your paper moves me to say to you something that has long been in my mind. Can't we get some concentration of thought on the problems of historical thinking and writing? Couldn't the A.H.A. appoint a committee and the S.S.R.C. finance modestly the cost of an inquiry into the questions you pose? This, it seems to me, is the most imperative intellectual problem now before us."[1]

As I was about to present my analysis of research in American history to the midsummer meeting of the problems and policy committee of the S.S.R.C., it immediately occurred to me to present Beard's letter too. I sent him a copy of the analysis which I was going to submit and asked him to enlarge his idea. This he did. The result was that the Social Science Research Council called a conference on Trends in Research in American History. Beard was the principal figure in it and the result was the appointment of a council committee of historiography. This committee and two which followed it produced three publications: *Theory and Practice in Historical Study* (S.S.R.C. Bulletin 54, 1946); *Social Sciences in Historical Study* (S.S.R.C. Bulletin 64, 1954); and Louis Gottschalk, ed., *Generalization in the Writing of History* (Chicago: University of Chicago Press; 1963).

During my service on the council I had several terms as a member of the problems and policy committee which gave direction to the group's thought and action, and for four years I presided as the council's chairman. I undertook to promote cooperation between the evolutionary thinking of historians and the modes of contemporary analysis which dominated the thought patterns of their fellows in the behavioral sciences. A common ground was being marked out upon which historians and their fellows could meet to consider the two basic fields of human behavior described as cooperation and competition. In these areas attempts were made to encourage historians to deal with long-term secular trends, cycles of

[1] C. A. Beard to author, July 12, 1942; quoted by permission of Miriam Vogts and William Beard.

behavior, recurring patterns of rivalry and adjustment in various fields of human activity. It was hoped that historians might be able to discover possible points of direction in the movement of human behavior over time and thus make time a factor aiding in the prediction of occurrence.

I believed that improved methodology might also emerge from this association. History scholars were literally becoming overwhelmed by quantities of data. If they were to handle these effectively, they must become more expert in statistics, in quantification, in sampling, and in cooperative study. Scientists and social scientists were making more use of computers and of the institute form of research organization and I thought historians might do the same. I was also much concerned lest the historians merely adopt the attitude of some social scientists that historians were convenient servants and useful hod carriers whose function was principally to fetch and carry, to bring out of the past in handy packages such items as the analysts of destiny might require.

When the Second World War broke out, several members of the Social Science Research Council, including the historians, secured the appointment of a committee to further Pendleton Herring's efforts to get the various government agencies at work in preserving records of their war activity and having them written up. This was stimulated by the fact that too few significant data regarding the national effort in the First World War had been preserved in usable form.

All during this service on the council the historians stressed the relationship of the interests of all concerned in the local place of happening, the locality where deeds were done, where patterns of behavior evolved. The development of this interest in locality was necessary to help the historian break himself of the habit of inversion, of doing things upside down. Patriotism and custom and the fact that in recent centuries nationalism had been so pervasive, all these had combined to focus historical attention upon national and international behavior to the neglect of the local basic history where the solutions of behavioral problems and the necessary data must be found. These national historians viewed phenomena from above, so to speak, and neglected local developments as antiquarian and insignificant. We kept Parker's *Local History* in print and for a long time it continued to be distributed. In certain social-science fields wider interest in community studies appeared, some on an elaborate scale. And among historians there was an increase in local historical societies; and as there was an ever greater demand for teachers of history, and more doctoral candidates therefore required, local history subjects became more viable in graduate schools.

My association with the Social Science Research Council served as yet another influence toward reorientation. Had I remained immersed in teaching and research within a purely historical frame of reference, I would have missed the give and take, the sense of the need for maintaining the significance of history, the compulsory experience with social-science glossalalia which at times proved so puzzling but the sum total of which taught me so much. Just as my experience with my colleagues in Columbia College in teaching Contemporary Civilization had done so much to educate me, so for these twenty years in middle life I had the continuing education provided by my brethren in the other social sciences. There is much to be said for continuing education, and likewise for having a cause to promote.

VII

PERSISTENT RESEARCH

As my activities and responsibilities were expanding and as I prospected in new relationships, I was still very much engrossed in historical research and teaching. Since the publication of *Franklin Pierce,* between intervals of textbook writing I had continued to work in the field I had chosen in 1919, the history of the Democratic party, 1850–60. Pierce's administration ended in 1857 so I proceeded from there. I would analyze the situation in the final years of the decade. I devised a plan for a more elaborate study which would require a deeper and more rigorous methodology than either my thesis or the biography. I was also conscious of a secondary motivation. As I was ransacking various collections of sources I had been rather unconsciously developing a frame of reference and formulating some ideas on the philosophical responsibility of a historian.

I felt that history needed an interpretative unity to make it significant, for to me unselective descriptive chronicles were coming to have a minimum of meaning. The historians of any society should be under obligation to discover a fundamental principle or principles of interpretation which would identify the image of the society in question, would define this individual quality and present the reasons for it. I was stimulated to this more strongly because I, as a political historian, found myself at work at a time when political history was in competition with the rising interest in, and influence of, social history. Political history must be better defined and its significance better comprehended, and I began to attempt a definition of the relations between political and social history. I believed that the growing disinterest in political history had developed out of an older interpretation, largely functional and concerned with patterns of behavior too narrow in scope. However, political history was in process of changing its definition to such an extent as to blur the distinction which had been so sharply drawn. For my part, I felt that political historians should be less interested in *function* and more intrigued by essence.

The United States defines itself as a democracy which is as complex as the motives and behavior of humanity. Its government has never existed in a vacuum but is forever the creation of society, and a society of rare self-consciousness. The historian should be able to understand and interpret this democratic self-consciousness which in reality permeates the society in which he lives and in a sense is its essence. When the Greeks invented the word from which "democracy" was derived, it meant the self-government achieved by their city-states. When twentieth-century Americans use "democracy" they generally intend to refer to their own complex system of government and the nature of their own social relationships and opportunities. The Founding Fathers saw no need to use the term in the official language describing their handiwork. As the nation grew, the United States, usually then a plural name, "were" referred to as a federal system, a confederacy, or a republic, but not as a democracy.

American democracy as it developed showed need of a special history. The so-called political history of the United States was inadequate, the politicians had been studied without sufficient knowledge of their true constituencies, politics as a form of social behavior too often had been considered without reference to its parent society. Ironically enough, the historians of this great democracy, as Whitman said of its literary men, had seldom recognized the people. If the political historian could do this, I believed he might awaken to a great opportunity. He might provide the great synthetic principle still undiscovered or at least still undeveloped by historians, whatever their label. For perhaps this great principle could be the evolution of the self-consciousness of a keenly self-conscious people. If there was any one idea which has stimulated the intellectual and, even more importantly, the emotional reactions of the American people, it was the idea that they compose a democracy capable of orderly self-government and infinite progress.

The character of the evolution of this idea should be a guide to all historians of the republic. The United States has evolved because of, or in spite of, a series of forces let loose with no particular order of importance or sequence. The real history of American democracy should be the story of a series of pressures of the human will stirred by conscience or self-interest rising from masses of people. These pressures have compelled politicians who in turn have impressed, even frightened, overweening interests. On the other hand, various interests and pressure groups representing small minorities have sought to stimulate and even to manipulate public opinion for their own ends, often creating a perversion of democracy. Such pressures have been exerted not only on the grand stage of national politics, but more significantly in the less noticed arenas of the states. I was becoming increasingly aware that society was much more complex than I had realized when I started and that because of this complexity those practicing the art of self-government had become subject to greater responsibilities and the pressures upon them were bound to increase.

As I worked over this problem I needed a new frame of reference for which I had no pattern. I began of necessity, though quite unconsciously, planning a model. In those days I had never heard of models or model building and I never realized I was constructing one until I came to write these pages. This leads me to confess or boast of a methodology which has been prominent in my work. From the standpoint of logical operation I originally did everything wrong, using a method which may be called "going it blind." Its definition is the discovery and use of as many sources as possible, taking notes and then seeking to discover meaning from the notes taken during the exploration. An initial pattern or, if you will, model is then constructed. During this process other information is found to be required, new research results, and the model may then be reconstructed. Looking over the *"Disruption"* I can now discover a model which emerged and can describe it "after the fact." The structure that I eventually achieved and which I could recognize only after the fact had seven features which, combined, were designed to furnish a pattern of analysis that could be applied to the study of the strain upon the process of American self-government which for a time in the mid-nineteenth century wrecked it.

The first of the seven elements was the axiom that politics in the United States by that period had become a profession. Secondly, this system of politics operated under the mandate of an artificially contrived program of periodic elections which, thirdly, in turn could be said to be controlled by a species of cycle operating in that particular century. The fourth element was the operation of this profession in a federal system which had to function on two levels of society, thereby inducing somewhat schizophrenic behavior. Fifthly, this federalism was not merely political federalism, an association of states, of bodies politic, but by a more fundamental diversity of behavior a cultural federalism. This feature was complicated by a sixth feature, which was a broader diversity of behavior that offered political operators certain useful instruments which they could with profit select and use without any logical relationship. The seventh element seemed to be the fact that at this time of approaching crisis the rules appeared to be in the process of change. These seven features of the structure of American democracy worked together to produce an emotional tension too strong to be borne upon behavior in such fashion that the system of politics disintegrated under the strain.

Foremost among the elements shaping the structure of the American system of self-government was the fact that it had come to be operated by a new and unique profession, one skilled in responding to the needs of society. This expert group was made up of many able and resourceful men and even a few women who had been attracted to its ranks by a variety of very human desires and interests. They had become something of an American ruling class, an elite who dominated the American establishment. They devoted their lives to gaining and retaining power. Those in office must be continually on the alert to keep from being shelved by rivals, by representatives of other interests, by candidates of other parties, or by prophets of other enthusiasms. Some of them were independent and did the leading; others were subservient, taking orders. Even more frequently they could assume either role. They might be clever psychologists, great showmen, supersalesmen, gifted in speech, schooled in diplomacy, frequently unscrupulous, often sincerely attached to the American traditions. Generally they have been organized in a two-group pattern variously called Federalists, Democratic-Republicans, Whigs, the American Democracy, Democrats, or Republicans. These shifting groups with changing names meant that any given aggregate would have difficulty in keeping its unity let alone its power amid such confusion. It was to be vital that party machinery be maintained in continuous and reasonably efficient operation, for the running of popular government in the United States is never more efficient than its politics. If its machinery is not reasonably smooth-running, the processes of self-government are correspondingly hampered. So swift has been the growth of the nation that the behavior of this profession has had to be adjusted constantly to perform more complex operations.

One of the principal influences which shape the behavior of the profession of politician has been the fact that those who hold public office have no tenure and must continually be aware that they stand or fall by the count of ballots. They must go before the people to gain and keep their places. To be sure, there are many practices which can influence the result, but if the mass of voters in a community has a preference or a prejudice, it can be carried by weight of numbers. However, there are in this large population so many politicians representing so many different sections and interests that it is seldom possible that any occupational or business group, any racial or religious combination, let alone any individual, can gain control of the government when it is to the self-interest of such a numerous and resourceful profession to keep a balance of interests, to play one against the other. Popular interest is indeed ever fluctuating. In time of prosperity, freedom is the watchword; in time of stress, security becomes the absorbing need. American popular opinion is a canny cross between the daring and the cautious, with a tradition of equal opportunity ever present to stimulate conscience. I was attempting to understand and interpret the behavior of this profession.

A second characteristic of the model was the factor of periodic elections. The American system of politics operated under a mandate of an artificially contrived program of recurring opportunities to choose governments. For much of the time after 1789, elections had been held not as now, generally in November of even years, but at various times in different states. And the recurrence of these elections has been relentless. By constitutional prescription political contests must take place at stated intervals, regardless of the condition of public affairs. The calendar rather than the need of the moment has summoned voters to the polls.

The incessant procession of artificially ordered electoral conflicts frequently has meant nothing more than the routine return of pleasurable electioneering excitement; but in the 1850's it had become dangerous. The campaigns of that critical decade focused public attention too sharply upon conflicting attitudes, exaggerated them to perilous proportions, and generated dangerous power conflicts in the course of the political maneuvering. These aroused passion to such a pitch that bloodletting, occasional or wholesale, seemed necessary to relieve the tension. Election campaigns thus became the catalytic agents which fatally hastened the processes that brought on secession and civil war.

The frequent and periodically recurrent political contests were the more fraught with danger because of the loose and unwieldy construction of party machinery in that day. This machinery rattled, creaked, and groaned partly because it was patterned by the federal system of thirty-one state governments under which the nation lived and worked. The gears were not well meshed. Coherent central direction had not yet been achieved; and without it the most effective organization could not be created. The national parties then, much more than now, were but loose federations of state machines. As there were at least two parties in each of the thirty-one states in the early fifties, and three in sixteen of them, elections involved seventy-eight practically independent state organizations, uniting into three national aggregations only for presidential campaign purposes. Thirty-one of these state parties, plus some more or less fluid groups in the territories, acknowledged the name Democrat, and in national conventions styled themselves the "American Democracy." Yet each represented a separate state with its individual social organization, personal antagonisms, economic interests, and political issues. Each was subject to local attitudes and prejudices, to internal rivalries and struggles for leadership.

The state political organizations maintained election calendars which made contests much more frequent, and therefore potentially more disturbing, than they are today. In the fifties, the first Tuesday after the first Monday in November, now so universally an electoral climax, was general only for the choice of presidential electors every four years. Some few states used it as a local election day, but they were exceptions rather than the rule. Each state has its own appointed times and seasons. In fact there were elections, somewhere, in every month of every year, save January, February, and July.

This federal, as distinguished from national, electoral procedure had certain chaotic implications. It meant that campaigning was going on in the United States almost all the time; political agitation seldom quieted. The urge for office was widespread, and as nominating and electioneering methods were inexpensive and informal many indulged their taste. Naturally the multitude of contenders took the most stirring issue they could find. In local campaigns, particularly, it was good politics to emphasize the dangers threatening from the nefarious conduct or designs of dwellers in more remote regions. Particularly effective were demonstrations that the federal government was imposing unjustly upon local interests. Efforts were constantly being exerted to arouse enthusiasm or distrust, to point with pride or, with even more vehemence, to view with alarm. This was the more unfortunate because the rapid growth of the country was ever raising the stakes of elections higher and creating a new and dangerous power politics. As new territories approached statehood they presented new interests and new, or revamped, personalities to be fitted into the congressional and party convention circles.

There was a rising appreciation of the profit which might be realized from government policies favorable to rapid development. There were insistent demands for appropriations, land grants, and protective tariff policies, all of which went counter to the democracy's pet principles of laisser-faire, of refusal to vote subsidies from the public treasury. In these years the lobby became an institution; agents were everywhere. The nature of Congress was almost as much political as it was legislative. Whenever national campaigns approached, political interests dominated purely legislative concerns. Similar pressures affected the executive branch and even sought to operate on the judiciary.

Success at elections was the more intensively sought as the rewards of power became greater. Campaign methods therefore grew more ruthless, and corruption more frequent. The temptation grew to seek advantage by arousing passions. It was harder for the statesmen at the capital city to calm the emotions stirred in these countless local contests when their representatives brought them to Washington. They had to spend much time formulating compromises to subdue the wrath so heedlessly roused. As the fifties advanced, these adjustments were harder to negotiate, and fewer legislative leaders were either sufficiently interested, or able, to write formulas of peace.

The extreme danger in these frequent elections arose partly from the skill with which local campaigners and candidates could exploit prevailing conflicts of interests, conditioned by geography and custom and by the traditions, needs, and hopes of a mobile and expanding population. These antagonisms, it is true, were occasionally sponsored by statesmen or party leaders but usually dictated to them. Politicos prospered or failed in the degree to which they consciously or unconsciously recognized, understood, and utilized the opportunities which these enthusiasms and prejudices afforded. The peculiar and ofttimes conflicting qualities of popular attitudes made their constant exaggeration dangerous, never more so than on the eve of the Civil War.

A third concept which influenced my analysis and my model building was the significance of recurring phenomena other than elections, not only in homogeneous cycles but more spectacularly in a coincidence or concurrence of dissimilar cycles. Three types of cyclical behavior patterns had been reappearing, at irregular intervals, affecting mounting tensions almost simultaneously. In the 1850's they coincided in a fashion hitherto not duplicated. The first of these cycles was political. In this realm of behavior, popular interest is subject to fluctuations. There are years of calm, of political relaxation; then periodically interest quickens, the electorate becomes more highly emotional, and tension develops. Such fluctuation recurs with singular regularity in the United States. Two other forms of behavior move conspicuously in somewhat similar patterns. In the nineteenth century both business panics and religious revivals recurred at more or less regular intervals, accompanied by emotional instability contributing to the unsettlement.

Such a strange and dangerous conjunction occurred during the middle fifties in America. Since the beginning of politics in the new republic there had been a pattern roughly resembling a twenty-year cycle of power aggregation. The Virginia dynasty associated with

Washington, Jefferson, Madison, and Monroe had remained in power for twenty-four years. Then there had been a period of chaos out of which had come a Jacksonian organization. It had reached its twenty years of life in the mid-fifties and then the Republican party appeared. As the consequent political frictions mounted, the panic of 1857 and the religious revival of 1858 followed. The nation was strongly moved by these political, economic, and emotional upheavals, its nerves were shattered and popular interest became hyperemotional. This triple conjunction of tensions in politics, business, and religion generated great force and made for a period of possible drastic political reshuffling.

The fourth element in the model is the fact that as the United States is a federal system, its politics must of necessity be operated on two levels, state and federal, and to that degree is much more complex and difficult to study and understand. For federalism in the United States has always been much more than a system of government set forth in the Constitution. It has been and continues to be a pattern of living and thinking ingrained in the general behavior of the nation. It has invested each American with a dual loyalty; he is at the same time a resident of a state and a citizen of a federal republic. Each citizen owes allegiance to both state and nation.

This dualism permits local peculiarities and national patriotism to exist simultaneously for long periods of time without too much friction. Certain communities, such as South Carolina, upon occasion have maintained a very definite sense of individualism while remaining within the Union. Economic conditions in various states and regions have continued different and business has been conducted under two procedures, interstate and intrastate. Likewise two systems of law are in effect.

The political dualism which has been created thereby must be understood by the political profession. All voters must take sides in controversies both state and federal; all are responsible for decisions in each. Therefore they become dual partisans. Their situation has produced a federalized partisanship which often confuses issues with a confusion that has woeful consequences.

This federalized partisanship, developing almost simultaneously with the organization of the federal system, had become firmly established and even mechanized by the 1840's. It was marked by multiple political organization. Each party had a national organization but its influence and significance were slight compared with the separate units in each of the states. State party managers were largely independent of the shadowy national committees. So it may be said that by 1850, when there were thirty-one states, there were not two parties but sixy-four, with a complexity of organization and variety of leadership which had momentous consequences.

Party leaders, and in fact all participants, had two interests to consider in making campaigns: the national will, with the issues which might gain support and victory on that level, and state and local interests with the appeal necessary for success in the more restricted geographical area. Such divided interest invited a type of political legerdemain which was to be exceedingly dangerous. State and federal campaigners juggled state and federal issues with surprising dexterity and in a fashion to deceive and to excite rather than to enlighten. Partisanship was in constant, active operation at the various elections, which in the days we speak of were much more frequent than now.

About these fundamental procedures the Constitution is almost silent. Section 4 of Article I makes certain provisions for congressional revision of local regulations, but leaves in general to the states as in section 4 "the Times, Places and Manner of holding Elections." The all important question of who should vote was originally left in large part to the states. Yet the federal system made it necessary to have two sets of officials, state and federal, and often some of each were elected at the same time and place. Therefore, both powers were involved in the conduct of voting and both had to exercise authority over the elections, generally through party operators.

The task of model building which intrigued me suggested the definition of a fifth element and led me to discard the well-known concepts of national, sectional, and federal political divisions as inadequate to explain the political behavior of the period. Vastly more complex than the struggle between two regionalized opponents was the basic political situation faced by the party managers in almost any campaign in this period. Their problem was more involved than any of them realized. They were well aware that they were operating the political mechanism of a federal republic composed of thirty-one states; but they scarcely comprehended that the most powerful conditioner of voting behavior was not political but "cultural" federalism. It harbored a greater threat to the success of the Democratic party and to the permanence of the United States government than did the sectional rivalries inherent in political federalism. In truth cultural federalism is a primary fact in American history, too little appreciated.

The association of people and communities exhibiting various contrasting attitudes has constituted this cultural federalism. Each attitude has contributed its quota to the national complex of feeling, thought, and behavior. But attitudes are never wholly confined to one group, state, or region. Different attitudes may exist side by side in a given community, on the same street, or within a single family. The task of the political leaders therefore was more subtle than keeping slave and free states in a political union; it was the task of finding ways and means to hold citizens dominated by a variety of attitudes in one body politic. The elements of conflict bred by these attitudes must be eliminated or restrained. Politicians must forever be busy composing formulas, organizing through legislation, patronage, and power, political combinations strong enough to insure continued cooperation in the federal union.

Of the countless attitudes composing this cultural federalism, ten were most influential in conditioning political behavior at this time. These I classified according to their nature and type of influence and then explained each individually. Two of them I classed as pervasive, five as divisive, and three as cohesive. The pervasive group—attitudes which vitally affected the behavior of most people—were dominated by ideas and modes of thought traditional and common in occidental civilization, with few or no native roots. They were American only insofar as they were sharpened by certain local circumstances. These attitudes were Protestantism and romanticism. The divisive group—attitudes fomenting antagonism—were for the most part indigenous, the products of American conditions, but were also intensified by Protestantism and romanticism. This group embraced metropolitanism, territorialism, southernism,

New Englandism, and antislaveryism. Finally, the cohesive group—attitudes tending to unite—were less well defined and were only partly developed; but if they had been spread more widely they might have proved sufficiently attractive to offset the divisive second group. These soothing cohesive ideas were nationalism, regionalism, and democracy. Many people who realized the danger in the divisive attitudes were striving to promote this cohesive group, so that common adoption of one or more of them might overcome the perilously accumulating antagonisms.

In the 1850's the sectional quarrel over the organization of new territories produced the disputed formula of popular or squatter sovereignty, which in its most extreme meaning was democracy in the form of congressional authorization to the early settlers to decide the question of the institutional patterns of the embryo states by mere majority votes. Finally in the midst of this prolonged territorial sovereignty debate appeared a more startling concept: questions of broad national policy should be decided by the will of the popular majority in the nation at large, without regard to the equality of the states.

The opponents of the Democrats were beginning to make this appeal. Pleas were heard for the acceptance of the democratic principle as the means of substituting fair play for the fractious negativism of minorities; there was no more equitable rule than the will of the majority. Such sporting words, however, did not make southerners forget the warning of the census. If the voice of the majority became the will of the republic, they might well be at the mercy of their free-state neighbors. They feared the tyranny of numbers. Plainly the effort by northern spokesmen to make democracy a cohesive formula would have only slightly more chance of success than the labor of their southern antagonists to secure the acceptance of regionalism and the recognition of the right of minority veto.

Thus the three general concepts, nationalism, regionalism, and democracy, which some people hoped would overcome the divisive strains, were themselves accentuating conflict. The very efforts to avert strife in vital respects stimulated it. Protagonists of nationalism and democracy could not, even by appealing to the grandeur or force of their ideas, divert the attention of the advocates of regionalism from their concern with minority rights and the need of regional veto power.

The leaders of the democracy and the rank and file of their followers were hardly equipped to understand the subtle implications of the cultural federalism with which they had to cope. They were in reality going blindly into the maze of opinion and attitudes which were its constituents. Their blindness was not their fault but their lack of culpability made their blunders nonetheless dangerous.

Other elements had to be included in the model of the history I was devising, elements even more difficult to define. The sixth feature was one of cultural selection, by which I sought to sort out from the mass of actions, motivations, and the infinite variety of patterns that make up society's behavior those that particularly influenced the politics of that particular time and attempt to assemble them in some association that would make their influences understandable. It was my task to choose such details of the process of cultural evolution as were determining and to describe their influence.

Having selected them, I used them as a background sketched in so that the politicos would not strut on an empty stage. These particular elements were population movement, economic panic, religious ferment, romantic trends of thought, and hyperemotionalism which acted as dynamic forces as potent to effect the behavior of the politicians as the latter were unconscious of their real nature.

In performing this task, it was not difficult to realize that the relation between political behavior and social and economic forces is not at all clear and simple. The classic tradition is that parties represent interests or groups which can be neatly isolated and ticketed. This is too simple. Parties are conglomerations of individuals in association who represent attitudes conditioned by prevailing prejudices, passions, idealisms, and loyalties. They often are made up of people of the most diverse interests who for various reasons find temporary satisfaction in a common name, association, or action program.

The contemporary influences that surround these parties may be so confused that any definite measure of their relative strength must be difficult to estimate. Truth concerning them can be more nearly approximated by suggestion than by any attempt at dogmatic statement. But it is important to remember that a party develops a complex behavior which is more than a reflection of influences surrounding it. This pattern of behavior is made up of customs and habits which are self-perpetuating and dominating. They are not weakly dependent upon economic or cultural influences; in fact they become cultural influences themselves which at times determine social and economic behavior.

The seventh characteristic of the model was the fact that American politics, on the eve of the conflict, was being operated under a new set of rules. One of these was to abandon a practice which had been resorted to increasingly by the major parties, the practice of avoiding dangerous issues and omitting reference to them in party contests. This practice had been painfully invented as a safety device by those directing the organization of national governing. Those who had built the political machinery that ran the national parties had learned that in a country as large as the United States and constantly growing, success could be most surely obtained on a negative platform. So varied were the attitudes that positive attention to any major interest would draw down the opposition of the others and court defeat. The Democrats had been the first to learn this, and when they came to write their platforms in the thirties they chose two ideas admirably suited to this purpose, laisser faire regarding controversial domestic issues and a spread-eagle foreign policy attractive to most interests. Also they had abandoned broadly popular leadership in the executive. After Jackson's retirement, they had nominated only professionals for the Presidency.

Their opponents had not learned quite so easily. Under Clay's guidance the National Republicans and the Whigs had tried a positive program, an American system, only to meet defeat. Their accidental and short-lived successes had been won with hand-picked "heroes" like Harrison and Taylor, who in no sense led the party, and who were given no platform at all. On the eve of the conflict, however, when the Whigs were played out they gave way to the Republicans, an affirmative type of party, exploiting differences and thriving on controversy, who would also distribute federal largess in a manner designed to attract to their banner those who were eager for national subsidies to railroads, industry, education, or for a general free distribution of land.

They were likewise determined to destroy the political power of the South by decreeing that slavery should spread no further. They would forge an iron ring around the existing slave states and impose upon the South a constantly shrinking status in the national power structure. The Republicans made little effort to compromise. They deliberately sought to capitalize the divisive attitudes. Their direct approach forced the Democrats into a position of untenable ambiguity. The northern wing led by Douglas proposed a principle of popular sovereignty which ostensibly left the question of slavery extension in the territories to the people on the frontiers. This sounded fine on the hustings or in legislative chambers but it was ambiguous as to the time when the status of slavery was to be settled in the territories and by whom. It could be interpreted as a device to promote freedom or to protect southern rights. Knowledge of this form of double talk filtered into the South, raising many a question there. Was the idea of the will of the majority, "the original and pure fountain of political power," to be used to deprive the South of rights of property in the territories? Was it not just as dangerous to their future power and safety as the "sentence of outlawry" contained in the Republican platform? Could the South have any more faith in the Democratic party than in the Republican? Now that the parties had taken on these new rules of operation, could the nation hold together? Was not the party system by its operation going to invite destruction?

The use of this model with its seven concepts enabled me to speculate not only about the intricacies of partisan behavior and their relation to the American Civil War but also about a problem of even greater moment. Had not popular government developed dangerous weaknesses and limitations—fewer perhaps than those of other forms, but nevertheless indubitable? In the changing times of the twentieth century when American political institutions may well be in the process of alteration, it seemed to me well to be conscious of the limitations of our historic system, so that ignorance of them might not at any future time contribute to the calamities of social disruption. Furthermore, if the United Nations were ever to develop an approximation of world federation, its managers must become more expert in the operation of the complexities of federalism. The founding fathers of this new order need skill in counteracting divisive attitudes, so that they may not nourish the fears and frustrations that breed secession and war. It would be well to heed today and in the future the uncomprehended danger signals which in the 1850's lined the road leading to the disruption of the American democracy.

In view of all this, I found that the paramount responsibility which I had thus assumed was the necessity of avoiding the pitfalls of simple interpretation, of failing to comprehend the variety of factors determining a given confusion, and for this purpose it was essential to acquire greater skill in identifying, sorting out, arranging in significant order the factors determining political behavior, assigning them their degrees of importance, and in so doing, discarding any that might be really irrelevant.

The truth was that the democracy, old and faction-scarred, had become institutionalized; being no longer spurred by pristine enthusiasm, it was in no shape to meet the demands of the new rules. Despite the efforts of the southern senatorial junto, which controlled it, the party was lacking in the most vital essential of power; national leadership recognized in all sections. Modern organization technique had not yet been fully created, although the structure was essentially there.

The campaign of 1856, the first in a new political cycle marked by further evidences of the operation of new rules, presented portentous new omens. A threat loomed behind the Democratic victory, made apparent by the statistics of the election. If the Republicans could gain but two more states, Pennsylvania and either Indiana or Illinois, the doom of Democratic power was sealed, at least for four years. It mattered not that the Republicans had no southern wing, they had now votes enough in the East and West. And if the Democrats were beaten, what of the future of both party and Union?

Nor were these statistics the only threatening signs. Threats of a southern secession in the event of Republican victory were ominous. If a large section of the nation were to assume the attitude that defeat at an election would destroy the republic, self-government was in a perilous situation indeed. Furthermore, there were indications that the narrow margin of the Democratic victory in 1856 was obtained by fraud in several close states. The use of so much money to carry an election was alarming. Was the growth of corruption inevitable? Was self-government to be manipulated through graft and bribery? Such rottenness like threats of secession boded ill for the future of the great experiment.

Unconsciously using this research model, I pursued the study of the power aggregate, the Democratic party during the years 1856-61. Because the confusion of those years was so great and the innumerable factors which affected, deflected, and obscured the onrush of events were so various, I undertook to place the situation under a microscope in more than a score of the thirty-four states. This was necessary because I found that the party disorganization could not be explained accurately by any concise formula expressed in national terms. The party, like the nation, was a federal system; it was not so much a national organization as a federation of state machines. It could be understood only by a microscopic examination of the particular relations of the three elements which were its most important constituents—the voters, the machines, and the leaders—both in their national and in their state relations. The internecine quarrel within the Democratic party, the rapid growth of the Republican party, and the northern-inspired John Brown's raid in slaveholding Virginia—all were disturbing factors which boded no good for the continued effectiveness of the ruling party or its success in 1860. Its directing junto dominated by Senators, mostly from the South, with whom the administration was closely allied could not meet the misfortunes that were piling up by any effective, constructive devices, so in their frustration they adopted policies which in 1860 destroyed the Democratic party. The nation might be on the brink of disaster, but there seemed to be insufficient strength or understanding in the ruling party, nor was there any staff or machinery able to prevent the threatened calamity. The Democratic leadership itself, by its own lack of resourcefulness despite its long experience, in effect destroyed its own party. The disruption of the American democracy, once the successful organization of Jackson's followers, was followed shortly by the election of the Republican President, Abraham Lincoln, and then the guns of civil war.

When I asked myself in 1946 the question "Why?" this was my answer. People fight under the stress of hyperemotionalism. When compelling drives, whether ambition, fear, anger, or hunger, become supercharged, violence and bloodletting thus far in human history have proved seemingly "inevitable." Now why was emotion in the United States in 1861 supercharged?

The basic reasons for this hyperemotionalism cannot be neatly formulated and weighed. Fundamentally the process was an illustration of what Machiavelli describes as the "confusion of a growing state." The population of the United States was rapidly multiplying, partly by natural increase and partly by foreign immigration, at the same time that it was arranging itself in rapidly changing patterns. Many Americans were creating new communities, others were crowding together into older urban centers. In old and new, change was continual, with a ceaseless moving out and coming in. The rate of growth, however, could not be uniform; for it was determined in large part by physiographical considerations and the republic extended from the temperate into the semitropical zone. In the semitropical-to-temperate agricultural South, enterprise was less active, mobility less noticeable. In the northerly states, on the other hand, the variety of realized and potential wealth was greater, the stimulus from climate was sharper, the interest in projects of all sorts was more dynamic. There the vision of wealth and of the needs of the growing society continually inspired the creation of new and more powerful interests, under zealous and ambitious leaders.

So rapid and uneven a rate of social growth was bound to inflict upon Americans this "confusion." Characteristic of it and dominant in it were the pervasive, divisive, and cohesive attitudes which, as Whitman put it, were "significant of a grand upheaval of ideas and reconstruction of many things on new bases." This social "confusion" was the great problem confronting statesmen and politicians. Turn where they would, they could not escape it; they must wrestle with it, weakened by their own confusion.

The political system which was in the process of evolving reflected their predicament. They knew that they were operating a federal system, but they oversimplified their problem by believing that it was only a political federalism. They did not grasp the fact that it was a cultural federalism as well. Not only were they dealing with a political federation of states, they must understand this cultural federation of attitudes. Their inability to understand this contributed much to their failure to organize the partisanship and the political machinery adequate to deal with these cultural complexities.

This lack of understanding was accompanied by a deep-seated enjoyment of political activity by Americans which became dangerous. They gave themselves so many opportunities to gratify their desire for this sport. There were so many elections and such constant agitation. A great disruptive fact was the baneful influence of elections almost continuously in progress, of campaigns never over, and of political uproar endlessly arousing emotions. The system of the Fathers might possibly bear within itself the seeds of its own destruction.

This constant agitation certainly furnishes one of the primary clues to why the war came. It raised to ever higher pitch the passion-rousing oratory of rivals. They egged one another on to make more and more exaggerated statements to a people pervasively romantic, isolated, and confused. The men and women exhibiting these different attitudes were not isolated and separated by boundaries—they dwelt side by side, and the same person might be moved by more than one attitude at a time, or by different attitudes at different times. The baffling problem was not how to maintain a balance among states but how to preserve a balance among a number of emotional units or attitudes. It was this that proved beyond the political capacity of the time.

Under the stimulus of constant agitation the leaders of the southern branch of the democracy forbade the voters to elect a Republican president unless they wished him to preside over a shattered government. A number of voters sufficient to create a Republican majority in the Electoral College defied the prohibition. Then southerners, in a state of hyperemotion, moved by pride, self-interest, a sense of honor and fear, rushed to action; they were numerous enough and effective enough to force secession. They would flee the peril; in the spirit of 1776, they would organize a second American revolution, this time against the tyranny not of a monarch but of "a mob." They would create a reformed confederacy free from corruption and centralization in which their social and economic institutions would be made safe because the South was at last "free."

Also under the stimulus of constant agitation, the newly organized Republican administration decided to put down what it called the "Rebellion." Backed by an angered constituency including most northern Democrats, it determined to fight rather than permit the seceding states to break up a profitable partnership, a source of wealth and power, and an experiment in liberty and equality which Lincoln felt was the hope of the world. It undertook a "people's contest" to insure that "government of the people, by the people, for the people" should "not perish from the earth."

Thus war came when the American people for the first time refused to abide by a national election. The parties which had been promoting the cohesive attitudes had broken down, and their disorganization had permitted the new Republican organization to win through direct appeal to the divisive attitudes.

War broke out because no means had been devised to curb the extravagant use of the divisive forces. Statesmanship seemed poverty-stricken. The work of the nationalists who sought to find a formula with which to overcome the divisive attitudes was vain. Too few even saw the need for the formula; they ran heedlessly down the path to disruption. The war was the product of the chaotic lack of system in ascertaining and directing the public will, a chaos exploited with little regard for the welfare of the general public by irresponsible and blind operators of local political machinery unchecked by any adequate central organization.

Finally, carrying the analysis even further, it may be postulated that the war came because of certain interests and activities characterized for convenience as the processes of human behavior, in which individual and general attitudes and emotional drives are constantly interacting—provoking and conditioning one another. At certain times and in certain circumstances, cooperative behavior predominates; but competitive behavior is seldom if ever absent, and when too vigorously aroused leads to a strife which ranges from argument to war. Indeed argument is itself a form of conflict short of war, more or less, and if pressed without checks and restraints easily passes over into war.

The American democracy sought from 1850 to 1860 to keep in power by encouraging cooperative behavior. But, deeply affected by the shocks of the collisions occurring within the society in which it operated and of which it was a part, the party failed to overcome the divisive attitudes and was shattered. The disruption of the American democracy eventuated in defeat, secession, and civil war.

The research for this book had been undertaken in twenty-six states and Canada. My headquarters was always in Philadelphia but I was so situated that I could spend half of many weeks in Washington. I arranged sojourns of various lengths at Columbia, at Duke University, at California, at Oregon, at Harvard, at Stanford, at the University of Chicago and the University of Illinois, and at various state historical societies in Springfield, Illinois, St. Louis, and in Albany. The University of Georgia acquired the Howell Cobb Manuscripts, and I found other papers in private hands. I spent a month in Kansas covering its great collection of territorial sources. Finally, by Commencement, 1942, I felt I had my material in hand. So we eschewed any travel that year and I sat down to write. The end of the summer found the back of the work broken and then came the typing and the checking of notes and the bibliography. Charles A. Beard did me the honor to read the manuscript and to write of it in flattering terms. Then I sent it to Macmillan. In April, 1946, came the welcome word from Charles E. Cuningham of that firm that contracts were ready, and in the spring of 1948 the book was out. The reviews were very heartening and in the end, one evening in May, 1949, when I returned to my rooms in Cambridge at Trinity, I found two little brown envelopes from the post-telegraph office and then I knew that I had been awarded the Pulitzer Prize. But this is anticipating the story a little.

VIII

THE ANGLO-AMERICAN CONCEPT

DURING THE YEARS of the Second World War cultural relations between the United States and Great Britain became more tightly knit. For some years an American scholar had occupied the Harmsworth chair in American history at Oxford. During the conflict Cambridge took up the idea and established what was to become the Pitt professorship to be occupied by a succession of American historians, each serving for a year. An invitation had come to me in the early years of the war to go over to the university on the Cam to lecture for a term before the chair itself had been established. This I could not undertake, but at war's end through Professor Denis W. Brogan I was invited again, this time to be visiting professor for a year. After some negotiation over the date, I accepted for the academic year 1948–9.

In the course of the correspondence, I received a letter from Dr. George Macaulay Trevelyan, Master of Trinity College, inviting me to be a professorial fellow and to live in the college. Jeannette was invited by the University of Birmingham to lecture there during the Michaelmas term. We both felt that the English experience would be most meaningful to me if I lived in the college association, which I could not do if we took a house in Cambridge; and as Jeannette wanted to pursue her research in international monetary diplomacy at the Public Record Office in London, she therefore decided to live in London at Crosby Hall, the headquarters of the English branch of the Association of University Women, commute to Birmingham for the term in question, and spend most of her time at her research at the Record Office. Brogan, who had initiated the correspondence with me about the Cambridge professorship, came to visit us and I undertook to write an inaugural lecture.

In preparing it, I became even more impressed with the relationship between British and American politics. I encompassed it in an address which in due time I delivered before the vice-chancellor and an audience, including the historians, the masters of Trinity and St. Johns.

I defined my own particular interest in the study of Anglo-American political institutions to be the evolution of their mechanism of operation and control. I offered my opinion that despite the fact that so much attention had been devoted to political and constitutional history, too little thought had been given to the evolution of the basic patterns of political behavior.

Judging by political history in the United States I reported my view that there was no adequate analysis of the evolution of the real instruments of democratic behavior, namely, the parties. Though there was much in the way of political biography, despite this concentration on the leaders, little or no attention had been paid to the led. It was knowledge of the political behavior of the mass, and the reasons therefor, not of the few in positions of party leadership or in legislative position, that was needed.

I wished to make a fresh study of the two-party system, that achievement almost unique of the Anglo-American endeavor. I felt that it was the chief mechanism of democracy, but that unfortunately the practical working of this system had been much distorted in historical writing. Political historians had been more interested in personalities, in the artificial dialectic of political debate, and in certain spectacular political events than they had been concerned with the history of actual political behavior and operation. In place of exclusive interest in prominent leaders, so-called political issues, and the incidents and statistics of campaigning, I would seek the more intricate causes of mass political behavior. Instead of so much emphasis upon what might be called the formal and visible history of government as operated by party in executive and legislative functioning, I would seek the less visible, in fact often hidden, operation of party machinery, using patterns which I had learned to believe were in some instances of great age and English origin.

In this inaugural lecture[1] I discussed the potentialities of the chair and offered a suggestion. In view of the fact that new ideas and varying points of view would be brought over each year, it might be well to conserve some cumulative result from these visits. Cambridge historians had always been noted for their cooperative endeavors. Could not some Cambridge scholar act as co-

[1] Roy F. Nichols: *The Historical Study of Anglo-American Democracy* (Cambridge, England: Cambridge University Press, 1949).

operator with the successive American visitors? He could work with those who were to come there on a new series in the notable Cambridge histories, each to be responsible for a particular section or series of chapters; there might emerge a "Cambridge History of Democracy." This plan of writing did not bear fruit, but a variation of the idea of the "cooperator" was adopted later.

Finally I felt the comparative study of political history could do much to overcome the handicap which nationalism had enforced upon those who were seeking such understanding. All during the nineteenth century, when history took such impressive strides ahead, the historians were working in an atmosphere heavy with rising nationalism. Almost unconsciously the histories of the various states had taken on that coloring, and that coloring emphasized separateness and uniqueness. Rivalries and jealousies were reflected consciously or unconsciously, and too often those in one society thought of others only as aliens who, like their language, must be understood in a different medium of thought, expression, and interpretation—with little concept of anything common or kindred. American historians had been much the slaves of this nationalism.

Also, particularly in the two democracies, there had been such great weight given to a particular color of political influence and tradition in a fashion which had at times partially obscured the truth. In Great Britain and in the United States it had been a commonplace, for those who had given heed to such things, to consider the trend of national development generally in terms of righteous striving with a great degree of success toward moral and social progress. This had produced in Great Britain the Whig tradition matched by the populist or the progressive tradition in the United States. The historians in these two societies had been almost constantly operating with beams in their eyes, sometimes conscious of motes in the eyes of their contemporaries elsewhere, but almost never aware of the hindrance to their own sight. I believed that truth in history demanded a conscious effort to consider the narrowing effect of employing such interpretive concepts and to discover more comprehensive interpretations. This I was going to attempt to accomplish.

Here I was in England, in the atmosphere and among the monuments of British politics, prepared for extensive exploration of the record of our political origins. I was to be admirably situated to carry on this work. As a professorial fellow at Trinity College I was assigned a set of rooms in Nevile's Court overlooking the Wren Library. Jeannette often came to Cambridge or I went to London. We spent our London weekends together at Dartmouth House, the clubhouse of the English Speaking Union in Mayfair. The situation in Cambridge was with another pattern. The colleges at the university had only bachelor quarters. Jeannette could visit me in my rooms, but at a discreet hour of the evening I must escort her to other lodgings. Occasionally we stayed at local hotels but they were often "booked up" long in advance and therefor inconvenient, so Jeannette shortly found some pleasant people in an ancient dwelling, once a mansion, not far from Trinity who on occasion would accommodate her with "bed and breakfast" and "two-thirds of a bath."

I had a fine degree of freedom for my searching and thinking. During the Michaelmas and Lent terms I gave two courses of lectures and in the short Easter term only one. There was a month's interval between the first and second and second and third terms. In Cambridge I had the riches of the Trinity and other college libraries, the Seeley Library of History, and the great new University Library. We, particularly Jeannette, worked a good deal in the British Museum and in the Public Record Office. In the latter depository she had the great good fortune of the advice and guidance of Ronald Latham in her use of British diplomatic and financial archives in the Round Room. I accompanied her in monetary explorations at Manchester, Dublin, and other former centers of British bimetallic activity and to some French bimetallic sources. Between terms we went to Switzerland and Holland, and I was privileged to visit the refuges of the English Protestants, particularly in Zurich, Geneva, and Leyden.

I was aware of the fact that there was a close relation between religion and English politics in the era of colonial migration and I soon went to work in the extensive collection of sixteenth- and seventeenth-century pamphlets on the shelves of the Trinity Library, which included many political tracts. I found the Cambridge Platonists of the seventeenth century particularly interesting. Cambridge was a political as well as a religious seed bed. Here was significant activity in the organization of something resembling a Puritan political party which eventually contested for seats in Parliament in the days of Elizabeth. This politics certainly made itself felt in her reign in the effort to curb the Queen's religious authority and that of her bishops and to secure a presbyterian form of church government independent of the Crown. Living in Trinity and often visiting Emmanuel, the center of this Puritan striving for liberty of worship, I became conscious of an "experience," an environmental experience of great historical significance.

It was one thing to read about this age of political disputation, it was another thing to walk where these disputants had walked, to work where they had worked, to worship where they had preached, to live where they had lived in an environment which still preserved some of the reminders of their existence, places such as Erasmus' tower at Queens' and Milton's mulberry tree at Christ's, and which had kept so much of what they knew. At this time I was fresh from experience with Croce and Collingwood and I was much in the spirit of the dogma that history existed in the mind of the historian. I was having a vivid experience of mental recreation of this people.

All told, my year in England taught me much, and one of the advantages was that it filled my mind with images from the parent cultures. I had always visited the American scenes but now I had gained a sense of origin, adaptation, and continuity that came not just from tourist visiting but from living, mingling, working, talking with those who were native to these scenes and this culture.

There was a daily ritual which encouraged pleasant acquaintance, after mid-morning, for it was recognized that privacy was a man's prerogative until after he had faced the daily problem of resuming contact with the world. My breakfast was brought to me from kitchens and laid out for me by my bed maker after she had brought in my hot water and lighted my fire. She thought I was missing something when I refused morning tea in bed. By ten thirty I was ready to sally forth in gown and "square" to lecture at the Examination School or at the Mill Lane lecture hall. Unlike some of my colleagues I did not fare forth, so garbed, on a bicycle, but walked.

After lecture I returned to Trinity, hung up my gown, in a nook off the fellows' parlor, and joined them at lunch at the buffet laid out in the Great Hall. At four there was a general gathering for a second time in the fellows' parlor where individual tea was brought. I soon had discovered that if I drank all the tea that it was my privilege to command, I would achieve a highly undesirable nervous tension, so I resorted to a saving device. Tea was brought to each on an individual tray, in a pot, together with a pitcher of hot water, a pitcher of milk, a small allowance of sugar—for this was one of the winters of austerity, bread and butter, and cake. I soon learned to fill my teacup with hot water and milk, sugar it, and leave the teapot exactly as I found it. I could therefore enjoy the bread and cake, for with rationing and no dinner until eight in the evening, one became conscious of an interior void at teatime. The great and final assembly of the day occurred once again in the fellows' parlor shortly before eight, when we assembled in our gowns for the climactic social office of the day. Promptly at that hour the chief porter appeared in morning dress and silk hat and ushered us up the stairway to the Great Hall, where under the watchful eyes of Henry VIII and the Duke of Gloucester we took our places on the dais well above the throng of undergraduates. The master and the vice-master then said a Latin grace antiphonally—*"Oculi omnium in te sperant, Domine"*—and we sat down to high table. If for some reason there was need of haste, the grace could be condensed: *"Benedictus, benedicat."* Then the waiters in white tie and tails brought us the three courses. As we dined later than any other college, I suspected the waiters on occasion of attempting in very dignified fashion to hurry us a little. This was always a very pleasant meal with conversation flowing free, though shop was never talked. The well-known American gambit "How is your work going?" was just not used.

After dinner and the benediction, *"Benedicto, benedicatur,"* a varying number went up to the combination room where, around a shining mahogany table, the fellows drank port. If three requested it, claret was also brought to the board and circulated. Then there were biscuits, on occasion fruit and nuts, and always snuff, a commodity which added to the hubbub and sometimes punctuated the flow of conversation. With these frequent occasions for meeting in so relaxed an atmosphere, splendid opportunities were offered to improve acquaintance.

This acquaintance had begun at the moment of my arrival. As I got out of the taxi at the Great Gate I was met by David Hinks, the junior bursar, who had arranged and furnished my quarters and now directed the porters to take my luggage thereto. As we were crossing the Great Court to go to my rooms we met the master, Dr. Trevelyan, who welcomed me and straightway invited me to lunch at the lodge with Mrs. Trevelyan and himself on Sunday. It was a very pleasant introduction to my new living.

Trinity proved to be a most pleasant place for a historian. There I had the great privilege of almost daily meetings with three of its fellows, Trevelyan, its master, the Regius professor of modern history, J. R. M. Butler and G. S. R. Kitson Clark. The master had the pleasant custom of frequently inviting the fellows to the Lodge after high table on Sunday evenings for talk and a drink. On occasion he would discuss with me the problems of Anglo-American political history to my great advantage. During the year I read a number of his books, including his inspiring autobiography which was published during my residence. Professor Butler was very hospitable and quite frequently invited me to have coffee in his rooms after lunch and I had the privilege of talking over my inaugural with him and of hearing him deliver his own. Kitson Clark acted as my mentor in Cambridge ways and our meetings in the fellows' parlor and in the combination room and our numerous walks around Cambridge and the colleges gave me an intimate view of the university and its customs, as well as insights into English political history of which he is a master.

Another of my happy Cambridge experiences was close friendship with another Trinity fellow, Tressilian C. Nicholas, the senior bursar of the college and a geologist. He and Mrs. Nicholas and their daughter Jean, an undergraduate at Newnham, lived in a delightful home on Park Terrace. I met Mr. Nicholas on the afternoon of my arrival and from then until this writing we have continued an association that has represented to me the depth and cordiality of English friendship. I saw him daily at Trinity and was often invited to their home or to be a guest with them at various Cambridge events, particularly of a musical nature. Mrs. Nicholas and their daughter were accomplished musicians and I enjoyed their talent. Frequently at the end of the day or after some Cambridge gathering I would be invited to their home for tea. Mr. Nicholas guided Jeannette and me to the boat races in the spring, and together with Dean Henry A. Hollond, through the delightful social intricacies of May week which, incidentally, is in June.

Our association with Dean Hollond was also very pleasant. One of my predecessors at Pennsylvania in the history department had been Gaillard Lapsley who, after a sojourn in our department, had gone to Cambridge as a fellow of Trinity and had become an institution, more English, it was said, than any Englishman. Dean Hollond had known him well and now lived in his quarters. Shortly after my arrival he invited me to his rooms and gave me a list of the fellows, with comments about them that made it easier for me to get acquainted. He was always doing pleasant things for me. One among the many I remember was connected with a royal visit. The year of my Cambridge sojourn was the year women were admitted to full degree standing at the university. So to celebrate the event the Queen was invited to receive an honorary degree. Dean Hollond arranged for me to be present with my colleagues in the Senate House as a member of the procession to witness the ceremony.

During the terms I was invited to dine at the high tables of the various colleges, generally by the teachers of history, and I made a number of delightful acquaintances. High tables, combination rooms, fellows' parlors, and the beautifully kept college gardens provided a frame for notable hospitality. Also, I sat with the history board on occasion and attended certain sessions of the University History Club and the history clubs of the various colleges. Likewise I had interesting visits with the historians at Oxford, London, and Birmingham. Because of my membership in the Social Science Research Council, the Rockefeller Foundation through Joseph H. Willits, the director of its Social Science division, had given me a generous grant enabling me to visit social scientists in English, Scottish, and Irish universities to learn of their research interests, and I made a report of these conversations to the Social Science Research Council on my return home.

The idea that British scholars were aloof and distant

was completely dispelled and my fellowship with my Cambridge hosts and many others that I met in the British Isles proved them to be most generous and outgoing. No visitor could ever have experienced a warmer welcome or have been made to feel more completely at home.

My sojourn in England gave me the opportunity and the inspiration to carry on a new study which had been germinating while I was engrossed with *The Disruption of American Democracy*. One of the problems which any historian may face is where to begin his research. His choice can be arbitrary and uncomplicated, but on the other hand it may take much thought and some imagination. When in 1919 I began the study of the ante-bellum Democratic party, I had no difficulty in choosing 1850 as the starting point. There was an obvious series of events leading from the successful achievement of compromise in 1850 to the failure to adopt one in 1860–1. But the more I continued working with the data and thinking about them, the more obvious it became that the significance of political behavior in that decade could only be properly interpreted by going deep into antecedent conditions, and even before I had finished *The Disruption* I had begun a long-range exploration, backward in time.

I had come to the conclusion that historians tend to work and think in terms of time spans, often denoted as epochs and eras, which are too short to enable them to define meaningful stages in the history of the evolution of human behavior. The real patterns in this evolution are often very ancient, and to ignore this fact by circumscribing their study and analysis within "epochs" which are too short and defined in an earlier day for reasons perhaps no longer valid, vitiates much of the significance of the work. One reason for this inadequacy is the fact that the general outline of history has depended largely upon the philosophical competence and educational prescriptions of textbook writers. In other words, much of the organizational pattern of history has been and continues to be dictated by the needs of high school students and college and university freshmen and sophomores. In fact, we have too generally depended upon Ph.D. candidates to supply the data, and textbook writers the overall pattern, of our historiography.

Yet behavior patterns, like everything else organic, develop in time; man has been forming and re-forming his ways of behaving over perhaps some half million years. The significance of this long time span of evolution has become more evident as we have gained greater insight into behavioral mechanisms. The better we understand what some of our colleagues tell us of the importance, in the forming of personality, of the experiences of childhood, of the survival of patterns of behavior learned in preadolescent years, and of the persistence of immaturity into later life, the more we see how thin a veneer of rational action and deliberation has been barely hiding a series of traits which are still basically primitive, even savage and very old. At a time when men seem to be stripping off that veneer and philosophers are discarding the concept of progress, it should be apparent that it is vital to think more in terms of time. We need to search diligently for more light on the process of change, even if it carries us out into that fog so impenetrable to some, the fog beyond the census.

Historical understanding of time is essential because one of our prime concerns is the measure of the social validity of institutions. The validity of institutions almost invariably depends upon their capacity to satisfy fundamental human needs, and the length of time during which they have satisfied them is a vital item of knowledge. This is so because sound modification of institutions depends upon knowledge of what is likely to work, and this knowledge can only be obtained from some kind of measurement or judgment of the success with which institutions have met the human needs for which they were designed. It must be understood that things take much longer to happen than we sometimes think. Patterns of behavior need to be traced through centuries, not merely over decades. The historians' interests should be fitted into a long chronology.

Continuing study of the history of the development of American political behavior patterns increased my consciousness of a pre-American background, particularly in the matter of evolving political machinery and the party system. In the study of these data categories, "by observation," as the mathematicians say, I had concluded that a two-party system rarely existed outside of the Anglo-American experience. But why had it happened in this culture and hardly anywhere else? I proposed, as an initial hypothesis, that it was basically conditioned by the fact that between 55 B.C. and 1066 the British Isles had suffered four major invasions and had been conquered four times, by the Romans, the Anglo-Saxons, the Danes, and the Normans. Of these conquerors, the Romans had remained for centuries, and the Anglo-Saxons and the Normans permanently. Consequently for a thousand years the inhabitants of England had naturally divided into two groups of political significance, the conquerors and the conquered, and a major cultural adjustment had had to be made on the basis of an accommodation between two interests. Later on the Protestant Reformation had produced another deep-seated two-party division between Catholics and

Protestants which had eventually been followed by another one between the Cavaliers and Roundheads. Later a fourth had developed between the Whigs and Tories during the seventeenth-century upheavals.

I had, in fact, begun working out these ideas in a graduate lecture course which I gave occasionally in the 1930's and thereafter, entitled "The Beginning of American Democracy," which I brought down chronologically to 1845. I projected my thinking farther and farther back, exploring the ancient behavior patterns of English self-government from the tribal days and tracing shire and borough government, the growth of Parliament, the evolution of elections, and the various peaceful or violent changes in the executive over the centuries. I had a vague plan of writing something that would show the evolution of the American political party and one of its instruments of operation, the democratic machine. Across the seas I turned to this project under the renewed impetus of my Cambridge year.

My work on this new study engrossed me from the time I began to plan my English lectures. They were to be two series. One was to embrace general United States history from 1763 to the present, and the other short course was to treat of American political thought and action. In this latter group I undertook to go back into British political behavior even before the age of written history and to try out the ideas that were engrossing me. My research and writing began almost immediately and were stimulated when Michael Oakeshott, fellow of Caius, invited me to write an article in the *Cambridge Journal.*

I was tracing the evolution of the operating mechanism of the republic of the United States, a self-governing society designed in the form of a federal system.

This polity was unique because it created and maintained self-government in a region so large, so varied in its physiographic features. and with a population so mobile that it was constantly expanding in all directions. During its relatively short history this society had grown in number from a few score souls to over 180 million people, still self-governing.

I set myself the task of studying the development of this process and art of self-government over a millennium. During some nineteen centuries a mechanism, a collection of folkways, a political machine had been constructed. I was not going to be satisfied with merely a narrative of its experience. Rather I sought to devise for myself a method of interpretation, some form of analysis which would produce an understanding of the process of its evolution. Not events, but steps or phases of an unfolding process must be defined, with a major objective the detection of the determinism, the force producing them. The emphasis was to be more on the "why" than on the "what," for obsession with "what" to the exclusion of "why" is too often the historian's intellectual limitation. My analysis enabled me to identify a series of steps in an evolutionary process which was to provide the outline for my study.

The actual writing of this book began on a May day in 1949 in Trinity's library. In its quiet dignity designed by Christopher Wren and decorated by Grinling Gibbons, I began to set down an analysis of the long process by which Anglo-American political customs evolved over the centuries. At Cambridge, in London, and on the continent I found so much to remind me of the age of these behavior patterns that were old even when those who crossed the Atlantic transported them for use in the new society then in the founding.

IX

GENEALOGY: A HISTORIAN'S HOBBY

I HAVE NEVER BEEN ABLE to separate my profession from a hobby implication. The connection has been genealogy. There should be no methodological difference between history and genealogy. Those who work or even dabble in genealogy should be, from the standpoint of craftsmanship, intellectual exercise, materials used, and thought processes, doing the same things in the same way as the historians. The only difference is that what they are doing is narrower and more highly specialized, with a much higher degree of personal identification. I have used genealogy as a hobby, a sort of a historian's busman's holiday. Again and again for nearly sixty years I have returned to certain persistent, entrancing, fascinating, exasperating genealogical problems for recreation as others turn to crossword puzzles or bridge, and I have found relaxation and mental renewal in this pastime.

When I was thirteen my grandmother Nichols died and the homestead at 359 Washington Street, Newark,

New Jersey, was dismantled and sold. In the course of disposing of the household effects, the accumulation of sixty years of living in one house, a collection of daguerreotypes must be disposed of. For some reason I wanted them and nobody else did. Also there were some family Bibles. My uncle wanted to keep his father's but two others, older ones, I coveted and received. At this time I began to ask questions about my forebears, and as nobody could answer them, I was referred to the New Jersey Historical Society housed in an ancient church building on West Park Street, right opposite my dentist's office. My uncle sought to discourage me somewhat by telling me if I looked too hard I might well find some ancestor who had been hanged. Parenthetically I might add I never had this excitement but I did find one who had built a gallows. My mother, who was apt to share my interests, encouraged me because she knew as little about her ancestry as my father did about his.

So one Saturday I went to West Park Street, not as usual to the dentist but to the Historical Society. This quiet library was presided over by a kindly lady, Miss Maude Johnson, who immediately placed in my hands Samuel H. Congar's "Genealogical Notices of the First Settlers of Newark,"[1] and with no trouble at all I found a listing of my Newark Nichols ancestors, learned that they had come from Connecticut in mid-eighteenth century, and that I was a descendant of a Revolutionary soldier. Upon that occasion or on a similar one, an elderly gentleman told me that when I reached my twenty-first birthday I would be eligible for membership in the Sons of the American Revolution and provided me with lineage papers against that day. Also on

[1] *Collections of the New Jersey Historical Society,* VI Supplement (Newark, 1866), 105–53.

one of my countless visits to the Newark Public Library I found a grand volume, *The Ogden Family in America, Elizabethtown Branch,* by William Ogden Wheeler, Philadelphia, 1907, devoted to the family of my great-grandmother Nichols, and from its pages I gleaned the prideful knowledge that I was related to a governor of New Jersey and President Millard Fillmore. I gained something of a sense of status.

My mother's interest grew and she encouraged me to explore her family. Her grandparents had migrated to this country later than my father's. His were English, Huguenot, Dutch, and had come to Newark and Piscataway town in New Jersey in the seventeenth century from New York City, Long Island, and Connecticut. Hers had come from Scotland and Germany in the eighteenth and early nineteenth century. My mother's mother and her sister told a confused story about their father's conscription in Hesse during the Napoleonic Wars and his migration to the United States after the end of these conflicts and the death of his mother, moved by a determination to seek a home where there was no conscription. However, all the documentation that I could then discover were two family Bibles which contained only vital statistics. So one Saturday my mother and I and a mutual friend, a lady who encouraged my historical interests by buying me books and discussing them with me and by taking me on Saturday-afternoon visits to interesting places in New York City, undertook to go to the Lenox Library, November 12, 1910, in that metropolis and make inquiries in their genealogical department. As we had very few data, the best the attendants could think of was to bring out New York City directories for the early nineteenth century. Our efforts were rewarded by finding the names and addresses of my two sets of great-grandparents which we duly copied out and which my mother recorded in her diary on our return home. In the course of this excursion and our discussions post and ante, she told me all she knew. We duly recorded her recollections of her grandparents and I undertook to interview my very few relatives and record what I learned.

When I went to college in New Brunswick I was next door to Piscataway town, which was the home of one quarter of my ancestry, for my grandmother Nichols had been born there in 1823. She united in her blood stream the contributions of a complicated network of relationships which had been cumulating in that one spot since its founding in 1666. I worked in the Rutgers Library and took occasion to explore the shelves for local data. I met a number of "woodpile relatives" who had similar interests, I explored burying grounds, I joined the S.A.R. as soon as I was twenty-one, and on my father's side I accumulated quite a store of ancestors. But on my mother's lines we had gotten nowhere, although she had looked through certain recent telephone directories in New York and New Jersey and corresponded with those listed who bore her family name of Cairns.

Then a genealogist contacted me. One of our family, a very distant cousin, was dissatisfied with the Nichols genealogy. There was seemingly no line discoverable back of that which Miss Johnson had showed me in 1909. He therefore engaged a cousin of his to make an exhaustive search and to fill in the missing links. It was well known and generally accepted that the original settler of the name was Francis Nichols who was in Stratford, Connecticut, by 1639, but how the New Jersey branch was connected with Francis of Stratford was as yet an unfathomed mystery. So Mr. Frederic C. Torrey undertook to solve the problem and to write a comprehensive genealogy. He contacted everyone he could find, seeking data. I gathered all I had found, corresponded with some I had not known before, and pumped my uncle who had a good memory and had lived in the family neighborhood all his life. While I was in college, Mr. Torrey completed his work. He had found posthumous twins registered in another Connecticut town and this discovery, he concluded, supplied the missing link in the person of one of the twins, Isaac Nichols, 3rd, of Stratford, who he maintained was the missing father of the Humphrey who established the New Jersey branch. In 1917 he published a book, *Ancestors and Descendants of Humphrey Nichols of Newark, New Jersey* (Lakehurst, N.J., 1917), which to his satisfaction established a complete line on the American shore and identified the Connecticut Nicholses with the Ampthill Nicholses in England. He believed he had resolved the doubts and put us all on sound foundation back as far as Charlemagne, who could now be accepted as a distinguished ancestor together with the Norman kings of England and Robert Bruce of Scotland. I rejoiced in a presentation copy which I had bound in blue morocco with black decoration and gold lettering. Genealogically, I had arrived. I was descended from kings, I was an S.A.R., I was also sprung from the loins of descendants of the first white child born in New York City. I was a member of English, Scottish, French, Dutch, German, Norwegian families, a truly representative American polyglot.

When I went to New York City to graduate school at Columbia, I spent much time in the New York Public Library and returned occasionally to the genealogical room to seek more data about my mother's lines. Also I discovered the Sixteenth Baptist Church attended by her Cairns grandparents and searched the records. These were curious because of a peculiar circumstance in the history of the congregation. When the builders of this church excavated for the foundations, they discovered a large deposit of excellent sand which could be sold at a good price to builders. The result was that they decided to dig down much deeper than planned and build brick burial vaults in tiers under the church. These vaults would have a capacity for numerous coffins. My great-grandfather Cairns had the misfortune to lose his wife and six children in the 1840's and their bodies were placed in these vaults. However, in course of time the New York City Board of Health forbade further burial in this manner and ordered the vaults sealed. In the meantime, my great-grandfather had removed to two other churches and had finally retired to live in Bloomfield, New Jersey. Some time during the 1850's he acquired a cemetery lot in the Oranges and sought to move thither the bodies from New York City, only to discover that they were sealed up by bricks and mortar and could not be moved. Now in 1920 I found myself sitting in a pew almost literally on top of their remains. My research in the New York Public Library uncovered very little. Incidentally, twenty years later I was in New York over the weekend attending Social Science Research Council meetings and I walked along Sixteenth Street—but there was no longer any church there; an apartment house occupied the site. Where were the bones of my great-grandmother and her brood? Not long afterward I stopped in at the office of the Baptist City Mission Society who had owned the building and learned the sequel. The church authorities, when they sold the church, had been mindful of their responsibilities and had acquired a lot in a Yonkers cemetery whither all that remained had been removed for reinterment. My informant rather callously called it "repacking" and removing. From a clerk I learned that one of the bodies had been mummified. I have always wondered if it were my great-grandmother.

Soon after our marriage it was my pleasure to go out to Michigan and Illinois to be introduced to Jeannette's family. In one way or another the conversations drifted to old furniture, old homesteads, pictures, family lore, and the like. One Sunday afternoon we began looking over old letters and family Bibles. No genealogical work had been done except in fragmentary fashion, and before long we were visiting graveyards and churches, and on occasion courthouses. In Michigan, Illinois, northern New York, and in the Hudson valley, particularly in the neighborhood of Kingston and Saugerties, we called on relatives of varying degree. Jeannette's father and mother were to celebrate their fiftieth wedding anniversary as we were nearing our tenth and there was to be a celebration. Jeannette got all the data together for the occasion and eventually she published it in book form: *James Styles of Kingston, N. Y., and George Stuart of Schoolcraft, Michigan, Their Descendants and Allied Families* (Swarthmore, Pa., 1936). While she was working on this I revived my own interest and found a few more items about my mother's antecedents. This was stimulated by the accident of finding mention of a familiar name in a news item. My mother wrote this man, who proved to be a distant cousin who was very cooperative and supplied some missing links and burial places.

On our visit to England, I went little realizing that I

was on the eve of a great disillusionment. There was an elaborate and what seemed to be a well-documented account of the Nichols family in England. I was particularly intrigued as a historian by the documentary citations and somewhat moved because a Connecticut authority had questioned the validity of the "line." So I would see for myself by looking at the originals of the documents. The principal items were wills at Somerset House. One fine day I went there, asked for the documents, paid my shillings, and there they were. But the quotations were not. Someone had manufactured the few words necessary to prove the line and then cited these documents as the source. I then took steps. I joined the Society of Genealogists at Chaucer House, where it then was, and began searching its collections. I went to Ampthill in Bedfordshire, where there was a monument in the church and where I was introduced to a gentleman who was living in a mansion on the site of a house where the presumed Nichols Ampthill ancestors lived. Then I retained a professional and finally had the benefit of the expert research of the Garter King at Arms at the Royal College of Arms. But all to no avail. There was no countervailing proof to offset this genealogical counterfeiting. At the same time, however, Jeannette was turning up English and Scottish ancestors right and left.

In pursuit of her forebears, she visited English parish churches and established connections. Then we took a delightful trip to Scotland. She had received from a cousin an account which placed the Scottish homestead at a farm called Greystone Leas in the parish of Ayton, to the south of Edinburgh. She got in touch with the minister of the Church of Scotland, who was very much interested, but from everything he and we could discover we were in the wrong place. However, we had arranged to visit the farm that had been the reputed homestead, so this we did. Our hosts were preparing for a wedding of one of the daughters and were in a very cheerful state of hospitality. We had the highest of high teas. With the family was another minister of the kirk and we talked the matter over with him, telling him of our disappointment at finding no stones in the churchyard, no names in the records. "Aye," he said, "but there were Stuarts in Fogo." Next day we were going to Registry House in Edinburgh, where the parish registers of all Scotland are under one roof, so on arrival, instead of pursuing the Ayton records any further, Jeannette asked for Fogo, and there they were. Eventually we went to Fogo and Greenlaw beyond the Lammermuir Hills and found gravestones and houses, were hospitably received, and partook of more high teas. Jeannette had bridged the genealogical barrier presented by the Atlantic Ocean.

Shortly before we left for England I had become president of the Genealogical Society of Pennsylvania and now and again I sought to use the horrible example of the Nichols swindle to impress upon those interested in Philadelphia of the need for standards of excellence, yea for plain common honesty and insistence upon proof based on valid evidence. Several of us in the society established a course in genealogy and conducted a weekly workshop in which the students produced papers and at the end of the season those whose work merited it received certificates of proficiency.

In the meantime, with my hard-won skepticism I reexamined the work done on this side of the water. I came to the conclusion that there were certain discrepancies here, the chronology was an unlikely one, and that the documents cited did not mean what the genealogist of 1917 had hoped they meant. Also I ran across other problems involving divorce hiding in clerical families, and chronological obscurantism due to anticipating marital vows. Here I enlisted further professional help but at present writing, officially things genealogical are in a mess. However, as far as my mother's relations are concerned, I can take satisfaction in a little progress. When my great-aunt died, her garret gave up some interesting evidence which led me to certain Hessian parishes. But here professional help seemed helpless. Even in the height of Nazi enthusiasm when masses of data were assembled, I had no better luck. Professionals, advertisements in German genealogical media, and chance all failed me.

The sum total of all this put me professionally in an embarrassing position, that is as far as the Nicholses' dilemmas are concerned. I think I know what the line should be from 1500 to the present on both sides of the Atlantic, but two of the steps are based on hypotheses which up to this date I cannot prove. This on the face of it seems frustrating but I have had a great deal of exercise, mental and physical, I have visited numerous historical repositories and become acquainted with many interesting people including some of my own relatives. It has been a relaxing and refreshing hobby which has sharpened my professional wits. Also, someday I may find the answers.

X

A NEW DIRECTION

SOME TIME AFTER I returned home in 1948, there came a diversion. I had settled down amidst my usual university responsibilities to finish the work started in England, but a change had taken place in the administration. In fact, there seemed an effort in the making to have history repeat itself. When I had come to the University of Pennsylvania in 1925 it had been seeking new leadership. Provost Edgar Fahs Smith had retired in 1920 and a bold stroke had been attempted to secure the vigorous direction required to meet the postwar problems of the university. Major General Leonard Wood had been chosen President. His popularity, together with the sympathy which Wilson's neglect of him during the war had aroused, led some of Wood's friends and certain of the trustees and alumni to think that he was just the man to guide Pennsylvania. Woodrow Wilson's career was fresh in everyone's mind. Various supporters of Wood thought that a successful university presidency might make the general the occupant of the White House when Harding's service there ended. Wood had accepted the invitation but he had never served; President Harding sent him to the Philippines instead. For a while the trustees had permitted him to remain away on leave, but before I came to the university he had been advised that he was needed here and he resigned. He had been succeeded as head by Dr. Josiah H. Penniman, acting provost and professor of English.

Dr. Penniman took as a major interest developing the research potential of the university. The First World War had stirred up a sense of the nation's lack of scientific preparation. Certain responsible citizens such as Herbert Hoover called upon the universities to be more concerned with research and the discovery of the new knowledge, particularly in the realm of science, which was so necessary. Conferences were suggested by Hoover to make plans for raising $20,000,000 for needed projects. Provost Penniman called one at the university in 1926 which resulted in the creation of a committee on research for the university of which Dr. Cheyney had been a member. As a result of plans made by this committee a grant of $80,000 was secured from the Rockefeller Foundation, to be administered over five years in the form of grants-in-aid to faculty research. And a board of graduate education and research was set up by the trustees, composed of some of their own members who co-opted people of influence from the community to work toward securing more funds when the five-year period of the Rockefeller grant had expired. I found the research committee interested in my research plans and my applications for funds for expenses in gathering material were very helpful, particularly in my work, which became *The Disruption of American Democracy.*

At this time ambitious plans were formulated for creating a new university which included a romantic project to move out to Valley Forge and to organize there a training school for leadership. However, the Panic of 1929 soon immersed the administration in the difficult though less inspiring task of keeping financially afloat and meeting payrolls. To do this the university was fortunate in persuading one of the trustees an able financier, a recent Morgan partner, chairman of its finance committee, Thomas S. Gates, to come out to the university and assume financial direction. Dr. Penniman remained as provost and educational leader while Mr. Gates was made President, concerning himself primarily with finance and public relations. For the first five years (1930-35) of his service he devoted himself principally to finance. Under the circumstances the university could and did seem to fail to advance. However, as soon as its head was above water financially Mr. Gates and his associates turned to reactivate a plan conceived in the previous decade to carry out an educational development and fund raising campaign to redefine and refinance the university so that it would present a new image in the intellectual world by the time of the bicentennial that it was planned to celebrate in 1940.

One of the phases of this reorientation was the rebuilding of departments. The biological and medical departments had been urging that some basic re-creation was necessary in physics and chemistry, particularly in physics, and the retirement of the chairman of that field made a convenient opportunity. In 1938 Gaylord P. Harnwell was called from Princeton. This was but one of several such moves.

The plans for the bicentennial were well worked out and effectively implemented. They came to climax in a series of successful symposia which brought so many from the scholarly world that I for one, and I am sure many others, got a sense of pride and effectiveness which for me, at least, had been previously lacking. After the long period of immobilization in the depression years, we were in motion. And then came the Second World War. Immediately I and my colleagues in the history department organized a special course to show how the war came. By 1943 the university was occupied in training programs. We were called on to organize various courses for Army, Navy, and Air force R.O.T.C. They all had American history requirements and it fell to my lot to design the courses which my colleagues were to teach the multitude of cadets, and to help some of my colleagues do it. Faculty in certain departments in social sciences and ancient languages no longer had many students, so they turned to teaching American history and I had the pleasure of coaching some of them. Then it fell to my lot to teach naval history to naval trainees. Also, Jeannette and I prepared a textbook adapted in shorter form from our college text. During 1943 I taught steadily through the twelve months. Fortunately I had the very effective assistance of two of our graduate students, John J. Reed and Joseph G. Tregle, Jr., who labored tirelessly in the various teaching programs.

By 1945 the conflict was obviously nearly over and we went up to Columbia to teach in the summer session. While we were there, the atomic bomb was exploded at Hiroshima and the war was soon ended. Jeannette and I retired to Eaglesmere for a few weeks of rest and freedom from war responsibility. It was very welcome.

In the academic years that followed the veterans began to return under the stimulus of the G.I. Bill of Rights. A new teaching experience was in store. These men were older, more mature, they had seen service, a number had been wounded or suffered battle fatigue. There were many problems involving space. Nothing of importance had been built at the university since the mid-twenties and then there had been calls from government for research. Now a number who had been away on war service came back, including many of our leading scientists with new ideas and new needs. Contracts were being offered for research projects, particularly by the government, though support was coming from industry as well. Then foundation interest in interdisciplinary area-language study, such as South Asia, American civilization, and linguistic analysis, caused new teaching groups to mobilize. It was time for new leadership.

In 1948 the Republican National Convention had held its sessions at Convention Hall just a few hundred yards from the campus. A young political leader came out of the West in the person of Governor Harold E. Stassen of Minnesota, who made a vivid impression as a leader of youth. Sometime during the summer of 1948 arrangements were completed to invite him to become president of the university while Dr. McClelland succeeded to the place left vacant when Mr. Gates retired as chairman of the university. In a manner the university was going to seek a leader in Stassen, as in Wood, from among public figures.

When I returned from Cambridge, Mr. Stassen was at work with plans to increase the university's resources and to improve its image. He arranged for the refinancing of the university's debt and projected impressive new buildings: the physics, mathematics, and astronomy housing; a new Wharton School; the Gates Pavilion in the medical school–hospital complex; and a new Library. Then Edwin B. Williams, dean of the graduate school, was appointed provost and in 1952 I succeeded him in the deanship.

It was at that time that politics concluded Mr. Stassen's administration of the university. Although he himself was not nominated in 1952 he had played a prominent role in the choice of Eisenhower, and on inauguration day he left the university for service in Washington. By May the university had chosen a successor in the person of the chairman of the physics department, Gaylord P. Harnwell.

For myself, I also had turned a corner in 1952 which involved a calculated risk. The risk was this. If I assumed administrative responsibility and became dean of the Graduate School of Arts and Sciences, would this mean the end of my functioning as a historian, the end of teaching, writing and research—in sum, the end of intellectual contribution as a scholar? I knew it was a risk but I decided to take it, in part because the university administration assured me that they would give me every facility to continue my historical contributions—a promise which they scrupulously kept.

The question was, however, despite facilities and encouragement, could writing survive the change of duty? Hitherto I had concentrated my teaching on Monday through Wednesday of each week and had spent the rest of the time in research, writing, and other professional activities. Now I would be in my office five days in the week. Certain changes in behavior were indicated if I wished to continue historical contributions. We had been living out in the suburbs; now we moved back to the university neighborhood within ten blocks of my office. I found it helpful to wake up early, sometimes five a.m., and work for two hours before breakfast, before any of the day's administrative duties and diversions began. Furthermore, I undertook writing that was more interpretive in character, which could be done in

Philadelphia and which did not involve much travel to repositories of material elsewhere. Besides, the day of microfilm and other inexpensive reproduction had dawned.

As I was to continue graduate teaching I proceeded to develop my study of the American political machine in my Wednesday afternoon graduate classes. I wrote these lectures out as I could find the time but I did not confine myself to them, and got a good deal published after 1952 because of certain adventitious circumstances.

The most significant encouragement to new writing came from the calendar. Just about the time that I entered my administrative duties there began the long series of historical anniversaries mostly connected with the Civil War, climaxing in 1961–5. For more than a decade occasional addresses were called for and from my multiple response came a series of essays and two books interpreting the years 1860–5, which had always been my keen interest. In doing these pieces I undertook to rethink and to reinterpret.

My rethinking along this line had really begun in the late 1940's. While in Cambridge I had received an invitation to join Avery Craven in a session of the Southern Historical Association to be held at Williamsburg in November, 1949. I prepared a paper which I entitled "1461–1861: The American Civil War in Perspective." I applied the fruits of my English research and reflections to the problem of the Civil War. I pointed out that from 1066 to 1861 there had been a period of violence first in English and then in American experience about once in every century. Therefore the cumulation of events seemed to make the conflict of 1861–5 likely to happen regardless of any immediate and particular circumstances.

Then the first of a series of anniversaries continuing down to 1965 began to occur in 1954 when the passage of the Kansas-Nebraska Bill was commemorated. During these commemorative years I was speaking in Virginia, North Carolina, South Carolina, Florida, Louisiana, and Texas of the seceded states and in Delaware, Maryland, Kentucky, and Missouri of the border states, as well as in the north. These talks were made before university and college audiences, before alumni groups, and at Civil War round tables. I spoke before the American Historical Association and the American Philosophical Society.

In the course of this writing and speaking I formulated certain ideas and concepts interpreting the so-called Civil War era. I became closely associated in university administration with the anthropologist and social philosopher, Loren Eiseley, and in the course of our frequent discussions I conceived the idea of a book which he thought Hiram Haydn of Atheneum Publishers might be interested in. As the dynamics of human behavior, particularly in its political phase, had always intrigued me, I made use of Thomas Hobbes's fanciful biomechanical concept of Leviathan, an "artificiall" organism or engine with "artificiall" life, to illustrate my concept that Anglo-American society had gradually constructed a viable instrument of self-government. The specifications of this mechanism had been set forth in the constantly accumulating file of constitutional documents which were drawn up as its various elements were invented to meet the needs of a constantly burgeoning society. When this society reached a point in 1860–1 when it could not contrive the parts necessary to prevent the breakdown of the "engine," the war came. During its course and in the reconstruction that followed, the process of political invention was resumed. My history of this institutional ingenuity appeared as *Blue Prints for Leviathan: American Style* on the Atheneum list in 1963. In it I undertook to account not only for the construction of the engine but for its failure just a century previously.

In approaching the problem of this failure I could find no simple explanation. The ecology and the demography of the United States had prescribed the evolution of a cultural pluralism within the swiftly growing society. Within this pluralism tensions had been present since the very early years, and one of the skills which the political engineers had been required by circumstances to develop had been that of contriving devices to secure an accommodation, a consensus. The device of political compromise introduced in the Constitutional Convention of 1787 had been subsequently utilized in Congress at various crucial times such as 1820, 1833, 1850, and in a sense in 1854 and 1858. However, these accommodations had proved increasingly difficult to negotiate.

The questions confronting the historian as he endeavors to analyze this problem are most difficult. As he examines the course of the South, some of the many puzzles he must consider are: Just how far did the southern leaders go in 1860 in planning for action in the event of the expected Republican victory? And if they were organizing secession and a new confederacy this early, just what were their motives? There was conference and a certain amount of militia organizing during that summer, ostensibly as protection against other possible John Browns. Presumably there were correspondence and the drafting of specifications. Was this treasonable conspiracy? Because of the accident of South Carolina's antiquated method of choosing electors, the governor and legislature of that state were in session and in a position to take immediate action when the news of Lincoln's election flashed over the wires. What were their real plans? Was this treason, a resurgence of the patriotic spirit of 1776, or a plan of direct action to secure reform and security?

And what of the Republicans? For the time being they were of no use at all in seeking accommodation, for they refused to acknowledge that there was a crisis to face. As a result their leaders were not in any kind of realistic communication; in fact they seem to have been in a state of euphoria. Some of them recognized no danger; they felt the South was just bluff, loud talk, and alcoholic exaggeration. The members of a more responsible group were confident that they could negotiate any danger away. Among these latter was Seward, who believed Lincoln to be a cipher and that he, Seward, was to be premier and party leader. There was a further unexpected complication. The Republicans had not carried Congress and so must be doubtful of their power and their responsibility.

In view of later developments too little attention has been paid to the operations of a third force. For there were not merely two alternatives, union and secession. Those of the third force, in attempting accommodation, had a task of almost impossible complexity, and it can hardly be said they understood it. The most commonly held definition of the function of this third force was the contrivance of another Congressional accommodation, a Compromise of 1860–1 that would allay southern fears. But at that moment was there any South, and if so, which of the paths prescribed by its various groups of activists was it following? There was a really horrible confusion with no group, not even the southerners, with any clear-cut plan upon which there was agreement. And was there any North?

South Carolina appeared to be moving straight out of the Union, but for what purpose and how many of the other fourteen slave states would follow? Eight of them seemed flatly refusing to secede. By Christmas it was clear that six others, the gulf states, when it was becoming apparent that Lincoln and the Republicans would accept no compromise, were joining South Carolina in secession, probably under direction from the Senatorial junto that now took over in Washington. In various meetings at Washington this body, rather resentful of South Carolina's precipitate haste, prepared a schedule designed to organize a Southern Confederacy which would be in operation before Lincoln's inauguration. This schedule was sent south seemingly from Buchanan's advisers, by Cobb and perhaps Thompson, and emissaries of South Carolina seem to have distributed it among the slave states. Some of the more vigorous hoped to enlist northern states, particularly outside of New England, to join. There were rumors that Buchanan might be persuaded to resign, even kidnapped, and then Breckinridge would be in power, ready to call a convention to organize a new republic at Washington which would include most of the Union except New England. Armed forces were reported to be assembling and General Scott was certainly apprehensive. A confederacy was achieved but not in Washington and then only seven of the slave states and none of the free had any part in it. Here again is a question of motive. Did these secessionists really want independence, or was this move designed to persuade the calling of a constitutional convention in which some plan of reorganization guaranteeing southern autonomy might be adopted?

Were the organizers of the Confederacy seceding from the nation as they had from the Democratic National Convention so as to establish a basis for negotiating a republic reorganized in some fashion such as suggested by Calhoun, whose plan for two presidents and sectional consensus in Congress Senator Hunter had recently resurrected? Was there hope that Seward, who expected to be the new Secretary of State and who had recently spoken in the Senate about the possibility of a constitutional convention, might be willing to negotiate with his old Senatorial cronies now established at Montgomery? In the new Confederate capital there was a certain amount of discussion of the possibility of reconstruction. Was there some such expectation? Is that why Senator Benjamin remarked before he left Washington that he might soon be back, why Mrs. Slidell left her clothes in Washington, and why European diplomats sent home dispatches reporting the possibility?

That this third force existed is obvious, but it is difficult to trace the details of its operation with as much clarity as might be desired because there was so much confusion, so many plans, and because so much of the record has been lost or destroyed. For when the possibility of an accommodation faded, when war broke out and when new loyalties were created, it became convenient to forget about this effort toward accommodation, and lamentably so little of the documentation of the period seems to have survived.

The existence and behavior of this third force points up a problem in historiography. So often complexity culminates in the precipitation of a conflict between what seem to be two groups, such as the Union and the Confederacy. This, history records as a controversy between simple alternatives, yet up until the last moment in this cultural pluralism so many others were possible. Yet as they failed, knowledge of the variant forces in the pluralism can and does largely disappear. Recognition of the existence of this third force, despite its rapid disappearance without leaving many traces, can be an aid to understanding not only why the war came but also some of the many problems of the Confederacy. The significance of this third force in 1860–1 and in the war experience of the Confederacy is particularly subtle and elusive and can be better understood in the light of some of the concepts of behavioral science.

In tracing the development of the third force I concluded that thinking of social conflicts as contests between two elements is generally too simple. This contest and often others are more complex than a simple one against one. There are always complicating alternatives and the concept of the universal third force is a useful symbol for the complexity of competitive situations. For the conflict which culminated in 1861–5 was not entirely unique nor confined to those years. It was one of a class of social wars, a complicated conflict among kinfolk, a brothers' war in which there were more than two brothers. An analysis of this type of contest should be formulated in somewhat different terms from those used in studying conflicts between foreign nations, wars between different ethnic groups. In such an analysis certain behavioral concepts proved to be convenient and enlightening. The Union and the Confederate societies were closely bound by cultural ties; they were members of the same society with a common tongue and a common history. They and their ancestors had created an image which, though it was variously conceived, was their common possession.

Even the most fiery secessionists took some precautions not to destroy their ideal of a republic but to protect and improve their interpretation of it. A significant number probably really thought of secession as an instrument of ultimate reconstruction. And when fighting broke out it took on the characteristics of family infighting or feuding. The fact that kinsmen were shedding each others blood probably had a stultifying influence on some of their efforts. Neither Confederacy nor Union seemed to be able to summon its full strength, and during the years of the contest there was much evidence of lagging enthusiasm, foot dragging, and even open opposition.

Those promoting the Confederacy were not free agents, in a position to adopt a simple political program of secession or either reconstruction or the formation of an independent polity. They did not understand to what extent they were controlled by the nature of the common and complex cultural relationship, the syndrome of pluralism. Rather, they attempted to follow a behavior pattern that might be effective between feuding tribes or rival national groups with a long-standing history of hate and conflicting objectives. But the North and South were neither hostile tribes nor rival nations. They were partners in a complex culture with a history of affection, common interest, and achievement.

Within this cultural complex the third force reappears in both the Union and the Confederacy. In the North a war spirit unexpected by the Confederacy was kindled because of this family situation. It appeared in the free states that their southern kinsmen were becoming more unreasonable and dictatorial, they were demanding that instead of the harmony of interest that had hitherto prevailed, the southern interest must predominate. This reaction produced a feeling resembling family resentment which would cause the northern members to fight the unreasonable South in order to preserve the integrity of the family structure. Likewise in the Confederacy, the divided initial objective took its toll. A segment of the Southern population, large enough to be significant, i.e. the third force, may not really have wanted independence as much as it wanted a reorganized United States in which its section would thereafter function with security insured by the autonomy prescribed by Calhoun.

Because of this divided objective, it can be seen that it was doubtful whether the South could contrive sufficient singleness of purpose or a motivation strong enough to achieve an independence that basically many of the southern people did not want. Inhibited by an ambivalence of this nature, the South, unlike its revolutionary forebears, failed to create the power necessary to win. Otherwise it is difficult to interpret the fumbling and indecisiveness put on daily display by a group of experienced politicians backed by a tradition of success. They talked of one thing while thinking of another, for as this was in fact a family quarrel, the last thing that many in the South may really have wanted was to leave home or to be compelled to leave home—that is, to gain final independence.

Many of the designers of the Confederacy had really not wanted to construct a new government; they had hoped to continue the old model without certain new functions, certain "improvements" that rival planners had insisted on incorporating, or, at the most, to be permitted to go their own way. Failing that, they had contrived a smaller-sized copy, which proved hardly adequate for the occasion. It could not function effectively in a war for which it was not planned and, because of a lack of compelling motivation, for which its designers did not muster sufficient ingenuity to make the necessary structural changes.

Therefore, when it began to be apparent that what the South was achieving was not security and a controlling influence in the home, but at best an uncomfortable seat on the doorstep, signs are discernible which suggest a possibility that is highly speculative and cannot be presented as a finding, merely offered for consideration as a stimulant to further thinking. If it were true that many in the South, the third force, never really wanted independence, but reconstruction, it can be suggested at least that the discovery of the impossibility of carrying out their original purpose may have deprived a significant number of a compelling motive for enduring further suffering to obtain what appeared to be unattainable. Rather, these turned to the idea of returning home and making the best of their position, still strong, in the federal system. For the freeing of the slaves, they would realize, would increase southern power in the Congress and in party conventions, because all of the Negroes, rather than three-fifths, would hereafter be counted. It has been suggested that this third force may, after a certain point, unconsciously at least, have wanted to lose, so that they could the sooner return to the home they deeply loved.

Such return was made easier because the possible sting of acknowledged defeat was lessened by the ties of common history. While there was a good deal of hatred of the "damyankee" and there was fear of slave reprisals, there are nevertheless indications of a feeling that if the fighting would stop and everyone go home, there could be a resumption of the old relationship. After all, these opponents were not marauding foreigners, they were people of the same culture, with whom there had been an experience of long association, often very fruitful. Why not resume it? Enough of independence; here was the prodigal son's refuge. Why not seek it? There might even be some species of fatted calf. Because of the cultural ties, it was possible to accept defeat without suicidal despair. After all, the family would again be intact, the brothers reunited, and they could turn to the tasks, not only of repairing the damage, but of combining energies to make their structure larger and finer.

A significant element therefore in my analysis was this conceptualization of the third force developing out of psychiatry and the behavioral sciences. Generalizations regarding kinship systems of social organization and their influence upon political behavior were derived from social anthropology. Such kin and family concepts invited certain psychiatric explanations of behavior, together with classifications of subtle forms of motivation arising from the unconscious.

The study of this conflict likewise brought me to grips with certain historiographical problems other than that of identifying the third force, which were illustrated in the process of interpreting additional phenomena involved in the conflict. I had come to the conclusion that those studying the American Civil War would gain much by considering it in its setting in the history of Western civilization as a whole. For in so doing they would find that the conflict was not unique but one of a class of social wars which may occur anywhere in any epoch. Some such phenomenon has been an element in the Anglo-American experience about once in every century. At various times in the nineteenth and twentieth centuries there have recurred types of national unifications generally including some phase of political conflict, notably in Germany, Italy, and the Dual Monarchy. Similar struggles on the field of battle or over the negotiation table had resulted in division as well as unification, in such instances as the separation of Belgium from Holland and of Norway from Sweden and as the breakup of the Ottoman Empire, the Russia of the tsars, and the Austro-Hungarian monarchy. There had been revolutions in Germany, the Balkans, Portugal, Spain, and China. The British Empire has become the British Commonwealth of Nations, and a process of separation is going on in Asia and Africa in various areas of British and French influence. The American Civil War was perhaps only an example of this type of "metanationalistic" action.

There appears indeed to be a continuous process of cultural integration and disintegration, marked by revolution, social wars, and other phenomena which are phases of a seemingly universal experience. Comparison of these produces new concepts of the history of cultural unity and particularly of the nature of the process which promotes, discourages, or destroys it. Answers to new general questions about civil war are constantly being sought. At what points are tensions likely to cause disruption? What means best promote unity? How can tension be relaxed? Is it true that the process of operating democratic government or any other kind of government invites disintegration? How can group hostility be overcome? Must internal conflicts and bloodlettings recur with a certain degree of regularity just as do international conflicts?

In the instance of the American Civil War was it inevitable that a democracy so huge and with such ecological and demographic diversity should develop so much social tension as to threaten its growing nationalism and in the course of this growth produce two incompatible patriotisms and two moralities? Did the armed conflict that ensued so mark the restored culture that it is still really two cultures, with certain degrees of incompatibility? The end of the conflict left another difficult problem for historians. The basic phase of the analysis of the anatomy of the conflict which I found difficult was the problem of the cultural limitations not only for those who attempted to deal with it but also for such of the American people in general as have since shown interest in their labors. These cultural limitations have been imposed by birth, environment, association, and tradition. Most of those with such interest have opinion shaped by circumstances outside themselves. Each has started life with a geographical relationship to the Mason-Dixon line, either north of it, south of it, or west of it, unless he is of foreign origin. Even those who have moved from their places of birth and dwell in a different cultural atmosphere have carried inherited tradition to their new abodes. If a historian marries on the other side of the line, he may be confused by harboring two cultures under one roof. But no matter how confused his experience with the conflict may be, it is not easy, though it may be possible, for him to release himself from external influences that will determine his interpretation and restrict his understanding.

Is it true that dwellers in these two cultures have not yet been able to free themselves sufficiently from their birthright bias to generalize objectively? Or can the scholar by constructing a table of comparative northern and southern generalizations achieve a balance of interpretation which may establish an objective generalization? Can he compare generalizations relating to the American conflict with others formulated in regard to similar experiences outside American culture? With these comparisons in mind can he construct a calculus of generalization which will enable him to correct for bias and produce a new series of more valid concepts?

I came to the conclusion that if the history of the conflict were to be written with even an approximation of truth, it would be essential for those concerned to understand the nature of their cultural limitations. This seemed particularly important because those who were shaping the government of the United States were circumscribed by these same limitations. I emphasize these cultural determinants because there is an almost irresistible impulse in the moralistic intellectual world in which so many Americans dwell to speak instinctively in terms of praise or blame, to condemn or to justify. The extent to which the balance is in favor of condemnation or commendation seems to depend largely upon the accident of who is making the analysis, upon his cultural definition. Do these limitations make inevitable a moral judgment, the casting up of an account? Is it not possible to accept the hypothesis that in the conduct of great masses of people there must, be some law of behavioral average, be as much to praise as to blame? In the long run, will not these judgments decree some sort of balance of virtue? Is there parity or, as parity has been questioned in the universe, can it be considered in human nature?

It seems to be a fact that emotions appear in pairs, and thus contrast like negative and positive charges of electricity, like the two sexes, like yin and yang. Where there is idealism there is sordid self-seeking, where there is loyalty there is callous disregard for the cause, where there is patriotism there is cynical disdain for the commonweal, where there is bravery there is cowardice, where there is unselfish sacrifice there is refusal to contribute a moment's discomfort or an ounce of effort. Where there is chivalry there is contempt for the foe. Where there is eagerness to serve there is heartless ambition. Where there is a favorable interpretation there is one to the contrary. There are always love and hate, hope and despair.

These contrasts, operating in both sections, suggest the hypothesis that the North American ecology decreed the evolution of two different societies in an environment and a cultural organization that would encourage a mutual desire for union—something akin to matrimony—in which two obviously different individuals sought the satisfaction of a primal urge stronger than their individual wills in a union that in this instance was crowned with the fruits of their own creation: something new, a nation. This nationalism in the end proved stronger than their individual wills, and after an emotional crisis that drove them to the brink of destruction, the strength of their own creation, their nationalism, saved them from annihilation. When the historian applies the dry scientific concepts of the behavioral sciences to an analysis of this war, it becomes difficult to assign praise or blame or to award victory or defeat.

The problem is further complicated by the puzzling possibility that the contestants were fighting for the same aim and that both achieved it. The war was a conflict to conserve the federal system and this end, which both sides really desired, was achieved. The Union forces were fighting for a federal system, in which the principle was to govern that the rule of the majority should prevail. The South on its part was dedicated to a federal system in which the autonomy of a minority should be recognized. It fought primarily to ensure the South a veto in the system.

Ostensibly the northern interpretation triumphed; but did it? The South certainly did not achieve a veto or an autonomy to the degree to which it desired, but its achievement even in defeat was no mean one. When the Confederacy returned to its allegiance after Appomattox, the states came back eventually to positions of no small power. The abolition of slavery increased their representation in the House because all the Negroes, rather than three-fifths, were now counted in apportioning representatives. Likewise these states contrived to keep senators and representatives in Congress for longer terms than on the average their northern counterparts were allowed, and so their resultant seniority gave them real control in the congressional committees. The southern representation has frequently exercised a veto and even control. Power in the nation is still divided, and the government is still a federal system. The war at length came to its end when there was no compelling reason for it to be fought any longer. It was perhaps a war that in a sense nobody won.

In conclusion I had become convinced that the historian had incurred a new type of responsibility. He cannot always depend upon finding direct evidence or binding himself within its limits. He must make responsible use of hypotheses as instruments of projecting his thought and suggest possibilities of explanation which he cannot prove. He must risk making more use of hypothesis in order to induce in others the trial of new interpretation and intuition. He may frequently be frustrated by a "not proven" but his suggestions may on occasion result in significant discoveries. Historians do not fulfill their obligations by supplying simple answers to abstruse questions but by endeavoring to make complexity comprehensible.

Though it had taken four years of civil war, a particularly significant question had been resolved—the question whether the federal system could continue to function under strain on its two specified strata; whether legislators on two levels, state and federal, could cooperate; whether state legislatures, state governors, and state courts could operate in sufficient correlation with Congress, the president and federal courts to make possible the bringing of such a full-scale war to a conclusion. This test was met. The Union was restored, and the nation rebuilt its government. It was a tribute to the capacity of the American political designers that they could repair damage largely of their own creation.

The varied consideration which I had given to the Civil War period thus had led me to pass through several phases of interpretation. When I had finished *The Disruption of American Democracy* I was most favorable to the idea that democracy carries within itself the seeds of its possible destruction. The complexity of the nation in physiographic influence and demography; mobility of the population; the romantic nature of the current emotional expression; some of the characteristics of the physical and mental health of the American society; the political, economic, and religious trauma of the time, the frequency of elections, occurring somewhere nine months in each year; the clocklike recurrence, the need of periodic contests, and the accompanying artificial crises were becoming cumulatively dangerous. And that this hyperemotionalism at length precipitated what was in effect an inevitable conflict.

My theory was that one might as well think of anything that happened as inevitable because it was not humanly possible to prove it wasn't.

This last decade of intensive study brought me to the conclusion that the conflict might be better understood in a broader context. I found certain interesting indicators. The American experience could be better understood by careful study of many of our institutional patterns. Some of these are of great age, for our political behavior is in many respects English. Likewise I came to the conclusion that the complex confusions of a growing state, including the remote influence of the introduction of a new power into society, the power of steam driven machinery, and the emotional complexity of the romantic age which had succeeded the Age of Reason had produced stresses and strains greater than any hitherto known in the American society, stresses and strains which could not have been foreseen by the creators of the republic and which were getting beyond the power of the statesmen to manage. They were producing an emotional confusion which taxed to the limit the self-governing capacity of the republic to handle by composing documents of accommodation.

Now, in the twentieth century, when the United States is two world wars and a cold war away from the turn of the century and the Progressive Era, is the republic in the throes of constructing, quite unconsciously perhaps, a new Leviathan, which no one has yet described? Is this a Leviathan of another sort, being designed by a people who are becoming preoccupied with such concepts as international insecurity, the welfare state, the new conservatism, social conformity, racial antagonism? In this period of mid-twentieth-century reconstruction it is well to remember that there are times in the history of men when they accumulate energy and release force that it seems beyond their intellectual power to control. Mankind today stands in all probability in such an age. Men have learned some of the secrets of genetic information; they have released the energy in the atom, they have created the atomic bomb, and they are poised on the edge of space. It may well be questioned whether human intellectual power as at present developed is equal to the challenge. Were Henry Adams alive today, he might again talk in terms of some destructive dynamic theory. However, it is not necessary to conclude that humanity does not have the intellectual potential; but it does mean that if society is to survive, all concerned must work tirelessly to understand, increase, and mobilize it.

A century ago Americans stood in a somewhat similar position. They had a vast continent largely unpossessed but very rich in unrealized resources and opportunities. They had new sources of power, new population, and a new treasure. They had a neat but old-fashioned system of control. They had a newly released set of emotions, driven wild by recently unbridled imaginations. This situation created a confusion almost certain to create conflict, which in Whitman's phrase was "significant of a grand upheaval of ideas and reconstruction of many things on new bases." If people are truly to comprehend and account for the conflict of 1861–5 and to apply their knowledge to the tasks of the twentieth century, they must do it in some such grand frame, summoning all they can of the available knowledge of why men behave as they do, as still a century later the process of adjusting the American government continues. Fifty-one legislatures are constantly at work studying the adaptations necessary to keep the design adequate to cope with constant change.

In April 1965, on the anniversary of Lincoln's assassination, I concluded my speaking on the Civil War Commemoration addressing the student body of Rutgers University in Camden. Four years of bloodshed and blundering had produced an ostensible victory that was hollow, for now a hundred years later, the basic issues are not yet settled and in a sense the struggle still continues. Two parties still vie for the control of the government but there are always third forces which seek to operate in the interest of easing or increasing tension, and the strains in this cultural pluralism seem again dangerous. The force of consensus has never failed but once when it did not arrest secession in 1860–1. In one way or another it has otherwise been able to arrange an agreement and is not the least of the elements of strength in the republic. It is the element in the dynamics of the federal system which guides the convergence of forces into the equilibrium necessary for continuous operation.

XI

THE MEANING OF POLITICS

DURING THIS SEASON of commemorative writing I was also continuing my history of American political parties which as a graduate student I had begun, so to speak, in the middle. During my fourteen years in the dean's office I finished *The Invention of the American Political Parties: A Study of Political Improvisation* and I sent it to the publishers almost literally as I was leaving office.

This particular book which I had begun writing in the library of Trinity had finally taken shape as an analysis of the processes of the evolution of political parties, one phase of which was the political machine which I had undertaken to study in 1919. I traced this history through five stages.

The first of the several stages of this process which I identified was the stage of English origins, the long course of the evolution of certain patterns of self-government which the English had achieved prior to the seventeenth century and which in significant part determined the political behavior of the colonists. It is not possible to be precise about the point in time at which to begin seeking for the origins of these patterns, for they are prehistoric, appearing somehow originally among the folkways of the British tribes. But somewhere in this primitive society unknown designers began the construction of the political machinery necessary to enable significant elements among the people to participate in the various community choices which self-government requires. The British were island people subject for a thousand years to either the threat or the actuality of invasion from the continent. They had to cope not only with the problems of ordering their island societies by local customs but they were forced to be constantly on the alert against invaders and to prize good leadership. They learned that self-government does not last very long unless it is structured; there must be contrivances.

So during these centuries the British constructed the necessary devices, various inventions such as elections in the shires, boroughs and parishes, and rule-making by representatives of the estates in Parliament, in the borough councils, in the vestries, and in the county courts. Men learned to draw lots and cast ballots. Very gradually certain extralegal customs and behavior patterns emerged foreshadowing political parties and the art of politics. Most of these were related to the contests which registering of choices for lawmakers frequently involved, including efforts to convince and persuade, particularly if any large numbers of participants were involved. In the realm of the executive, elements of choice by voice or by force were sometimes involved in determining the succession of kings. Such were the bases of political action which the colonists knew before they came to America. The striking features of this pattern were its age and its intricacy. Tracing it took me far back in time, for some of its elements were more than a thousand years old in 1607.

The second stage was the process of invention and adaptation in America by government, organized groups and individuals, carrying expedition after expedition across the formidable Atlantic and setting up new societies in hostile environment. They brought with them English concepts of the executive branch, of lawmaking, of justice, and of the transplanting of the rights of Englishmen. They also knew something about elections, embryonic parties, and political change by violence as well. In the seventeenth and eighteenth centuries something appeared resembling an alternating cycle of equilibrium and revolution, but by mid-eighteenth century equilibrium and the customs of self-government seem to have been established. In the process there was in fact much more of adaptation than invention.

The achievement of this political equilibrium together with the political demands upon the colonies of the world wars of the eighteenth century determined the development of a third stage. The colonies were acquiring an increasing capacity for independent action which in turn, in part stimulated by international events, induced a growing desire for autonomy. At first these new motivations did not interfere with loyalty to the Crown but as this loyalty was strained, patriotic zeal changed into revolution and the hoped-for autonomy was achieved by the creation of the United States of America, a self-governing federal polity.

This third stage was that in which a new politics was created together with the machinery essential to insure autonomy and create an American establishment. Here again the promoters of the new enterprise depended largely upon what they knew. The mechanisms and behavior patterns to which they were accustomed as colonies now were adjusted. There were mass meetings and petitions, organizations were formed. The local militia drilled for action. The lower houses of the legislatures or in some instances the legislatures themselves, became political conventions. Intercolonial intercourse was carried on by committees of correspondence. Eventually Continental Congresses assembled and a Continental army was organized. The leaders of these civil and military orders became leaders in a Patriot organization, designed at first to protect their rights and then to secure their independence. All this was done in an Age of Reason and carefully set down in writing in a series of petitions, declarations, and articles of agreement which carefully spelled out their intentions and their plans. As the population was not a unit, the Patriots found themselves in conflict with a considerable body of Tories or Loyalists. The Revolution was not only a civil war but a civilian political contest as well.

The successful establishment of the new republic by the adoption of the Constitution in 1787 invited the identification of a fourth stage, that of creating a new surrogate to take the place of the Empire. They constructed a federal republic. Federal politics was something novel and it proved intricate, with few precedents to guide it. Each colony, now a state, had its own politics based on its many decades of operation. But a new experience had been created, an experience of joint or federal endeavor which was now systematized permanently under the Constitution. New patterns of political behavior had to be created. These patterns arose from the activity of a relatively small number of people chosen as representatives of local elites and establishments who traveled from their localities to a central place of political experiment and while there created the new designs. During a series of sessions of the Continental Congresses, the Constitutional Convention, and the Federal Congress, groups of men, orignally fifty or more, though increasing in size, developed modes of action determined by what may be called the "dynamics of small groups." The American people had changed surrogates, they had substituted for the British Empire a political organization of their own making. They had also faced the problem of creating a power structure. The legislative instrument in this system was reasonably easy to construct, using the British model, but when it came to the executive there were few precedents. They rejected both a sovereign or a long-term executive. There was to be a president selected for a relatively short term. Through some intriguing turn of fate arising probably from the peculiar quality of the eighteenth century mind, and produced by the Age of Reason and the dynamics of the revolutionary process, the Founders decided to submit the question of who was to exercise power to the hazard of election every four years. As occidental civilization was at that time so largely committed to hereditary executives, this was a decision with momentous consequences, some of which were not discovered until some time had elapsed.

But how should the executive be chosen? The imaginations of the members of the Constitutional Convention contrived a peculiarly original and unworkable instrument, the Electoral College, which rarely could be used as planned and once, at least, with danger. At first the choice of the executive did not seem difficult. The Patriot elite contributed three of their number, Washington, Adams and Jefferson, to the ranks of presidents. Then Jefferson together with certain members of Congress undertook to guide the selection by means of Congressional caucuses, but these aroused no popular interest and, worse, they stimulated some distrust. Then the Electoral College, even after the XII Amendment, still proved to be clumsy. For a few years this awkwardness did not seem to matter much. The original executives were not possessed of much power and the president of the United States for a while in the early nineteenth century was not a figure of political national interest nor was the task of selection very difficult. But as the nation grew and became ever greater and more powerful, ever more wealthy and more elaborately organized, the question of the power of government became more important. The rapid growth and the increasing complexities of communities and interests made the authority of the executive progressively greater, the office more sought after, and the task of procuring agreement upon who should exercise it much more complex.

These changes were to require a new politics which were to be devised during a fifth phase of the evolution of American political behavior. This fifth stage began after the coming of peace in the occident at the conclusion of the Napoleonic Wars and the War of 1812, when American society inaugurated a great period of expansion within its huge estate. It was then that a new phase of our political evolution was shaped by the radically changing cultural pattern. Novel conditioning factors were particularly supplied by the mobility of the rapidly growing population. This migration was not one of simple pattern. For not only was the early design of westward movement to continue but in these early years of the nineteenth century the population began to contract as well as expand, to cluster in urban areas of industrial and commercial concentration. The rural simplicity of life in the older areas began to give way to urban complexity. People in fact were moving in all directions.

This intricate mobility produced a new dynamics which affected political as well as other forms of behavior. The individuals, families, and large groups as they moved from place to place generated forces of various intensities in many new ways. The process of deciding to move, of making the change, of determining where to stop, of creating a new community, or of contributing to one already established required the expenditure of much energy. The energy available in the republic was constantly redistributed during the process. Older communities lost as new ones gained. Since this was a society of self-governing communities working on several levels —local, territorial, state and federal—power was created in each of them based upon the aggregate of the participating individuals and the influences which determined the quality of their contribution. There was bound to be friction because few changes of pattern, unless specifically and mechanically channeled according to plans and specifications, could take place without forcing new routes or channels through resistant structures. These frictions might be dangerous—witness the calamity of 1861–5—but for decades this possibility appeared remote to those adapting the politics of self-government.

The changes characterizing the fifth stage of political evolution were slowly and with great difficulty created in the form of the contrived party machinery so well known today. The organization of this system was the final process which I undertook to analyze.

The original concept of the choice of the president by the Electoral College and Congress had proved inadequate to meet the changing conditions. It was evident that the process of adaptation must be continued beyond the specifications of the Constitution, so two or three ingenious devices were attempted, not so much inventions of something new as adaptations of something well known. National conventions were organized by party workers, which might be thought of as trade conferences of political professionals. These professionals got to work on a solution of the problem of choosing the president.

But in investigating this I was again puzzled by the question of origins. When did the American party system begin to operate? The commonly accepted idea is that it began with the Revolution or at latest after the drafting of the Constitution. At that point there appeared Federalists and Anti-Federalists, those for or against the Constitution. These two groups were then followed by the Federalists and Democratic-Republicans, the followers of Washington, Hamilton, and Adams on the one hand and Jefferson on the other. These some forty years later were followed by Democrats and National Republicans and Whigs and finally, after 1854, by Democrats and Republicans. All such groups are indiscriminately called parties and a sense of identity and continuity is implied which does not exist.

The word "parties" as it is commonly understood today means a highly organized group of politically minded operators who carry on often as a profession within an intricate pattern of a permanently structured behavior, marshaling the numerous voters in two major and some relatively minor groups. It is an extraconstitutional organization provided for in no chapters of the federal statutes. It is full-time in its operation with a continuous direction and permanent employees, supported from treasuries of varying repleteness. These parties operate on two levels, state and federal.

The first of the groups, frequently designated "parties," the Federalists and the Democratic-Republicans, were under such definition really not parties but factions, or interest groups, originating among the small number of people associated in creating and guiding the federal establishment. These men had connections with certain elite groups and associated operators in the states but with little formality or continuity. As the early functions of the federal government were soon confined to foreign affairs and military defense, popular interest in the practice of politics on the federal level dwindled down to an absolute minimum. Between 1815 and 1822 national contests practically disappeared in choosing the presidents.

It was at this point and in the fifth stage of political development that national parties and political machinery really began to appear. Responding to the basic changes and forces then operating, the emerging class of professional politicians who were creating state machines undertook to create and operate a federal two-party system which Richard P. McCormick has named "The Second American Party System." They used the emerging federal party conference system and in a series of trade conventions which they dominated they organized the party machine. A series of local committees operating in the several states constructed national conventions which nominated presidential candidates and national committees which sought to direct their elections. By 1848 the fifth process involved in constructing this mechanism was outlined on the drawing boards and has been in use ever since, doing much of the work which the Electoral College was designed to do. It had been achieved by the first organized party called "The American Democracy," which became the Democratic party. In this study, therefore, I included an analysis of the evolution of that democratic machine, the behavior of which from 1850 to 1860 had been my initial problem.

During the writing of this book I became ever more conscious of the existence of the pitfalls encountered when studying or concentrating on a much too simple, narrowly defined political history, and of the existence of a broader frame of reference, of a complex series of cultural determinants into which any analysis of our political evolution must be fitted. The total cultural picture as I conceived it was like a complex textile design made up of a great variety of colored threads. Despite the variegated shades and hues making up these patterns, one occasionally predominates. To use but two examples, Russia is a communistic society, the United States is a democratic community. The real history of such societies is the description of the process by which the prevailing institutional complex became dominant. There is a temptation, which too often prevails, to concentrate on minor threads and subordinate designs in any cultural aggregate and spend overmuch time in tracing and accounting for them, often without meaningful or comprehensive reference to the overall pattern. The main design may even be lost to sight.

The structure of American democracy has not been one which someone or some group invented, at any given time, not even in 1776–87. It is a pattern slowly created to meet certain needs which have arisen at various times and places. It was never designed at any point in time nor has it been prescribed in any contrived blueprint. It has been a slowly evolved complex pattern of behavior, a culture conditioned by folk experience, by the dynamics of migration and of community creation. It has certain characteristics which were never legislated into existence: they became accepted habits of behavior which in turn proved determinants of further development.

Its study has become ever more significant, particularly in this twentieth century, which has produced at least three situations which are such a challenge to historians, namely, a return to warfare, the emergence of totalitarian and collective systems which challenge democracy, and the threat of peril not only to democracy but to the human race. These are awakening a sense of the need of more knowledge of the basic behavior patterns which induce peril-producing phenomena and their origin and evolution; and of more information, accurate scientific information, regarding the actual operation in communities of the habits of cooperation and competition which are the basis of peace and war, of liberty and restraint, and of the actual ethical and religious behavior of men and women.

This American culture pattern, long in the weaving, was created in a definable area—it has yet to be shown that it is of universal application. It was not created entirely within the United States—in fact, most of its basic concepts came from elsewhere. They emerged during the transplanting of folkways over a millennium in a variety of regions and were the result of the adjustments required to meet the needs of migrants. The history of the creation of the American democratic image can have no meaning if it is held to begin in 1763 because so many of its features were in anterior operation.

In studying the evolution of this pattern of democratic culture in the light of these challenges and these needs, I had undertaken to build my analysis on my understanding of human behavior and the complex factors shaping it. Not only the intricacy of the demands of the fast-growing American society had determined this revised political procedure but a special demand, more subtle and difficult to isolate, was proposed to make of democracy a more viable system of government. The Progressive Age had produced a belief in ultimate and inevitable progress which proclaimed the "total reconciliation of men" in a type of ultimate Utopia. But a reaction was setting in against this optimism, for the belief in inevitable progress had presented the historical analyst with problems which persisted in urging him to seek a greater realism and thereby to modify the concepts of certain of his colleagues.

He learned from biologists and sociologists concepts that purported to "show races and perhaps classes and individuals unequally gifted, nations definitely singularized by their histories." These scientists stressed the unreality of unobtainable Utopia. They substituted a concept that "the proportion of goodness and wickedness, of unselfishness and egoism, in each and all is hardly likely to change, but individuals will show unequal qualities or faults. . . . They will accumulate fewer resentments . . . , if they free themselves from complexes arising from prejudices" based upon setting goals founded upon unreality and therefore unobtainable. If historians and society could be freed from this concept of progress, "the hope of improvement [would] become intelligible" not only to society but to history.[1] Tracing the implications of this revised attitude should be a primary concern to the historian, and if he accomplishes it he can be of great aid in showing how man may use his still unexhausted capacity to change, to be unfinished business, which the anthropologist reminds him he has. He will keep on inventing and exercising his judgment, which will enable him to continue to adjust his folkways so that he may survive and continue his pursuit of happiness with unequal degrees of success but with occasional startling insights and discoveries.

He can apply this skill to develop new uses of our very great capacity for self-government. Because our political behavior is very old, it is based on impulse structures much older than reason, therefore man needs to be re-educated emotionally to meet the demands of the cultural changes which are so marked today. But as yet we know too little about these impulse structures which are based upon emotion and about how they may be channeled and adjusted.

Man is ready to die for what he values and much of the danger in today's world is threatened because men following their good instincts may elect to destroy in order to defend that which they value. On occasion societies have followed suicidal courses defending values which they have held more important than survival. Rather than cherishing values for which circumstances may require us to fight and die, it may be more significant to achieve such values as will produce loyalties which require us to work and live in order to preserve them. If this be a revolutionary age, we are confronted by the problem of devising new political institutions

[1] Raymond Aron: *Introduction to the Philosophy of History,* trans. George I. Irwin (Boston, 1961), p. 340.

that will make it possible for us to transmute our biological capacities for sacrifice. Margaret Mead, after setting forth the above analysis, concludes, "If we can do it, then the journey ahead of man is incredibly more magnificent than the journey . . . from the Stone Age into the present."[2]

This possibility provides the historian his great opportunity. In this emotional age of quantification we are a long ways away from the Age of Reason. Democracy is now best justified not by Lockean logic but by the findings of today's pragmatic social science in its study of the question, Does it work? Many feel that it is better to be controlled by the mean will of society than by the erratic inspiration of genius. The chance consensus of the sentiments of the many has a greater possibility of achieving community acceptance than the perhaps capricious will of any elite few. It may be society's best hope that through its long experience in the art of self-government, this republic can continue to exercise it. It is time to speak up, to assume a new role and assert what we know. We have learned from our specialization how to define and practice self-government in an enormous society; we need now to put it to the greater use of mankind. We must fill larger canvases, we must courageously deal more effectively with generalizations. We must, if not prophesy, at least proclaim what we know has happened before, not only in monographs in depth but also in more narratives in breadth. The chief responsibility of the historian is to supply to society a knowledge of the long evolution of the process of self-government, of the age and validity of its patterns of behavior, so that mankind may never be ignorant of the

[2] Margaret Mead: "A Look at Human Capacities," *Lamp*, XLV (Summer 1963), 16-17.

nature of a republic and of that which is needed to maintain one. *Esto perpetua!*

In this vein I finished another volume of my study. From the *Democratic Machine* of 1923 to *The Invention of the American Political Parties: A Study of Political Improvisation* of 1967, I had worked out the evolution of the American process of self-government down to the middle of the nineteenth century. I had also lived through a cycle. When I started in 1919, political and constitutional history were declining in interest and yielding to the newer economic and social interpretations. But in the end this was of advantage. I watched a new generation emerge who benefited by these new insights and began a new series of sophisticated behavioral studies which I had found so helpful that I dedicated the book to their authors.

Also I had myself passed through a cycle of historiography. I had started when the end of the predominance of political and constitutional interest seemed at hand and was now working in an atmosphere of the renaissance of a new, more comprehensive, and more analytic political history.

XII

GRADUATE EDUCATION

I PRESUME I owe it to the profession to make some attempt to explain how a historian could ever get involved in educational administration. I am not too sure I understand it myself, but I shall at least make an attempt to communicate.

The Second World War had reoriented much of the educational system of the United States by the demands which it made upon its institutions of higher learning. By interesting chance it coincided with changes in leadership at the University of Pennsylvania where within the administration, trustees, and faculties a generation was passing. Figures which had been long in the front offices as presidents and provosts—Gates, Penniman, McClelland, Musser, and certain of the deans—were relinquishing their responsibilities and a new leadership must take over.

The bicentennial celebration of 1940 had in a sense prepared the way. Dr. Cheyney had brought before the university and the society it served, the history of its experience. The colloquia had brought many to the campus and a new sense of responsiblity and opportunity influenced those laboring in the vineyard. The time was ripe to consider the writing of a new commission. In 1948 Harold E. Stassen had been chosen president. Hon. Owen J. Roberts, recently Associate Justice of the United States Supreme Court, became a trustee and dean of the law school, Edwin B. Williams became provost, and Alfred H. Williams president of the board of trustees.

The appointment of Dean Williams of the graduate school as provost meant that a new dean must be found. Faculty were appointed to advise the provost and the president, and I was invited to occupy the post. After a period of hard thinking I accepted. Why did I do it? I was fifty-six. There had been no change in my responsibilities since I had been made a professor at the age of thirty-four. I had shown that I could write, teach, and occupy positions outside the university, in the world of learning and to a minor extent in public life. Perhaps I was interested in trying something new, in having an office and a staff, in being associated with authority, in having a new title. Besides, I would be closely associated with an old friend, the new provost, Edwin B. Williams. Somewhere among these words perhaps lies the answer. On September 15, 1952, I took my place in 101 Bennett Hall and began developing a job which had little precise definition. For the next fourteen years I was free to make of it what I could with only cooperation from my associates. I proceeded, aided in large part by a great many friends, old and new.

When I became dean, the program for the degree was operating about as it had when I was a graduate student thirty years before. The degree candidates certainly amassed a great deal of fact and covered much literature in the areas in which they were to be examined for admission to candidacy. In the fields of the humanities and social sciences they learned to be thorough in covering the sources in the field of the thesis, to be critical of the validity of the data, to be careful in note taking and in providing footnotes and bibliography for their writing. All of this was excellent but they also were prone to write too much and take too long. In so many instances there was an absence of literary style or depth of understanding, of capacity for interpretive analysis. Often there seemed more learning than understanding, more drudgery than inspiration. Too often what was designed to be the beginning of a life of search for new truth proved to be the end.

As I assumed office the graduate school was approaching its seventy-fifth anniversary; its student body had grown from four to 1,450, and the faculty from twelve to 350. The school had a small suite of offices and I was assisted by two vice-deans, a chief clerk, a secretary, and two clerks. By accident I had the department of Oriental studies and the South Asia Institute reporting and submitting their budgets to me. Almost immediately conditions changed; within a year President Stassen had gone to Washington, and after serving a period as acting president, William H. Du Barry was succeeded by Gaylord P. Harnwell as president. There was a certain amount of administrative reorganization. Also, a university survey was launched.

Joseph H. Willits, sometime dean of the Wharton School and more recently director at the Rockefeller Foundation for the Social Sciences, came to Penn and worked out with faculty committees a comprehensive plan whereby visiting teams surveyed each school and reported. These reports were then turned over to local committees who in turn studied them and formulated recommendations. Dr. Willits studied these reactions and then filed his final report. This in turn was submitted to a faculty planning committee.

Even before Willits presented his final report the plans were in the process of being implemented. The first to produce concrete results was that on the operation of the university press. At almost the same time the various faculties of the university studied those appropriate to them and a number of changes began to be consummated. I was much involved in planning and in recruiting new faculty. It seemed possible to see a new university emerging.

A second major interest of President Harnwell was the rehabilitation of the community in which the university played a major role. West Philadelphia was to be the scene of innovation and renewal. Federal, state, and city funds became available to aid in clearing the ground for construction by the university, Drexel, the Philadelphia College of Pharmacy, and certain hospitals. Slowly rows of small and inadequate houses disappeared and the physics building, a new woman's dormitory, a parking garage, and other structures were erected. Then the commonwealth enlarged the scope of its aid and a grand new library, buildings for the social sciences, including the Graduate School of Education, the School of Social Work and the Department of Psychology, an administration building, an auxiliary gymnasium, and the Graduate School of Fine Arts. Woodland Avenue was eliminated, certain streetcar lines were put underground, Locust Street was for one block made a walkway. On its original area the Gates Pavilion, the Alfred N. Richards Medical Laboratories, a new unit to the men's dormitories, a new biology building, an addition to the chemistry building, new units for medical and dental education, the notable Ravdin building and squash courts made their appearance. The new Wharton School building, Dietrich Hall, the Mayer dormitory for married Wharton graduate students, new elements in the engineering schools and in the physics area provided, among other things, for atom smashing and other phases of higher energy and solid-state research and instruction. The campus was transformed, it became a self-contained landscaped section of the community and not merely a way station for commuting students. Plans were in process of realization to give post-baccalaureate students facilities equal to those provided for undergraduates and to encourage students of all interests to come to the university as residents. Under President Harnwell's leadership Pennsylvania was learning what it meant to be a university.

A third interest which was intimately connected with this was a more effective organization of support from alumni and the public in general. A development plan was organized under the direction of a national council. Under its auspices meetings were held in all parts of the country where alumni and friends of the university gathered to spend time together and to discuss with members of the university administration, faculty, and students the needs and hopes of the university. The president, the provost, certain of the deans and members of the board of trustees traveled a great deal and many of the alumni gained a new interest in their alma mater.

Thus in the years between 1925 and 1965 I was to experience a sense of being part of an unusual concentration of institutional force and the achievement of significant change. A university amorphous and slow-paced, where so little seemed to happen, had achieved a new vision of itself and created a new image. Strength, vitality, and enterprise were transforming characteristics. These experiences I shared as I participated in this metamorphosis.

The chief role which I undertook to work on with the administration in the university was the promotion of the growth of the graduate school as a prestige center and a place of intellectual and educational adventuring, particularly in the realm of the discovery of new knowledge, understanding and truth. I had three particular advantages which aided me. The first was the university survey, the second the seventy-fifth anniversary of the graduate school, and the third the fact that under the Harnwell leadership the university was experiencing a renaissance.

The sixteen years of my administrative responsibility were years of steady growth. The student body increased in fourteen years from 1,449 to 2,470. The Ph.D.'s and masters degrees granted had grown from 129 and 250 to 231 and 376. Most spectacular was the change in the nature of the student body, for in 1952 only 180 of the 1,449 had been full-time students; in 1965, 1,636 of the 2,470 were so classified; in other words, what had been only 7 per cent had become over 67 per cent.

The growth in numbers of faculty and students had emphasized the division between those interested in science and in the humanities; their respective needs were on some occasions demonstrated to be different and at others in conflict. In 1936 there had been a reorganization. The faculty was divided into quadrants, biological and medical, humanities, physical science, and social sciences. Each quadrant annually elected its chairman, divisional committee, secretary, and three members of a new twelve-man council of the graduate school. The divisional chairmen, it was planned, would aid the dean by handling details appropriate to their respective quadrants.

This reorganization had not worked as hoped. The chairmanship of the divisions, and membership in the elected divisional committees had not generally become more than a minor interest of the persons elected; the dean spent some of his effort in getting them to perform their duties as specified, without obtaining the benefit of either effective leadership or entirely interested and constructive cooperation. The principal difficulty was that the elected personnel served generally for but short terms and there was a constant interruption in activity, a constant necessity for initiating new colleagues into unfamiliar roles, which frequently and unfortunately did not enlist their full effort.

I proposed a reorganization in order to secure a more concentrated and interested planning group. Instead of an elected chairman and a divisional committee for each of the quadrants I asked the divisional faculties to substitute committees on instruction, made up of the chairmen of the group committees in each quadrant plus two younger men nominated by those below the rank of full professor. This was agreed to, together with the stipulation that I should preside over these committees made up of the men who had the real responsibility for the program of the graduate school. I felt that the graduate school would profit by closer association with them on my part and from the opportunity which I would gain for discussing with them their plans and proposals for new faculty and new courses.

While developing this reorganization I undertook to enlist the aid of a series of vice deans who served for shorter or longer tours of duty for different purposes. When I took office Paul C. Kitchen continued and W.

Wallace Weaver joined us. Eugene Nixon, John Preer, William C. McDermott, William M. Protheroe, Gerard J. Brault, and Tristram P. Coffin followed. The vice deans assisted in revising and developing graduate school functioning for the ever growing student body: planning better methods of administration, securing larger quarters, better equipment, and more numerous staff. Preer revised the admissions procedures and McDermott the mechanics of awarding the increasing amounts of money available for scholarships and fellowships.

With the establishment and increase in government contractual connections, such as N.D.E.A., N.I.H., and other avenues of aid, came larger resources to be administered. In dealing with the various government bureaus for securing this aid, Vice Dean Protheroe took charge with a superb capacity for which countless graduate students should be grateful. Under the new procedure for awarding fellowships and scholarships a small interdivisional committee was appointed each year to read all the applications recommended by the group committees, rate them, and then recommend the awards to the council of the graduate school. This new system provided for a judicial review by a group who had read all the applications recommended by the departments and were thus aware of the whole picture and could insure uniform and consistent consideration. The successive committees reduced a chaotic and sometimes quixotic procedure to a real sense of order.

With the aid of the vice deans, the graduate students were encouraged to organize more regularly into clubs, generally by their respective disciplines, and a federation of these clubs was created to which each group sent representatives. A generous proportion of the students' activity fees were assigned to this federation which apportioned it among the clubs, primarily to aid them in organizing symposia, bringing in outside speakers, and providing social functions designed to give them some sense of school identification and opportunity for extracurricular intellectual and social participation. Among the alumni, after a number of years of effort, a greater interest was developed by promoting seminars during alumni weekend functions, at commencement time, and by encouraging annual giving.

An innovation of particular significance was the enlargement of the functioning of the dean of the graduate school by making him a vice provost. At the opening of President Harnwell's administration in 1954 he and Provost Williams worked out with a trustees' committee a new administrative chart. Hitherto there had been one vice provost; now there were to be two, one concerned with undergraduate matters and the other with graduate. I was to be the latter. Under the new plan, the old executive committee of the executive board of the trustees, which had passed on all matters of appointment, promotion, and administration in general, of which I had been a member, was superseded by a president's conference and a provost's conference and I was made a member of each.

The provost's conference considered all matters of faculty appointments and promotions. As the reports from the survey came in, the university administration, the various deans, and department chairman became increasingly concerned with recruiting faculty and reorganizing departments and schools. These Wednesday meetings, seldom omitted, became the scene of operations of a central task force and involved the dean of the graduate school intimately in this planning. I was included in the administrative conferences which met prospective faculty appointees and on numerous occasions cooperated with other deans in plans for reorganization and reconstruction of segments of the faculty.

At the president's Thursday conferences I participated in discussions of the many problems of general university policy and development. Furthermore, I was a member of the university press committee, and occasionally of the research and the budget committees and attended various meetings of the board of trustees and the constituent boards, principally the board of the humanities, and regularly the committee on educational policy of the trustees. Also I met with the board of libraries, the board of physical and biological sciences, and the boards of the schools of social work, education, and fine arts. During the course of the survey and after its completion I served on the committee which reviewed the findings and made recommendations as to their implementation and the priorities involved. The office of the graduate school was definitely involved in planning the new university. The history department had been working on this for some time. My colleagues as I had first known them were forced by age to withdraw from the scene shortly after I was promoted and I had participated actively in replacing them. In the course of the reorganization we invited Conyers Read, Arthur P. Whitaker, Richard H. Shryock, John La Monte, and Lynn M. Case to succeed Cheyney, Ames, Sioussat, Howland, and Lingelbach. Read was a distinguished Tudor historian of Harvard training and Chicago experience, who was executive secretary of the American Historical Association and was eventually to become its president. Whitaker was a Harvard Ph.D. whom we called from Cornell to develop the field of

Latin American history. Shryock was a Pennsylvania Ph.D. who was working in medical history at Duke. La Monte came from Cincinnati, an authority on the Crusades working in the medieval field. Case was one of Lingelbach's students who had been teaching at Rice and at Louisiana State University, working in the field of nineteenth-century French history.

While this reorganization was in process certain of the academic interests of the department were changing. The interest in interdisciplinary training was blossoming, encouraged by the needs developing during the Second World War for area language regional understanding. In the late 1930's under some impulse from scholars in American literature came a proposal for a new concentration, particularly in Ph.D. training, in American studies or American civilization. Professor Arthur H. Quinn had led the battle to introduce the teaching of American literature into the university English department, and he now led the move for this new interdisciplinary concentration. When he retired he was succeeded by Robert E. Spiller of Swarthmore, one of his students. He was even more enterprising in developing the field. So he and Shryock and I, with Sculley Bradley of the English department and several of our colleagues in both departments, developed a program for which Spiller obtained financial support in the form of fellowships, visiting professors, and specially trained members of the staff. The most active of those who joined us was Anthony N. B. Garvan, who came from Yale and developed an anthropocultural frame of reference and gave the course a more characteristic and unique, independent intellectual content than such programs hitherto had had. They had tended to be content with joining literature and history, rather than defining and interpreting culture.

During the Second World War a number of our faculty in Oriental studies, other language departments, and history were scattered all over the globe, and in government offices in Washington gathering much that was required by the war effort. Two of the most active in this field were Ephraim Speiser and W. Norman Brown, authorities in the Near East and in India. Soon after the war ended Brown devised a plan for and secured foundation support for a South Asia program which included language instruction and courses and degrees in history, art, music, economics, and geography. He enlisted the various departments to make appointments in these fields partially supported by South Asia funds. As its part, the history department invited Holden Furber of Harvard and Texas to join it and teach Indian history as part of his contribution. When I became dean of the graduate school these interdisciplinary interests had taken on new significance, for the war had stimulated closer interdisciplinary cooperation and the graduate school became an experiment station for them. They developed significantly and their range broadened to meet increasingly compelling social needs. They included economic history, engineering mechanics, city planning, regional science, biomedical electronic engineering, microbiology, molecular biology, religious thought, history and philosophy of science, operations research, applied mathematics, architecture, demography, and an institute of neurological sciences.

Under purposeful administrative direction following the recommendations of the university survey, departments continued to be systematically rebuilt. There were notable reorganizations in psychology, mathematics, economics, sociology, and English. This work was a constant process and the departments listed but illustrations of a broader program of university strengthening.

My responsibilities as dean as well as my service as Pitt professor at Cambridge brought further foreign contacts and caused us to undertake certain significant obligations abroad. When we had made our first trip to Europe we had planned to return every five years. However, we had not been able to follow this plan, and between our first trip and our tour of duty in England in 1948–9 we had returned but once. But after this experience we returned frequently. By this time the West had become more conscious of the dropping of the Iron and Bamboo curtains, of the Communist world, and of a new Asia and Africa. A new balance of civilization, culture, and power was being struck. So we began a new education.

We attended the International Congresses of the Historical Sciences in Paris, Rome, Stockholm, and Vienna and Unesco's International University Union at Istanbul. In 1960 we had a tour behind the Iron Curtain in Russia and Poland in an all too short fortnight.

The culmination of our traveling came in 1962 with a journey around the world in a few days over two months. Bob and Mary Spiller, Jeannette, and I were sent to India by the State Department on a cultural mission. We were all interested in the American Studies move. We had helped organize a Society of American Studies in Philadelphia, an American Studies Association in the United States and the European-American Studies Association. At the 1957 meeting of the latter in Paris Jeannette and I read papers. Now our cultural officers in India planned to get together some forty who were teaching or who were planning to teach American history or literature at the various Indian universities. We put our heads together and organized a three-weeks conference at a hill resort, Musoorie, and in due course appeared there as Fulbright lecturers. Bob and Mary came via Japan and we by way of Egypt and Bombay. We met on schedule and spent one of the most strenuous and satisfying periods in our lives. We outlined and discussed what we thought were the best methods of analyzing and teaching our culture in South Asia.

Jeannette and I then went on into the East while Bob and Mary returned to the West. We had planned an extensive tour to Delhi, Agra, Benares, Calcutta, Madras, Ceylon, Thailand, Cambodia, Hong Kong, and Japan. We returned to Delhi and on to the incomparable Taj Mahal and then, the heat being too severe, I flew directly to Japan, starting early one morning in Calcutta and arriving at Haneda airport and the cool and pleasant International House at Tokyo in one long day. While Jeannette carried out her schedule I remained in Tokyo. We stopped in Japan to do some lecturing for the State Department at the universities in Tokyo and to meet with Penn and Rutgers alumni. I spent two memorable days at our affiliated university at Kanazawa. We also went to Doshisha University at Kyoto where we spoke at an American Studies Conference under the auspices of the State Department. All this done, we left Tokyo one evening and arrived in Chicago next day, entering the United States via Anchorage, flying over the clearest possible view of our snow peaks ranging out from Mt. McKinley. We had traveled round the world in sixty-nine days.

After I had been in office six years the report of the

Survey of the University was completed and the seventy-fifth anniversary of the founding of the graduate school occurred. The council of the graduate school used this concurrence of events as an opportunity for reviewing its experiences and achievement and gave careful and extended consideration to the recommendations of the survey, particularly encouraged to do so because its findings emphasized the position of the school as the intellectual center of the university. To this end the various reports of the survey were considered by the council of the graduate school and the several committees of instruction. The anniversary celebration included an all-day meeting of the whole faculty organized to discuss the structure and educational policy of the school, and two symposia of two days each, one in the humanities and the social sciences and the other in the biological and physical sciences, were attended by the faculty and a number of invited guests who made significant contributions. Thereat the central theme was the creation of an atmosphere in which the students and their faculty associates would have the freest possible relationship in which to encourage independent study, self-development, and discovery.

The fact that the graduate school had been attached to undergraduate and professional school operations and had drawn its students, in the beginning at least, largely from employed persons who could attend classes only in the late afternoons, evenings, and Saturdays, had meant that many seeking graduate degrees were only part-time students, these were of necessity bound to pursue their degrees by courses rather than by term. Therefore, bookkeeping had been stressed. Too often the principal objective seemed to be the accumulation of forty-eight credits, representing so many hours of sitting in class.

Also there was something of a tendency to spend much time listening to lectures without any participation, save note taking and the writing of an occasional paper based on reading rather than research.

This situation was discussed in various forums and a change initiated. In place of credit hours, a number of courses was prescribed and an effort was made to break the customary two hours per week for each course. As too many graduate students were spending most of their time in short courses, which fragmentized their efforts, the new emphasis was designed to encourage more concentrated effort. Also a new category was introduced, denominated "independent study," which enabled students to work out programs of work with various members of the faculty on something like a tutorial or laboratory project basis, thus supplementing the opportunity for individual participation provided by the seminars.

Opportunities for acceleration were likewise offered and more undergraduates took graduate courses before the award of their baccalaureate degrees which could be counted toward masters and doctors degrees. Something of a breakthrough was recorded when a man got his A.B. and his M.A. on the same day at the end of four years' residence. New arrangements were approved to expedite the work of certain medical students who wished to secure the Ph.D. as well as the M.D.; courses which hitherto had had to be presented and repeated for each degree were now recognized as valid for both without the repetition.

Of equal or greater concern than administrative machinery was educational policy. Here the dean of the graduate school found himself, vis-à-vis his diaconal colleagues, in a unique position. He had no appreciable budget and his extensive faculties were almost all borrowed from the schools wherein their assignments were made and their salaries determined. Educational planning and innovation often therefore depended on whether someone else was willing to pay for change. Much of the graduate school's effectiveness therefore depended on the development of cooperative relationships with other schools. Through a series of pleasant personal relationships I never found this difficult.

But the success of the graduate school depended too much on the accidents of personality, for it had scarcely any power or money of its own. I had always had knowledge of the budgets of the schools in the provost's area and had every opportunity to make my wants and my recommendations known. Luckily I was usually fortunate in the support I received from the president, the provost, and various of my fellow deans.

One of the features of the graduate school had always been the autonomous character of its group committees and it was apparent that there had developed in some of the groups a concept of a departmental rather than a university degree. In a number of the disciplines the degrees were practically self-administered. The various group committees or departments prescribed the programs for the individual students, passed on their qualification, examined them, and decided on the validity of the theses, often without any reference to any but themselves. Therefore I deemed it fortunate when some years previously the treasurer had advised me that an anonymous benefactor had provided a fund upon which I might draw to pay fees and expenses to external examiners and readers of doctoral theses. When this fund was exhausted it was renewed and I was eventually able to establish a line item for this purpose in my deficit budget from university funds. A good start, I believed, was thus made in the direction of objective appraisal of the work of doctoral candidates by more frequent co-opting of outside specialists; but despite it the sense of local responsibility and autonomy remained still more general than I might wish.

During these years in which the graduate student body had been growing so steadily, its character had been changing. For so many years it was made up essentially of part-time students who came to the campus a few hours a week but whose primary interest was in some occupation, at first generally teaching but more latterly also in fields of industrial research. When I retired, the statistics showed that the students were some sixty-seven per cent full time. The true percentage was, however, really greater than our peculiar statistics recognized, for we defined as full time only those who were taking four or on occasion three courses. Those of our students who were teaching fellows and research assistants, and therefore could not take a full quota of course work because of their duties, were classified as part time. Actually, they might be on the campus constantly, spending a larger proportion of their time there than a number who were registered for a full quota of courses.

Early in my experience I became aware that graduate students were destined by university conditions to live lives on the campus which were unique and in a certain sense unfortunate; they were not as other students, who lived programed lives in a fashion strange to graduate students. In the pre-baccalaureate and in the other professional schools, educational programs definitely structured in time and in required courses were the rule.

The usual undergraduate had a four-year program, the law student three years, and medical students a longer prescription.

But graduate students could and did come and go from day to day almost at will until their scores on the record books were complete. No housing was offered to any but the merest fraction. No social or recreational facilities were available to them except such as were overrun by undergraduates; they had no eating facilities of their own. To some extent they were almost forgotten men and women, coming after hours to buildings and study facilities designed for undergraduates, and in the old university library there had not been much convenient, and hardly any comfortable, space allotted for their use. Something called the Graduate School of Arts and Sciences could be found in a few obscure and inadequate offices in Bennett Hall, established there because that was one of the few buildings on the campus where women could feel other than interlopers. Graduate students had no real place of identity.

Yet changing conditions in university life, as the modern trends asserted themselves, indicated with increasing clarity that there was a new community growing apace on the campus, though without adequate recognition and with too little attention paid to its needs. This was a post-baccalaureate community where graduate students in arts and sciences and in the various professional schools were increasing in numbers and changing what had long been the predominantly undergraduate image of the university. This community had certain essential needs. They needed library and laboratory space where they were not merely tolerated. They needed a center, a school headquarters, where they could study, eat, meet professionally, socialize, and find recreation. Finally, they needed housing of their own, not merely a few rooms allotted in undergraduate dorms subject to the diversions of "rowbottoms"[1] and the like.

These needs the university had now recognized among the great development campaigns which are the feature of its renaissance. More adequate libraries and laboratories have been achieved through the cooperation of the Commonwealth of Pennsylvania and the General State Authority, and through generous gifts and grants. Through the instrumentality of the commonwealth, plans for a graduate center have been developed by faculty, architects, and the university's development directors; ground will soon be broken for construction. Speaking personally, my great regret was that this could not be done before the turning in of my seals. But the project is in line of fulfillment and is about to come into being. It will owe much to a vigorous faculty committee headed by William M. Protheroe. Progress has likewise been made in the direction of housing and the need is definitely recognized. The university council, through the interest of the committee on post-baccalaureate affairs chaired by Robert Maddin, and one of its subcommittees whose leader was Andre Von Gronicka, has identified the post-baccalaur-

[1] In the spring of the year for no particular reason except tradition and animal spirits the students might surge out of their dormitory rooms into the night shouting "Rowbottom." Once in the dim past, student tradition had it, a convivial student was wont to return to the quadrangle after celebrating and became confused as to which of the dormitory houses contained his quarters. To resolve this confusion he yelled for his roommate, Rowbottom, to come and guide him up the proper staircase. "Hey Rowbottom" became the signal for a general rush down the stairs for jollification.

eate community. Henceforth it will have not only a name, but a definition and a place of identity.

And finally a new phase of university responsibility is on the threshold of the graduate school. The field of post-doctoral research and research training is closely allied to its interests and should be united with them in some significant and effective union. In planning the graduate center and post-baccalaureate housing, we had this in view and included in the plans for this community what could be called an institute of advanced study, a place of association of scholars in retreat for concentrated study. The responsibility of the university no longer ceases when scholars leave their twenties, but is becoming more apparent for those sometimes referred to as of riper years. And in such programing the Graduate School or Arts and Sciences has a very intimate interest.

In all this I and many of my colleagues in administration and faculty had certain principal objectives. One was to encourage the faculty of the Graduate School of Arts and Sciences to think corporatively as a school creating educational programs, to experiment in new forms of cooperation and educational synthesis, to evoke creative response from students in an atmosphere of freedom and sophistication. To that end, I sought to work with as many of my colleagues as possible.

Other objectives had been to give the graduate school a sense of a common purpose in the realm of discovery and to enlist cooperation in creating an image which would compare favorably with those of our peers. In all this I was conscious of a maximum of general university cooperation. Presently ranked at least among the first twenty of all the graduate schools in the United States, perhaps among the first fifteen, it will continue to progress in the pursuit of excellence, tolerating nothing less.

However, when I left office there was yet much to be done. The position of the graduate school was still constitutionally ill-defined and insecure. Too much depended upon the accidents of personal relationships. The dean must ask so much and can command so little. If he is among friends, his lot is reasonably pleasant, but a few enemies could make his position intolerable. To turn to things material, in the office we were hampered by lack of room and staff which on occasion prevented the prompt action we would like to take. The dean's budget was inadequate; he still needs funds to promote educational experiment, to secure released time for the development of new ideas, to encourage more intellectual exploration. In this day of new methods and new tools, of new library controls and the expansion of computer techniques for calculation, retrieval of information and the like, at a time when there are so many government and private contracts for research, the dean of the graduate school should be more involved in all these operations. And as the new phases of post-doctoral research and continuing education develop, the graduate dean should be cooperating in these aspects of university responsibility. Too much time has been spent to minimal advantage in record keeping, too little allowed for more direct planning for a future which should give every promise of possessing a significance for intellectual adventuring of which we have not yet dreamed.

The half-century mark of my association with graduate education in one form or another found me in a mood to advise. I had served as president of the Association of Graduate Schools, as chairman of the Council of Graduate Schools, and I was retiring as dean, so when addressing other graduate schools and my final faculty meetings I expressed some views, more general, of graduate education which had been long developing.

The Ph.D. often took candidates too long and they went forth after securing it tired and loath to pursue research any further. They had finished the subject assigned and their motivation for discovery was exhausted. I felt that the program adopted so widely but without much thought, beginning nearly a century before, should be restudied in the light of very different needs of today.

I suggested two ideas that might be given particular consideration. The first was that the degree program might be set up like the law program in three or four years and that during this definite term of years the students receive instruction in teaching and research with thesis topics designed to be finished and accepted as journal articles within the definite period. The thesis could therefore be the beginning rather than the end of discovery.

The second idea was a program of two doctorates. For those who were primarily interested in teaching, a program of instruction of three years in which there would be some research training, as in the above, but the second Ph.D. would be primarily in research and would be without course or other requirements subject to general administration. Students of research potential, if accepted, would then register with one sponsor and pursue a program set up by him or a supervisory committee. When his finished product was ready, he would be examined by a group who had read his work and, if they approved it, he would be given the degree on the basis of the excellence of his research rather than his work in courses or on his mastery of a field of learning as demonstrated by a general examination. The degree has suffered by being so widely used as a union card, as a guarantee of teaching employment.

The student should go from the university with a life's work ahead of him, not behind him, with the thrill of discovery and exciting adventuring as his motivation for future intellectual leadership. The graduate school should be a place where experiments are made in new methods, and the laboratory a place where efforts are made to assemble new divisions of learning and research, capable of coping with the increasing complexities of our knowledge. It should be the center of the intellectual life of the university, a place where the intellectually adventurous make new ideas contagious and constantly send waves of new explorers out to the frontiers of knowledge. Such had been the objectives of my efforts.

XIII

BREAKING DOWN LIMITATIONS

DURING MIDSUMMER 1964 the nominating committee of the American Historical Association reported me as their choice for vice-president. This action meant that at the Christmas meeting in 1965 I was elected president and therefore scheduled for a major address before the association at the next annual gathering. During these years I was concluding this book, in a sense reliving my life, reviewing what I had thought and why. Also, as I was retiring from the university at the statutory age, I had further impulse to take an appraising look.

As my labors in the historical vineyard over the years had cumulated, my conception of my professional responsibility had assumed forms increasingly more complex. I had at first viewed history as an established corpus of knowledge, ready for me to learn. Then it appeared as an incomplete mass of information which was to be enlarged by research and communicated by art. Later it assumed the form of a significant dimension of the science of society which was being formulated and interpreted by means of scientific analogies fashioned in terms of human dynamics. Through all this experience I had an increasingly sharp realization that history should be an intellectual instrument, a sophisticated method of identifying, accounting for, and interpreting the meaning of human behavior. History should contribute intellectual strength not only to those who discovered and mastered it, but to those who merely became aware of its substance.

My study of history likewise taught me the supreme importance of thinking in chronological depth. It has provided me with an instrument of behavioral analysis. Throughout the growth of my capacity to use this tool I have become conscious of situations governing my employment of it. My thinking has been conditioned most significantly by two circumstances, by being on my feet in front of a group or by sitting down with a pencil and paper. Thinking develops spontaneously in such surroundings and has not very frequently been contrived without them. In these circumstances "things come to me." Just thinking while walking or resting does not seem to produce much, and saying to myself "Think" can be inhibiting. Until recently I have not been too successful in dictating, but that device is now becoming more useful for thinking beyond the scope of letters.

There has really never been any more thought-encouraging medium than the pencil-and-paper combination. Under this influence I must confess I pile up pages, so many of which seem scattered, confused, inchoate. And then at some unpredictable point I discover that there is meaning and continuity lurking within the mass which I certainly never saw before. But lo! it is there seemingly induced by some unstructured unconscious; then it is time for a penciled fair copy and the secretary.

I admit this seems very wasteful and I often ask myself: Would it have been better to have thought before I wrote and done as they tried to teach me in my school days, to outline first? But this I never could manage; the outlines were always constructed after the essay had been written. Had I managed differently I certainly would have saved much paper and many drafts. Would the finished product have been any better? Who can answer that question?

In the course of outlining this process I leaned, likewise, as already has been suggested, that though one very often thinks and acts without conscious plan, the sequence of effort despite this fact can produce seemingly without direction a logical procession of thinking. It sometimes appeared uncanny—the result of some determinant either built in or imposed from without. So in conclusion I am undertaking a summation with the purpose of explaining, as well as I can discover it, the evolving structure of my thinking.

Although the theoretical nature of history had been of some concern to me as early as the thirties, I took more definite interest in it about the end of the Second World War. My experience as a member of the Social Science Research Council, particularly my association with certain scholars from other disciplines, had emphasized the fact that among them historians sometimes could be considered merely as chroniclers and compilers who found little need for, and could make less use of, any refined intellectual instruments. The war, however, had had an unsettling effect upon scholarship in the social sciences and the historians had been particularly reminded of the *Kriegschuldfrage* controversy current after the first world conflict had subsided. We on the council had endeavored to prepare for the war history by seeking to secure an adequate record and to commit scholars to the required analysis.

As the war came to its reputed end, I discerned signs of a reorientation of thinking which was making it possible for historians to raise new sights and develop modes of thinking of greater intellectual significance. They were becoming active in seeking a more sophisticated dialectic and a technique of analysis. But there were and continued to be habits or customs which in many instances set limitations on the historian's intellectual capacity. These limitations are more or less self-imposed by his definition of his functions and may hinder him from realizing his full intellectual potential.

Prominent among these limitations is the historian's natural preoccupation with nationalism. He takes on the coloration of the society in which he lives, and as the nineteenth and twentieth centuries were epochs of intense nationalism, these influences led him to patriotic concern for communicating the "truth" about his own people, sometimes for the purpose of confounding their rivals. This led him to indulge in an inversion. Instead of dealing with the basic processes of community behavior such as are discoverable by the study and analysis of the activities of people in their local communities, he came to employ national generalizations often based on insufficient knowledge of process.

A second of the historian's most serious limitations is his unrealistic attitude toward time, the chief determinant of his conceptualization. Particularly those historians who write textbooks for our schools and colleges have emphasized relatively short time spans or epochs, the boundaries of which are often conveniently chosen cataclysms, such as wars and so-called "revolutions," which hide the fact that it takes a long time for things to happen, that evolution is a very slow process, and that the beginning of any significant development is usually far back in the past not shaped by sharp distinctions before which these things were not.

A third outstanding limitation has been an increasing pattern of specialization. As the historian has become more conscious of a purpose larger than chronicling, he has been more desirous of developing a more exacting methodology to insure factual accuracy. This arose in part from the fact that in theology at the same universities in which the historians flourished there was much ingenuity displayed in "higher criticism" of the Scriptures, and scholars were subjecting historical data to intensive analysis to insure correct translation and use of documents often obscure and remote. The authenticity of the text became a watchword. This took so much time and preoccupation that vast areas of human behavior could not be treated in this fashion. So, areas of concentration were defined, initially—perhaps often—nationalistically, but within these, functionally. Historians were thought of not only as American historians but also as American political, economic, social, and other, historians. This specialization limited decidedly the historian's capacity to synthesize, for as he knew more and more about less and less he found it more difficult to keep his bearings in the larger field of the evolution of human behavior and his general understanding shrank.

Further, a subtle and very significant limitation determining historical thinking proved to be teleological. Historians searching out the meaning of things and the purpose of things had given the craft of writing history great stimulus at a time when the philosophical climate was rational and secular. To these writers history therefore had to be secular and rational, avoiding religious implications as sectarian and "unscientific." However, their determinism was not strong enough to eradicate the long-standing predilection for the normative, namely, history with a purpose, the improvement of morals, the reward of the "good" and the condemnation of the "evil"; or to translate, history should encourage that which is socially desirable and discourage that which is judged to be to society's detriment. These predilections asserted themselves in the late nineteenth and early twentieth centuries and influenced many to discover and explore the idea of progress. They chronicled mankind traveling an upward path leading to ever greater human welfare and happiness.

Finally, a rather subtle limitation was the historian's lack of understanding of his intellectual potential. Satisfied with narrative and specialization based upon accurate fact-finding and graced upon occasion by good writing, he could easily fail to realize that he had an analytical responsibility to explain and interpret, and when he did grasp this responsibility, he was intrigued by the generalizations of natural scientists and sought laws, dynamic theories, genetic determinants, or general concepts of the broadest possible scope. Thus he could and did seek inspiration in what could be described as *Geisteswissenschaft.* He was intrigued by analogies which seldom had anything directly to do with human behavior.

The problems confronted by historians attempting to transcend their limitations led into a search for certain altered concepts.

To overcome nationalism, we must correct for inversion. This involves study of the basic behavior patterns of communities. There are found the conditions determining so much of what man does. The interest here to be cultivated is a study and analysis of local history so as to secure adequate knowledge of the units which actually determine the aggregate. Where this basic principle has not been recognized, governments have failed to supply the leadership and the means necessary to solve insistent problems.

In the matter of the limiting concepts related to time, it is particularly desirable for the historian to attempt studies of longer chronological time range than he is accustomed to explore. Behavior patterns take longer to evolve than our current periodization of history would seem to recognize. Our use of the terms "ancient," "medieval," "modern European," and "American" history makes it a common practice to chop off segments of the evolutionary process by date or ocean and fail to think or search at any points in time and place beyond these boundaries. But process knows no time nor place, nationalism nor functional specialization; these are man-made devices which often have outgrown their usefulness and which have frequently hindered historical understanding.

Our present periodicity and the current forms of specialization should be superseded by forms of evolutionary analysis based upon much longer time spans and involving comparative study of behavioral patterns in much wider areas of social development. We need a more realistic concept of behavior in time.

Historians as they associate with other social scientists concerned with creating a science of society make a unique contribution to such a science. For any science, physical or social, is much concerned with direction of force and seeks to plot lines of past and present motion so that it may project them into the future and thus gain some knowledge of possible expectancy. Most of the natural sciences devise controlled experiments so that they can predict with some statistical accuracy what could happen under given circumstances. In joining with those looking for methods useful in studying the behavior of the human race, history stresses secular trends. Historians, however, should be cautious about the implications they draw from their use of time. They, like so many, are perhaps too much influenced by biological analogies, probably because they themselves are human organisms. As individuals begin and end and pass through a usually apparent rise and fall, it is man's second nature to personalize all this and to think of all social, even cosmic, experience in these subjective terms. But he has also developed the conception of eternity, of endless time, of what amounts to spontaneous generation, a sudden explosive creation and a continuous evolution. It is conceivable therefore that rise and fall, time itself, are relatively meaningless concepts and that the concept of eternity makes the beginning and the end of time without the bounds of any social experience and to be of practically no significance. If human existence has been going on so long that a concept of beginning cannot be reproduced even in the human imagination, it is meaningless as any guide for human thought, particularly in the form of historical interpretation. Consequently, the historian can in a sense make less use of such concepts of beginning and end, or of rise and fall, growth and decline; rather, he should have the consciousness of the probability of continuous existence, in a world which in some respects is now as it has been and ever shall be, time without end.

While achieving these concepts, I was struggling to find a behavioral generalization that would also be useful in overcoming the limitations of specialization. This I believed could be done by employing a more sophisticated, a more refined methodology to be used in achieving such generalization. During the years of my collegiate and graduate school training in history I had not been overburdened with instruction in method but I had learned thoroughness in search, care in compiling, and the critical use of data. I had been becoming increasingly conscious of the need of interpretative insight and synthesis. As a member of the Social Science Research Council's third committee on historiography. I brought my ideas together while participating in the discussions of generalization which this committee chose as its task. These ideas arose from my study of the politics of the middle period in American history and from my immediate association with the commemoration of the centennial of the Civil War period.

This conception of generalization was one of a more or less orderly succession of stages of evolution which could be likened to a genealogical order of generations. The first generation of the historians of any phenomenon or epoch is made up of those on the scene who for some reason are called upon to interpret or record what is happening. They are joined by participants who describe and interpret, sometimes justify, what they have done.

This first stage of generalization is followed by a second. A new generation comes forward after the record, in a sense, has been prepared by contemporaries and participants. This generation, brought up in the atmosphere of the event, has been affected by it but has taken little if any part in it. They approach the task with greater detachment even though the views of each of them must in general be largely dominated by his cultural situation. These men and women must make a selection from the mass of source material mobilized for them by those who labored in the primary phase. The sources of the second generation are the accounts prepared and the documents preserved by the first generation. The historians in this stage produce a full and comprehensive narrative dominated by generalization which they hope will be "definitive."

A third stage of generalization starts when such an extensive and inclusive narrative has been scientifically established. At this point, approximately half a century after the event, more sophisticated scholars begin to explore different paths of interpretation. They sometimes find new meanings. They may also revive earlier generalizations and give them fresh prominence, or set forth broader and more abstract concepts. Some sacred cows are slaughtered and what is known as "debunking" may appear. This third stage is a period of revision. The process becomes cumulative; it is never static, and it never ends.

The fact that the process of generalization never ceases and that the sequence of historical methods passes through identifiable stages invites the formulation of quasi-laws. One law is suggested by the tendency of generalization to expand and declares that this expansion appears to increase in direct proportion to the distance in time of the historical work from the event itself. This rate of expansion, often influenced by the persistence of past pronouncements and characterized by probability of recurrence at intervals of various older formulations, suggests a second rule of thought. The farther the student is distant in point of time from the phenomena in question, the more essential it is for him to study the genealogy of the discoverable generalizations.

The reason for insisting on rigorous "genealogical" thinking, on thorough research in the history of a given generalization, is that one of the few means which the historian has of judging the probable degree of validity of a generalization is to examine its age and the degree to which it has stood the scrutiny of succeeding generations. But this is no infallible criterion. The age of an idea may well provide a measure of its truth, but long life may indicate only respectability, i.e., that the generalization is acceptable to a particular culture. Such respectability does not necessarily insure truth, but it may supply a presumption to be tested.

The capacity of the historian to make effective generalizations depends in large part upon his skill in exploiting the genealogy of earlier generalizations. One of the hazards I have found blocking the historian's progress is the temptation to omit consideration of what his predecessors have done. We teach, and rightly so, that the investigator should start with the sources and only from them proceed to generalize, if he generalizes at all. Frequently, however, others have worked with the same sources and have likewise generalized, though in another context of time and environment. If the latest generalizer does not give attention to previous formulations and their reception, he may well miss implications which occurred to others nearer in time to the events in question but which he, because of his chronological distance, might not perceive. He ought to make a special effort to consider and judge these implications as well as his direct insights stimulated by study of the sources; thus he can decide whether and which previous generalizations should be part of his foundation or be disregarded as bare excrescences. The process of writing history merely by consulting the primary and original sources and omitting study of previous secondary treatments is like building a high-rise structure without enclosing or furnishing the middle stories.

Particularly to overcome the limitation imposed upon history by fragmentation of knowledge through specialization, I undertook to devise a further generalization, one that would aid me in achieving synthesis. I reverted to the civilization, the culture concept, which had been with me since I taught contemporary civilization at Columbia and which had been impressed upon me by the work of Toynbee and Charles and Mary Beard. This had developed as my work on the Social Science Research Council had brought me in closer touch with the culture concept used by social anthropologists.

The term "culture" used in this sense is all-inclusive, embracing as it does all the behavior patterns employed by any given society. It also supplies the concept of a unity greater than even the sum of its definable parts. Into such a synthesis can be fitted any specialized, any personal, or any nationl experience. Each of us can relate his interest to any such concept of image, national character, or *Gestalt* that appeals to the individual's sense of the all-embracing. Viewing any specific problems in the light of such overall interpretation supplies whatever each of us may do with a maximum of significance and interpretive meaning.

There are various types of cultural definitions, but one in particular can be especially useful: namely, I believe, the design most indicative of the nature and identity of any society. This is its plan of operation, the force or influence that organizes it and keeps within it a semblance of recognizable structure and order. In highly complicated societies this plan takes the form of government, the customs of rule, of the exercise of authority, of the structure of power. A culture therefore may be known as a democracy, an empire, a totalitarian state. Any such designation is not merely derived from constitutional institutions, but it embraces attitudes, ideas of community identification, and social as well as political relationshps. The distingushing characteristic of the society known as the United States of America is the fact that it is a democratic culture dedicated to a self-government in which all are technically involved and in which this interest is demonstrably central to the self-identification of the people. It can be used as the hallmark of the culture.

Finally, an even more difficult limitation to overcome is probably the teleological limitation, the difficuty of discovering the meaning of existence, the concept of purpose. In dealing with this constant there are certain considerations which are helpful. People can very early acquire institutional identifications which very definitely shape their thinking about history just as they do their self-identification. Certainly this was my experience. At the age of five I began to go to school—kindergarten and Sunday school. By the age of eight I was deeply interested in the politics of liberalism. At thirteen I joined the church. Sometime before I was fourteen I had begun to think of teaching history as my means of livelihood. Thus by my teens I had made major commitments to institutions. Even that early I had begun to function with a certain degree of official responsibility in organizational activity connected with school and church, and these were service rather than social associations. Politically I was a child of the Progressive Era and dedicated to reform.

All this combined to spell out a commitment to the objective of social improvement motivated by an altruistic selfishness that fed ambition and produced results, or a selfish altruism that enabled me to accomplish the goals which I set for myself. Whether my main object was to serve or to succeed has not always been clear to me. Perhaps they have been identical.

Controlling, perhaps, has been the fact that my identification with religion has been frequently pervasive, it came by inheritance and it began early. All my forebears appear to have been evangelical Protestants, mainly Baptist and Presbyterian. As a child, attendance at Sunday school and church were as much a part of my experience as going to day school. I was brought up a Baptist with neither creed nor catechism; our own congregation governed itself. My religious beliefs were of my own formulation, and as there was never any ecclesiastical authority to prescribe any statement, I always thought as I pleased. I was conscious of God, but a God who was unidentified except in such terms as creative, omnipresent, and omnipotent. The most significant characteristic of the Supreme Symbol of existence was as an undefined source of power, of wisdom, and of light. My earliest impression of this idea was visual and anthropomorphic, gained from my mother's illustrated Bible and the pictures used to illustrate my Sunday school lessons. But intellectually my theistic concept has long since been most effectively expressed in certain religious poetry set to music which I have always enjoyed singing.

Lord of all being; throned afar
Thy glory flames from sun and star
. . . . .

Lord of all life, below, above,
Whose light is truth, Whose warmth is love
. . . . .

Grant us Thy truth to make us free,
And kindling hearts that burn for Thee,
Till all Thy living altars claim,
One holy light, one heavenly flame.

Lead, kindly Light,
. . . . .
So long Thy power has blest me, sure it still
Will lead me on
O'er moor and fen, o'er crag and torrent, till
the night is gone;

Immortal Love, forever full
Forever flowing free
Forever shared, forever whole
A never ebbing sea . . .

God has therefore been the Logos, the Light, the Creative Force, all that part of existence which I cannot understand, and as I cannot claim to understand everything. I can therefore only accept the existence of God.

I have believed in being honest and in treating my fellow men with consideration. I have recognized a historic Jesus in whose name an institution was organized that has maintained a continuous existence for nearly two thousand years in all parts of the earth, with generations of followers more numerous than statistics have registered. I have always used prayer as a combination of petition and a form of affirmation of my beliefs and my faith in my ability to act effectively in patterns which I consider both desirable and valid. My experience over seventy years has taught me that behaving within these guidelines I seem to know what to do on most occasions and that I can achieve most of my objectives. Whether this determinism comes from without or is built in is probably an exercise in semantics. It emanates from the Light or is the Logos which the dynamics of the universe supplies and it is a determinism discovered by experience which gives meaning to existence, purpose to the individual, and power which will enable him to realize and mobilize his potential. Most significant, he can discover that this potential is greater than he may have ordinarily thought and thus he may on occasion astonish himself at his achievement.

Experience may shape a sure faith. Those who have had the experience know whereof they speak, those of less comprehensive years can discover that such faith exists and can the more quickly acquire it, the more assiduously they seek it. The efficacy of ethical conduct for many is demonstrable; it does not depend upon any belief in folklore; it is something that can be developed experimentally. And whatever is gained need not be lost, for intelligence is cumulative and adjustable. As the body changes, the intelligence can make the needed adjustments.

This personal experience has of necessity colored my historical interpretations. The progressivism and pragmatism of the years of my formal education shaped my mind and have been projected into the behavioral patterns of the relativism of my later experience. This analysis is as near as I can come to identifying myself. And this frame of reference, I am sure, has been the chief determinant in most of my acts and thoughts. The need of a timid child to gain social approbation created an optimistic normative member of the American education establishment of the mid-twentieth century. The pattern is still in operation despite the seeming confusion of the atomic age. But there have been other ages of confusion and man still labors on toward the goals he sets for himself in the light of his own inheritance and his own experience.

The historian can do well to understand that he must record, recover, and explain something not easy to find. As science and philosophy may be losing the historian's confidence, Aron reminds us, history can become "the principle of the movement which spans and carries along all man's works" and which can aid man "to penetrate that mysterious power, God, or the demiurge of those who have lost all faith in science and reason."[1] Free to make a commitment to search for knowledge and find truth in a world of unlimited and eternal change, the historian is free to triumph over nihilism by seeking objective knowledge and by engaging in thought. He must travel a path, not necessarily an upward one, but more probably a generally horizontal road with only occasional hills and hollows which by the law of averages level it so that it neither dips into depths nor scales heights. Cataclysm because of its startling crash tactics probably has made too great an appeal for attention. Man's behavior patterns are the product of long evolution and these crashes probably neither stimulate nor deter very markedly. Mankind has a way of behaving continuously with an inertia which compels

[1] Raymond Aron: *Introduction to the Philosophy of History,* trans. George I. Irwin (Boston, 1961), pp. 297–8.

an even pace that is not much altered by sudden incident.

The historian should concentrate on endless experience with variations that mark out a road which, by and large, proceeds along an average level so that at any given point humanity is neither higher up nor lower down in the scale of experience but within a calculable distance from the mean level that, over the millennia, man has maintained. If this concept eliminates consistent and uninterrupted progress and perfection, it also precludes complete degradation, disintegration, and destruction.

By adopting this concept historians are freed to proceed with the possibility of endless time in which to observe, record, and interpret the continuous stream of human experience. They can provide an intellectual balance wheel for a nervous, fearful, and erratic society in the form of a concept that good and evil, hope and fear, discovery and destruction will probably continue to strike an average of existence in a world of constant change, canceling out extremes such as perfection or destruction. For the philosopher this may be damn foolishness, but for the historian it makes sense, providing him with a secure position in eternity. Also it is a positon which is not likely to be proved wrong in the consciousness or the comprehension of any given historian.

XIV

THE DISCOVERY OF THE INTELLECTUAL POTENTIAL—THE GREAT OBJECTIVE

As I have pondered the limitations of the historian and the means at his disposal for freeing himself from them, my attention has constantly reverted to the basic, all-pervading limitation, namely, the historian's failure to define or even to realize his intellectual potential. The overcoming of this limitation should be his greatest achievement, an achievement which will enable him to grasp his creative opportunities and open the paths of discovery available to him as a man of thought and interpretation.

The possible realization that progress is not inevitable or predetermined, and that time may be endless, could conceivably require historians in the latter half of the twentieth century to come to a redefinition of function and thereby to remove this last of the limitations under discussion. The labor and thought of all those thinking in time, particularly of the cultural analysts, are essential to society. This is in large part due to the fact that the experience of these scholars is unique because they live on two planes of existence. They most certainly dwell in the present, and by definition they must also live in a world of the imagination which is past time reconstructed. They are confronted with the opportunity for constant comparison. They continually have to deal with two sets of phenomena, each of which gives meaning to the other. The harmonization of these two sets affords historians a unique experience which can equip them with unusual insight.

They can see better than anyone else how old the horizontal road is which mankind is traveling, how ancient and firmly established behavior patterns are, and therefore how unlikely they are to be obliterated. Also, because the road is a level one, not only without great heights but also without overwhelming depths, the lack of upward climbing may not be so desolating.

It is conceivable to think of men and women avoiding destruction and continuing to exist because advance and retrogression factor each other out and leave this very average continuity as the principle of existence. Under these circumstances the historian does well to have as a purpose the factoring out of his emotions, his hopes and fears, as he continues his search, his analysis, and his growth in understanding. Thus he can communicate his findings in the light of his wisdom, in a manner which shall show their depth and their inclusive character and convey the contagion of the confidence of understanding. He alone can do this.

He therefore has a special role to play which requires that he live under a discipline; he must develop a historical yoga or detachment from the present which will enable him to exclude, to a degree at least, the confusion of current experience, to rise above it and to relive the past in its *own terms.* To accomplish this he must develop a metaphysics that transcends most of his own immediate experience and adjusts his emotions so that he can correct his understanding by disregarding extraneous circumstances of the moment which only hinder his comprehension of the past. Living by discipline on a plane of existence in which past and present are blended, freed from domination by the unique or the immediate, the concept of the continuity of process can raise him above contemporary terrors or ecstatic hopes and reduce the variety of happenings to a line of direction which is horizontal.

These possibilities display to the historian the value of cultivating a new asceticism, based upon expectancy of an infinity of continuity. Such an asceticism will provide the historian with a new liberty and a new confidence in the validity of his labors. This intellectual and emotional readjustment, to a realization of the richness of experience, enables him to revise his methods of intellectual activity and the training which he imparts. Likewise he can acquire greater insight and understanding, view human behavior with a broader perspective, make more valid generalizations, and more convincingly report to society the findings which will guide thought and action in a fashion that may be described by the adjective "wiser."

The success of the scholar in the long run depends upon the richness of his experience, and no one with a rich experience can be pessimistic. If he leads a full intellectual life, this experience will be rich because it will be filled with understanding. If he is skilled in communication, the life of society will likewise be enriched. The German historian Dilthey believed that the historian, according to the measure of his own spiritual life, and in proportion to the intrinsic richness of that life, could infuse life into the dead materials with which he is confronted; he could far surpass the ancient role of the bard, the narrator of great deeds.

In the realm of the mind, historians are peers. We have a discipline and a series of unique functions of our own. These instruments of analysis, these forms of thought are our own, and we owe them to none but ourselves. Other scholars have neither devised them nor used them with any common degree of frequency. Too much attention during the novitiate has been placed upon critical apparatus for testing the validity of data, too little upon techniques for recasting the thought in terms of past situations. Many historians never get beyond producing a series of doctoral dissertations, each more careful and perhaps more specialized in a narrow field than the last. To a certain extent this is highly commendable, for the historian who can put a good narrative in literary form based upon a comprehensive survey of the sources and an accurate recording of facts has indeed done much.

But we can and should do more, and it is unfortunate that we do not. Simple, specialized narratives of limited national experience, though they produce much of interest, do not give the historian free play for the wide use of his mind or the development of his intellectual potential. The historian often stops too soon. His life can be, and I believe should be, one of growing capacity to discover, understand, and communicate satisfying analyses of human behavior, and not, as too often happens, an abdication of his most meaningful function. The historian should furthermore use his wisdom and his imagination to advance hypotheses, to project himself beyond his tested data and conclusions based thereon, and to establish advanced positions in the world of research, even at the risk of having to admit on occasion that he may be wrong.

These possibilities invite historians to be most vitally concerned with thought, man's unique intellectual instrument. They above all others think in terms of time. Few other scholars have this skill. Mankind in general has it hardly at all. Collingwood has defined history as the rethinking of men's thoughts, the thoughts of those who have gone before. In continually reconstructing situations in which man was called upon to act, the historian must think through with him the problem, thus reaching a better understanding of the actions in question and a greater ability to recount them. The historian must be able to relive, with understanding, human experience in varying epochs. He must do this with a realization that he is living at a different point of time, with contemporary compulsions dominating most of his behavior. He must strive, and this is his great task, to correct for those compulsions, so as to reconstruct the conceptual framework of the period he is studying, to know the conditions dominating thought and action in that time, and then to think in such terms rather than in those which his normal present-mindedness would dictate.

In achieving knowledge of what men were thinking as well as doing, the historian must have some inkling of why. Now to understand why, there must be more accurate understanding of what. In understanding the what and the why of the past it is essential to know circumstances, often subtle, which condition thought at any given epoch.

The historian must learn the reciprocal relationship

between environment and thinking. Therefore he must know some environment thoroughly and learn to observe how it affects and has affected thinking and how it has been affected by thinking. However, locality can be overemphasized—it can lead to overemphasis on nationality which has so long colored historical work that it has become accepted as essential, which it is not—and may even become a hindrance. The basis of historical study should be people, civilizations not nations, people in their various forms of association, people and their various types of behavior. Places are significant, in that people do not live in vacuums, in midair so to speak, but in some definite place; X marks the spot. Since environment has much influence on behavior, there is a reciprocity, for behavior influences environment. Some may go to a desert, draw back or pass hurriedly through it—others may stay and make it blossom. There is no fixed formula that desert plus man automatically either repels or attracts—the result is dependent upon other variables.

But to continue with the historian's intellectual responsibility. In using and developing his particular techniques of thought the historian should join the philosopher in demonstrating the validity of knowledge; he may do more than just train historians, by supplying the world of scholarship with methods that are of general utility. For his historical methods may be used universally regardless of the epoch or the people. The historian's tools can be employed to solve problems whether they arose in ancient Athens or in modern America. The chief instrument of the historian is the concept of behavior analysis by series over a long time range. Any event *x* or behavior pattern *y* or problem *z* is only the momentary pause in a series of situations which for the moment has culminated in *x, y,* or *z.* What history does, in a way that no other discipline can do, is to project the series far enough back in time so that by proper perspective into the antecedents one can gain a reasonable understanding of why *x, y,* or *z* emerged from time into this momentary present. Without such an understanding the present cannot have any valid meaning, and because the present has so little valid meaning we are in much of the trouble that now haunts the world.

By these methods of reorientation the historian may indeed produce a significant redirection of thought. Redirections of thought may not be as spectacular as the manufacture of atomic bombs but in the long run they may be more significant in the millennia of human existence.

First, as pointed out above, it is well to pay less heed to concepts of rising and falling, progress and decay. In history one can agree with Collingwood that every so-called decline is also a rise. "It is only the historian's personal failures of knowledge and sympathy . . . that prevent him from seeing the double character at once creative and destructive, of any historical process whatever."[1] Secondly, this reorientation can provide release from the slavery of present-mindedness and thus promote the possibility of that philosophical and ethical stabilization which we so much need today. The influence of present-mindedness is pernicious, subtle, all-pervasive. We undoubtedly live in the present, and all history has to be written in the present—there is no blinking these facts. Yet the present can be so pervasive

[1] R. G. Collingwood: *The Idea of History* (Oxford, England, 1946), p. 164.

that unless this pervasiveness is evaded it can destroy the validity of historical knowledge.

Thirdly, by rethinking and thus reliving the problems of local community development and presenting these problems effectively and forcefully, the historian develops another great potentiality. His work will enable society to recall and reinforce concepts of moral values, of strength, freedom, cooperation in danger. It will give that sense of the value of these concepts which is necessary if we are to have the will to preserve them, if we are to afford chaos a less recurrent opportunity to displace order in the state. Or again, it may prevent us from being swept along the lines of least resistance toward the destruction of individualism, by the too great exaltation of the state in the name of social security and justice for the many. A complex society has created a complex government. Must it be too complex for responsible democracy to understand or operate? A complex society undoubtedly produces problems which it takes power in the state to manage. But abuse of power is always a temptation, a temptation to which the most high-minded may succumb. Only the strongest sense of the value of individual strength, rather than autocratic power and mass weakness, will prevent the accumulation and then the abuse of power.

In sum, the intellectual energy released by the historian's study can contribute to the preservation of man's liberty. By his explorations in the past the historian should know as accurately as possible what has created any given situation and this knowledge should acquaint him with the possibilities and limits of current action. Therefore he can estimate within what limits man remains free to act. For man will find his freedom the greater the more clearly he understands its limits.

With this knowledge of limits he can define liberty. A new capacity for historical understanding and interpretation should help to restore man's freedom, permit him better to cope with catastrophe and to command that reasonable optimism so essential for continued achievement. If the historian abandons inversion and recognizes both his intellectual independence and his great responsibilities, he may reach a much higher level of intellectual dignity and social usefulness.

The consideration of most significance in my analysis of the nature and meaning of history was my conclusion that history is a form of thinking which stands by itself, one which must construct its own frame of reference and produce its own instruments. It is not art, science or literature; it is *sui generis,* philosophically independent, a unique form of intellectual activity. Historians to make the best use of their skills must construct a conceptualization of the significance of cultural evolution in their own terms as independent, creative thinkers who associate with other scholars but on a basis of reciprocal intellectual give and take. Since the historian has a unique contribution because he thinks in time and explains the slow processes of the evolution of cultures, he alone can protect society from present-mindedness.

The historian should subscribe to a declaration of intellectual independence. It is time for him to be more positive about his functions, his objectives, and his methods. It is time to stop living by other people's wits, by frantically seeking to adopt other people's jargon, by humbly seeking to be recognized as faithful and reasonably satisfactory handmaids worthy of Thursday afternoons and alternate Sundays on which to do what they really wish. Historians must become independent and self-confident again, and thereby assume a new importance in the intellectual world as scholars with unique functions of their own.

If our democratic culture is in the throes of a revolution, yet unnamed, it is so surely because of many influences which have a long history, a history of which we are still painfully ignorant. The dispelling of this ignorance is the historian's responsibility and certainly no one can conceive of a greater challenge. This challenge should inspire us. Society here and now needs something and the historian alone can provide a major element in it.

If American society is in the midst of such a convulsion, it is creating a new image which too many either ignore or fail to understand. We who were the product of a rational revolution may now be living in an age of visceral revolution, in which emotion rather than reason prevails, or we may be in the midst of supranational transformation. Nations are giving way to mass conglomerations of cultural patterns, different ideologies and power aggregates. Within American democracy fears are so obvious. The fear of the radical left stimulates a strengthening of the conservative right which has grown to such proportions that it has produced a militarism incompatible with traditional concepts of free institutions. If one person believes he sees signs of a Communist conspiracy, yet another becomes aware of fascistic utterance. One feeds the other.

This new responsibility involves a comprehensive synthesis of past behavior illuminating the present and the future. This synthesis will concentrate on a cultural conceptualization, to make possible the recording of the evolution of the image of American society, or of any civilization in question, and it is the joint responsibility of the historian and the cultural analyst. For this task there is a new intellectual orientation. Relativism takes on a new importance, as synthesis vies with specialization for the historian's attention.

The historian should have a new sense of discipline, a new metaphysics. He must have a new sense of the inevitability of history and the indispensability of the historian. For as Lincoln once said, we cannot escape history—any more than the normal individual can escape his memory. Historians are faced with the mighty challenge of living up to their intellectual responsibility, and if they strive to meet this challenge there can be a new sense of their own intellectual significance.

The inclusive function of the historian is to shoulder a dual responsibility, to understand and interpret the process of cultural change, and yet meanwhile to communicate effectively, not only with the learned world but with society in general; otherwise he has missed his greatest opportunity. While the historian must consider the past as past, seeking to recapture situations which cannot be observed and to reconstruct them in terms of the times in which they occurred, he must also rework the past in the light of present fashions of thought and action. The meaning of history has to be discovered and restated to every generation in terms of current behavior. Thus the historian must deal with what can never be complete and definitive.

This obligates the historian to sharpen his mind for the discovery of more complex methods of thought, for a full participation in the computer age. While retaining his own identity he must keep a sharp eye out for the inventions in other disciplines. This requires a mind with a much finer edge—a tool capable of far more incisive use than heretofore, if it is to do what is needed for society.

In the twentieth century new scholarly tools have become available, because the increasing sophistication of social scientists has enabled them to supply helpful concepts. The basic disciplines in his realm—anthropology, economics, political science, psychology, and sociology, together with the cognate fields of psychiatry and geography—have always had some degree of influence on historical thinking. Scholars in these areas have become more analytic and perceptive in their study of "behavioral sciences," particularly in cultural anthropology, social psychology, demography, and human ecology. Their knowledge of race, family, group dynamics, roles, and behavior of small groups has contributed new skills to generalizing. Further, their improved understanding of cooperation and competition and of the relation between personality and culture is providing broader concepts for historians who might choose to generalize about cultural conflict.

The perils and exactions of the two world wars of the twentieth century stimulated further insight. A school of psychiatrically oriented political scientists contributed an analysis of democracy which emphasized the influence which the American pattern of frequent elections may have had upon emotions—the reciprocal relation between frequent electoral choice and fear and ambition. The political contests may be viewed in terms of the operation of group dynamics, of role-playing and status-seeking. The acceleration of social-science conceptualization has produced many new generalizations which have come rather from certain social-science attitudes than from any compulsion caused by historians' mere temporal distance from the events. Perceptive historians have been absorbing such attitudes into their calculus.

Such concepts opened a vista of generalization in yet another direction, affecting the historical thinking which has been circumscribed by geographical and particularly national limits. The conditioning of American historical thinking by nationalism or nationalisms has been pervasive and oppressive. But American historians are becoming increasingly conscious of universal phenomena common in the analysis of behavior, untrammeled by nationalism, and which suggests a new realm of thought. As the philosophers found metaphysics essential in their search for meaning, so historians have discovered an area which can be thought of as metanationalistic. For in this mood historians can leap the barriers of nationalistic thinking, transcend cultural limitations,[2] and develop a conceptualization within a framework of universal history.

The historian should hold high among his intellectual priorities an endeavor to think of himself as seeking a species of social genetic code. If the cellular units of men's nervous systems contain the information necessary to direct the behavior of that cell—so that it can reproduce itself and/or join in cooperating with associated cells in producing the behavior of a complex organism which in turn can carry on the process of human evolution—can it not be suspected that the units of society, its communities of association of various types from tribe to nation, may have built-in codes determining behavior? And, if so, is it not the historian's responsibility to discover these codes? The great variety of men's behavior patterns have emerged in time. Mankind has been responsible for making, storing or rediscovering, and interpreting the records of ten thousand

[2] Robert Palmer: *The Age of Democratic Revolution* (Princeton, N.J., 1959), *passim.*

years of human behavior. Who has more data regarding human behavior, who is more capable of thinking in time? No one should be better equipped. But we are so slow, so careful, and so content to putter. We are already late. We are afraid of hypothesis, of daring attempts at discovery—so we do not find because we lack both the intellectual enterprise and the courage to seek.

There is no better time than the present to pursue new breakthroughs. The historian, if he will, has much that is new with which to work. There are computers, there are modes of projecting work such as those in use in systems engineering and operations research. There are concepts such as model building and research design. There is a new science of information retrieval. Demography, human ecology, regional science, to say nothing of social anthropology, social psychology, and psychiatry have concepts which if reduced to reasonable language can be helpful. There are an increasing number of buttons to be pushed which will seemingly summon genii from the atmosphere.

The historian may plot points through which a line can be projected beyond the moment which might indicate direction. He may discover a code which reveals the sequence of occurrence. He may be able to isolate units of synthesis and the nature of their relationship. He can ponder the techniques of generalization. He has discovered approximations of laws like Paul Schrecker's Principle of Least Change.[3] He can identify the usual existence of the third force. He should be able, and it is his responsibility, to design history to be an instrument of the intellect, a tool of thought. It is not sufficient to

[3] Paul Schrecker: *Work and History* (Princeton, 1948), pp. 238–50.

speak of truth, accuracy, the critical use of data. The question is, What does the historian do with data? It is not enough to let facts speak for themselves, or to be content with merely a graceful narrative. The historian must devise a method of analysis and synthesis which communicates to society the meaning of its actions and the processes of its change.

Time and space seem no longer to be limiting concepts; man not only stands on the verge of outer space, but on occasions walks in its vastness. A mechanism is replacing the human brain in some forms of computation. We are told that the genetic code has been broken and that the universe has lost its parity and is lopsided. We are reminded that upon occasion when some basic irregularity, operating contrary to the accepted laws of the universe, has been discovered, such observations can be the prelude to significant new knowledge. A drift in the perihelion of the orbit of the planet Mercury was eventually accounted for when the general theory of relativity was formulated, not until recently challenged. With all these aberrations and incongruities may we not be on the eve of certain discoveries in human knowledge? The time has come for the appearance of the metahistorian who goes out beyond the chronicles, even beyond the monographs of "scientific" historians, and in thought categories of his own creation analyzes the character and significance of the human adventure.

And now for a final word. The essence of what the study of history and of living a life devoted to its cultivation has taught me, as nearly as I can identify it, may be summed up as follows:

I have discovered that we are not living wholly in the present. Most of what we are conscious of is not only very old but will continue to have influence in the future. The moment in itself is never very important and never independent of its antecedents and its successors.

We are behaving because of intricate patterns which we are seldom able to understand fully but must always seek to comprehend as correctly as we can at the expense of great labor, hopefully on occasion guided by flashes of insight. We act as often blindly and instinctively as by reasoned acts based on judgment.

We are part of a society composed of numerous fellow men and women, who range all the way from members of the family to the neighbors and our colleagues, to chance acquaintances, those dwelling wherever we may travel and sojourn, the citizens of these United States, and mankind. A few of these we can know, fewer of them intimately, most of them never. A few we can influence, others we must be influenced by; perhaps there is a discoverable balance of influence. If it can be discovered it is well to know it, to come to some conclusion as to whether one is more likely to influence than to be influenced.

We can discover a great deal of knowledge and put it to our own use and to the use of others. Of much, however, we must be generally uncertain, about more we must remain completely ignorant, and without any comprehension of that which we do not know. About much we must be mistaken. But how can we recognize and correct for mistaken "knowledge"? How can we appraise the validity of what we know? If we are confident of our own accuracy, how justified are we in this confidence?

Those who have read the foregoing pages may have come to some conclusion. I think I have too. As a long-time student of what is going on and what has preceded it, to what extent do I understand the processes of human behavior, particularly of group behavior? To what extent should I commit myself to group activity, or should I seek to remain independent, and to believe myself capable of independence? Or shall I consider myself merely the creature of environment following genetic orders, swayed by my social group, living in time under circumstances which are never stable? I am obviously puzzled.

But nevertheless my answer is: I have been led to believe in a degree of independence, in a sort of built-in-inevitability about my behavior. I started out with an objective, namely, to be a historian, and as can be seen, I have never veered away from it. What produced this insistent determination to follow this course indicates the operation of a determinism made up of my physical inheritance, and of a series of fortuitous influences derived from physical surroundings and personal relationships. This determinism was so strong that I really never even thought of going in any other direction. I am accustomed to think of it in religious terms which have become more complex and mystical as I have grown older. But it is a concept learned in simple terms as a child which has grown more sophisticated as the years of experience have accumulated.

Thus the basic force in history I believe to be an undiscoverable sum total of individual determinisms which vary all the way from complete disorganization to highly concentrated personal mobilization of the resources of personality. Mankind under genetic direction and ecological influence has created his destiny whatever it may be and it is the product of his humanity, his concept of the universe in which he dwells, and his relation to it. His capacity to comprehend this complexity is the light that leads him. Certain deep yearnings may lead him to have faith that it is a "kindly light"; this has been my interpretation; but anyone's faith that this is so is often tried, and is by no means universal; it must be a matter of faith. The historian, with his constant preoccupation with life in time, should be better equipped to draw conclusions about this than the bulk of present-bound mankind.

In all this I have attempted to make complexity as comprehensible as I could, not by simplifying it but by developing techniques of analysis designed to make for better understanding. I have adopted by and large the behavioral approach relating where possible the individual to the mass. I have used the "culture" as the basic concept for analysis and have believed the American democratic culture to be dominated by an interest in self-government. The shaping of this political image is the logically correct and the identifying theme of the history I have written. Had I another life to live I would endeavor to master the history of another culture to use as a control.

Finally, there is very little "instant" happening. Contemporary behavior is generally but the result of a lengthy cumulation of experience. If you erase the "r" from any "revolution" you find that it is nine tenths "evolution." History never repeats itself, but patterns of behavior tend to be cyclical. History, like electricity, appears to be made up of positive and negative charges which maintain a simulation of equilibrium. The basic process is change in the form of continuous motion which fluctuates; falls are compensated for by rises. This makes for movement rather than progress. If there is little progress, by the same sign there is little regression, rather a mean average movement along what eventually proves to be, by the laws of averages, a reasonably level road. As long as man remains intelligent, I can see no ground to expect annihilation. He always has the means of his own safety at the command of his own nervous organization. I see no ground for pessimism unless man takes leave of his senses. Survival may not always be easy but it should never be impossible, unless mankind loses the will to command it. The historian, from his survey of the past, should know this better than anyone else and it is his duty to proclaim it.

A List of Works by Roy F. Nichols

BOOKS AND CONTRIBUTIONS TO BOOKS

THE DEMOCRATIC MACHINE, 1850–1854. *New York: Columbia University Press, 1923.*

SYLLABUS FOR THE HISTORY OF THE UNITED STATES. With John A. Krout. *New York: Columbia University Press, 1923.*

AN OUTLINE OF THE MIDDLE PERIOD OF AMERICAN HISTORY. With John A. Krout. *New York: Columbia University Press, 1926.*

SYLLABUS FOR THE HISTORY OF CIVILIZATION. With Witt Bowden. *New York: F.S. Crofts, 1928.*

"Jeremiah S. Black," in Samuel Bemis, ed.: AMERICAN SECRETARIES OF STATE AND THEIR DIPLOMACY, VI, 387–409. *New York: Knopf, 1928.*

SYLLABUS FOR THE SOCIAL AND ECONOMIC HISTORY OF THE UNITED STATES. With Julian P. Boyd. *Philadelphia: University of Pennsylvania Press, 1928.*

FRANKLIN PIERCE. *Philadelphia: University of Pennsylvania Press, 1931; 2d edn., 1958.*

"Latin American Guano Diplomacy," in A. Curtis Wilgus, ed.: MODERN HISPANIC AMERICA. *Washington, D.C.: George Washington University Press, 1933.*

MEMORIAL; HERMAN VANDENBURG AMES. Ed. with E. P. Cheyney. *Philadelphia: University of Pennsylvania Press, 1936.*

"A Political Historian Looks at Social History," in William E. Lingelbach, ed.: APPROACHES TO AMERICAN SOCIAL HISTORY. *New York: Appleton-Century, 1937*, pp. 14–34.

AMERICA YESTERDAY AND TODAY. With C. A. Beard and W. C. Bagley. *New York: Macmillan, 1938.*

OS ESTADOS UNIDOS DE ONTEM & DE HOJE. With C. A. Beard and W. C. Bagley. *São Paulo, Brazil: Companhia Editora Nacional, 1941, 1944.*

GROWTH OF AMERICAN DEMOCRACY. With Jeannette P. Nichols. *New York: Appleton-Century, 1939.*

REPUBLIC OF THE UNITED STATES. With Jeannette P. Nichols. *New York: Appleton-Century, 1942.*

A List of Works by Roy F. Nichols

"The Role of History," chapter in EDUCATION FOR CITIZENSHIP RESPONSIBILITIES. With Arthur C. Bining. *Princeton, N.J.: Princeton University Press, 1942.*

"Federalism vs. Democracy," chapter in FEDERALISM AS A DEMOCRATIC PROCESS. *New Brunswick, N.J.: Rutgers University Press, 1942.*

SHORT HISTORY OF AMERICAN DEMOCRACY. With Jeannette P. Nichols. *New York: Appleton-Century, 1943.*

DISRUPTION OF AMERICAN DEMOCRACY. *New York: Macmillan, 1948.* Available in two paperback editions.

HISTORICAL STUDY OF ANGLO-AMERICAN DEMOCRACY. *Cambridge: Cambridge University Press, 1949.*

Introduction to John Taylor: AN INQUIRY INTO THE PRINCIPLES AND POLICY OF THE GOVERNMENT OF THE UNITED STATES, reprint ed. W. Stark *(London: Routledge & Kegan Paul, Ltd., 1950; also New Haven, Conn.: Yale University Press, 1950),* pp. 7–29.

"James Buchanan: Lessons in Leadership in Trying Times," in BULWARK OF LIBERTY, Boyd Lee Spahr Lectures, Dickinson College. *New York, 1950.*

"History and the Science of Society: The Problem of Synthesis," in THE SOCIAL SCIENCES AT MID-CENTURY, ESSAYS IN HONOR OF GUY STANTON FORD *(Minneapolis: University of Minnesota Press, 1952),* pp. 84–94.

ADVANCE AGENTS OF AMERICAN DESTINY. *Philadelphia: University of Pennsylvania Press, 1956.*

Introduction to New Edition, Roy F. Nichols, ed.: BATTLES AND LEADERS OF THE CIVIL WAR. *New York, 1956.*

RELIGION AND AMERICAN DEMOCRACY. *Baton Rouge, La.: Louisiana State University Press, 1959.*

"Abraham Lincoln: Master Politician," in Ralph G. Newman and David C. Mearns, eds.: LINCOLN FOR THE AGES. *New York: Doubleday; 1960.*

"Mass Education in America," in Frederick C. Gruber, ed.: EDUCATION AND THE STATE. *Philadelphia: University of Pennsylvania Press, 1960.*

Introduction to Charles E. Boewe and Roy F. Nichols, eds.: BOTH HUMAN AND HUMANE. *Philadelphia: University of Pennsylvania Press, 1960.*

STAKES OF POWER. *New York: Hill and Wang, 1961.* Also available in paperback.

BLUEPRINTS FOR LEVIATHAN: AMERICAN STYLE. *New York: Atheneum, 1963.* Paperback edn. entitled AMERICAN LEVIATHAN.

"The Genealogy of Historical Generalizations," in Louis Gottschalk, ed.: GENERALIZATION IN THE WRITING OF HISTORY. *Chicago: University of Chicago Press, 1963.*

"Why the Democratic Party Divided," in George Harrison Knoles, ed.: THE CRISIS OF THE UNION, 1860–1861. *Baton Rouge, La.: Louisiana State University Press, 1965.*

"Lincoln's Second Annual Message to Congress, December 1, 1862," in Daniel J. Boorstin, ed.: AN AMERICAN PRIMER. *Chicago: University of Chicago Press, 1966.* Available in paperback.

INVENTION OF THE AMERICAN POLITICAL PARTIES. *New York: Macmillan, 1967.*

ARTICLES AND ADDRESSES

"Some Problems of the First Republican Presidential Campaign," AMERICAN HISTORICAL REVIEW, XXVIII, 492–6 *(April 1923).*

"United States versus Jefferson Davis, 1865–1869," AMERICAN HISTORICAL REVIEW, XXXI, 266–84 *(January 1926).*

"Biography: The 'Case' Method in History," HISTORICAL OUTLOOK, XVII, 270–2 *(October 1926).*

"Biography and the Teaching of History," PROCEEDINGS OF THE ASSOCIATION OF HISTORY TEACHERS OF THE MIDDLE STATES AND MARYLAND, XXV, 85–92 *(1927).*

"The Progress of the American Negro in Slavery," THE ANNALS OF THE AMERICAN ACADEMY OF POLITICAL AND SOCIAL SCIENCE, CXXXX, 116–22 *(November 1928).*

"Historical Research in Colleges," HISTORICAL OUTLOOK, XX, 280–2 *(October 1929).*

"Trade Relations and the Establishment of the United States Consulates in Spanish America, 1779–1809," HISPANIC AMERICAN HISTORICAL REVIEW, Vol. XII, No. 3, pp. 289–313 *(1933).*

"Navassa: A Forgotten Acquisition," AMERICAN HISTORICAL REVIEW, XXXVIII, 505–10 *(April 1933).*

A List of Works by Roy F. Nichols

"A Great Party Which Might Have Been Born in Philadelphia," PENNSYLVANIA MAGAZINE OF HISTORY AND BIOGRAPHY, LVII, 359–74 *(October 1933).*

"History Teaching in This Intellectual Crisis," HISTORICAL OUTLOOK, Vol. XXIV, No. 7, pp. 357–63 *(November 1933).* Also in PROCEEDINGS OF THE MIDDLE STATES ASSOCIATION OF HISTORY AND SOCIAL SCIENCE TEACHERS.

"Has the History of the Middle States Been Neglected?" PENNSYLVANIA HISTORY, II, 99–103 *(April 1935).*

"William Shaler, Early American Ambassador of Good Will," PROCEEDINGS SECOND GENERAL ASSEMBLY OF THE PAN AMERICAN INSTITUTE OF GEOGRAPHY AND HISTORY, OCT. 14–19, 1935 (Department of State, Conference Series #28, 1937), pp. 476–85.

"The Dynamic Interpretation of History," NEW ENGLAND QUARTERLY, VIII, 163–77 *(1935).*

"The Revolution and the Constitution," PROCEEDINGS PENNSYLVANIA SOCIETY SONS OF THE REVOLUTION, 1935–1936, pp. 83–7.

"William Shaler, New England Apostle of Rational Liberty," NEW ENGLAND QUARTERLY, Vol. IX, No. 1, pp. 71–96 *(1936).*

"Cuban Commercial Regulations in 1805," HISPANIC AMERICAN HISTORICAL REVIEW, XVI, 213–19 *(May 1936).*

"Dictionary of American Biography," PENNSYLVANIA MAGAZINE OF HISTORY AND BIOGRAPHY, LX, 323–9 *(October 1936).*

"The Wyoming Valley—a Great Laboratory of History," PROCEEDINGS WYOMING COMMEMORATIVE ASSOCIATION *(1937),* pp. 7–15.

"The Mission of the Liberal Arts," FRANKLIN AND MARSHALL PAPERS, Vol. 1, No. 12 *(December 1937).*

"Pennsylvania and the Constitution," PUB. GENEALOGICAL SOCIETY OF PENNSYLVANIA, XIII, 11–24 *(October 1938).*

"The Historian's Dilemma," PROCEEDINGS MIDDLE STATES ASSOCIATION OF HISTORY AND SOCIAL SCIENCE TEACHERS, 1940–41, pp. 1–8.

"Alice in Wonderland," AMERICAN ARCHIVIST, III, 149–58 *(July 1940).*

"Historical Society of Pennsylvania and the Two Commonwealths," PENNSYLVANIA MAGAZINE OF HISTORY AND BIOGRAPHY, LXV, 265–75 *(1941).*

A List of Works by Roy F. Nichols

"Confusions in Historical Thinking," JOURNAL SOCIAL PHILOSOPHY AND JURISPRUDENCE, VII, 334–43 *(1942)*.

"War and Research in Social Science," PROCEEDINGS AMERICAN PHILOSOPHICAL SOCIETY, Vol. LXXXVII *(1944)*.

"History and the Social Science Research Council," AMERICAN HISTORICAL REVIEW, L, 491–9 *(1944–5)*.

"Pennsylvania History's Long Road," PENNSYLVANIAN, III, 45–6 *(1946)*.

"Yesterday and Tomorrow in Ohio," OHIO STATE & ARCHEOLOGICAL QUARTERLY, LV, 201–11 *(1946)*.

"American Democracy and the Civil War," PROCEEDINGS AMERICAN PHILOSOPHICAL SOCIETY, XCI, 143–9 *(1948)*.

GENESIS OF THE MARSHALL PLAN, Montague Burton Lecture, University of Nottingham, Nottingham, England, 1949.

"Unfinished Business," PENNSYLVANIA MAGAZINE OF HISTORY AND BIOGRAPHY, Vol. LXXII *(1947–8)*.

"The Mystery of the Dallas Papers," PENNSYLVANIA MAGAZINE OF HISTORY AND BIOGRAPHY, Vol. LXXIII *(1949)*.

"Post War Reorientation of Historical Thinking," AMERICAN HISTORICAL REVIEW, Vol. LIV *(1948–9)*.

"Early Transatlantic Migration of Politics," CAMBRIDGE JOURNAL, II, 671–83 *(1948–9)*.

"Social Science Research in Britain, ITEMS, Vol. III *(1949)*.

"Diplomacy in Barbary," PENNSYLVANIA MAGAZINE OF HISTORY AND BIOGRAPHY, Vol. LXXIV *(January 1950)*.

"A Failing Century," GENERAL MAGAZINE & HISTORICAL CHRONICLE, Vol. LII, No. 2 *(1950)*.

"Birthpangs of American Democracy," AMERICAN HERITAGE, New Series, Vol. I *(Summer 1950)*.

"1461–1861: American Civil War in Perspective," JOURNAL SOUTHERN HISTORY, Vol. 16, pp. 143–60.

"Operation Reorientation," GENERAL MAGAZINE & HISTORICAL CHRONICLE, Vol. LIII, No. 2 *(1951)*.

"The Missing Diaries of George Mifflin Dallas," PENNSYLVANIA MAGAZINE OF HISTORY AND BIOGRAPHY, Vol. LXXV *(July 1951)*.

"If These Walls Could Speak," QUARTERLY BULLETIN OF THE NATIONAL SOCIETY OF THE SONS OF THE AMERICAN REVOLUTION, Vol. XLVI, No. 1 *(July 1951)*.

"English Origins of American Politics," PENNSYLVANIA MAGAZINE

OF HISTORY AND BIOGRAPHY, Vol. LXXVI, No. 1, pp. 5–29 *(January 1952)*.

"General William Tecumseh Sherman in 1850," PENNSYLVANIA MAGAZINE OF HISTORY AND BIOGRAPHY, Vol. LXXV, No. 4, pp. 424–35 *(October 1951)*.

"Past Presidents and Present Responsibilities," ANNUAL PROCEEDINGS MIDDLE STATES COUNCIL FOR THE SOCIAL STUDIES, Vol. 50, pp. 7–12 *(1953)*.

"The Territories: Seedbeds of Democracy," NEBRASKA HISTORY, Vol. 35, pp. 3–16 *(1954)*.

"The Louisiana Purchase: Challenge and Stimulus to American Democracy," LOUISIANA HISTORICAL QUARTERLY, Vol. 38, No. 2, pp. 1–25 *(1955)*.

POLITICS AS PLAYED WHEN PHILADELPHIA WAS THE NATIONAL CAPITAL, 1790–1800, Annual Address, Meeting Athenaeum of Philadelphia, February 6, 1956.

"Franklin's Message in the Twentieth Century," PROCEEDINGS OF THE AMERICAN PHILOSOPHICAL SOCIETY, Vol. 100, pp. 346–51 *(1956)*.

"It Happens Every Four Years," AMERICAN HERITAGE, Vol. 7, No. 4, pp. 20–33 *(1956)*.

"The Mind You Find May Be Your Own," GENERAL MAGAZINE AND HISTORICAL CHRONICLE, LIX, 35–41 *(Autumn 1956)*.

"The Kansas Nebraska Act: A Century of Historiography," MISSISSIPPI VALLEY HISTORICAL REVIEW, Vol. 43, No. 2, pp. 187–212 *(1956)*. Reproduced 1964, Bobbs-Merrill Reprint Series in History.

"Kansas Historiography: The Technique of Cultural Analysis," AMERICAN QUARTERLY, Vol. 9, pp. 85–91 *(1957)*.

"One Hundred Years Ago," NORTH CAROLINA HISTORICAL REVIEW, Vol. 34, pp. 225–69 *(1957)*.

"A United States Historian's Appraisal of the History of America Project," REVISTA DE HISTORIA DE AMERICA, Vol. 43, pp. 144–58 *(1957)*. Quoted in part in Lewis Hanke: DO THE AMERICAS HAVE A COMMON HISTORY? A CRITIQUE OF THE BOLTON THEORY *(New York: Knopf, 1964)*.

"The Meaning of History in This Democracy," TEXAS QUARTERLY, Vol. 1, No. 3, pp. 1–10 *(1958)*.

"The Ambiguous Position of the Graduate School Dean," THE JOURNAL OF HIGHER EDUCATION, *March 1959*, pp. 123–7.

A List of Works by Roy F. Nichols

"The Stimulus of Confusion," The Graduate School Record of Ohio State University, Vol. 12, No. 2, pp. 3–8 *(Winter 1959).*

"The Present State of Research on the American Frontier Problem," Proceedings of the Second Conference of the European Association for American Studies, Sept. 3–6, 1957, *(pub. 1959),* pp. 62–73.

"The Operation of American Democracy, 1861–1865: Some Questions," The Journal of Southern History, Vol. 25, p. 1 *(February 1959).*

"Alice in Wonderland After Eighteen Years," in The Present World of History. A Conference on Certain Problems in Historical Society Work *(Madison, Wisconsin, 1959),* pp. 26–33.

"The Teacher and the Times," Graduate Journal *(University of Texas),* IV, 434–49 *(Fall 1961).* James Henry Morgan lecture at Dickinson College.

"The Magic Square," Proceedings American Philosophical Society, CV, 237–43 *(June 1961).*

"Skill in History," The Literary Criterion (Mysore, India), Vol. V, No. 5 *(Winter 1962).*

"The Problem of Civil War Historiography," Proceedings American Philosophical Society, CVI, 36–40 *(February 1962).*

"Is the Graduate School in Step With the Times," Missouri Alumnus, Vol. LII, No. 1, pp. 10, 20–1 *(September 1963).*

"Fighting in North Carolina Waters," North Carolina Historical Review, XL, 75–84 *(Winter 1963).*

"Why So Much Pessimism?", in Marshall W. Fishwick, ed.: American Studies in Transition, pp. 314–29 (Philadelphia: University of Pennsylvania Press; 1964).

"Adaptation vs. Invention as Elements in Historical Analysis," Proceedings of the American Philosophical Society, Vol. 108, No. 5 *(October 1964).*

"A Reconsideration of the Ph.D.," Graduate Journal *(University of Texas), (Spring 1966).*

"History in a Self-Governing Culture," American Historical Review, Vol. LXII, No. 2 *(January 1967).* Presidential Address given December 1966.

"A Hundred Years Later: Perspectives on the Civil War," Journal of Southern History, Vol. XXXIII, No. 2 *(May 1967).*

THE PENNSYLVANIA HISTORICAL AND MUSEUM COMMISSION: A HISTORY (Commonwealth of Pennsylvania, Pennsylvania Historical and Museum Commission, Harrisburg, 1967).

"The Slow Evolution of American Politics," COTTON MEMORIAL PAPERS, 3 *(August 31, 1967),* Texas Western Papers. Robert L. Goff Lecture at the University of Texas at El Paso, Feb. 3, 1967.

A Note about the Author

ROY F. NICHOLS was born in Newark, N.J., in 1896 and received his A.B. from Rutgers University in 1918 and his Ph.D. from Columbia University in 1923. He taught at Columbia from 1922 to 1925 and then went to the University of Pennsylvania, where he was a faculty member for more than forty years, serving as professor of history, dean of the graduate school of arts and sciences, and vice provost. He was Pitt Professor of American History and Institutions at Cambridge University in 1948–9, and chairman of the Social Science Research Council from 1949 to 1953, of which he had been a member for twenty-two years. During his tenure as university administrator, he was president of the Association of Graduate Schools of the Association of American Universities, and Chairman of the Council of Graduate Schools of the United States. In 1966 he served as president of the American Historical Association. Mr. Nichols is the author of many distinguished books, including a biography of Franklin Pierce; *The Growth of American Democracy* (1939), written with his wife, Jeannette P. Nichols, herself an eminent historian; *The Disruption of American Democracy* (1948), which won the Pulitzer Prize for History in 1949; *The Stakes of Power* (1961); *Blueprints for Leviathan: American Style* (1963); and *The Invention of the American Political Parties* (1967). Now retired from the University of Pennsylvania, Mr. Nichols lives in Philadelphia with his wife.

A Note on the Type

THE TEXT of this book was set on the Linotype in a face called *Baskerville,* named for JOHN BASKERVILLE (1706-75), of Birmingham, England, who was a writing master with a special renown for cutting inscriptions in stone. About 1750 he began experimenting with punch-cutting and making typographical material, which led, in 1757, to the publication of his first work, a Vigil in royal quarto, with great primer letters, in which the types throughout had been designed by him. This was followed by his famous editions of Milton, the Bible, the Book of Common Prayer, and several Latin classic authors. His types foreshadowed what we know today as the "modern" group of type faces, and these and his printing became greatly admired. After his death Baskerville's widow sold all his punches and matrices to the SOCIÉTÉ PHILOSOPHIQUE, LITTÉRAIRE ET TYPOGRAPHIQUE (totally embodied in the person of Beaumarchais, author of THE MARRIAGE OF FIGARO and THE BARBER OF SEVILLE), which used some of the types to print the seventy-volume edition, at Kehl, of Voltaire's works. After a checkered career on the Continent, where they dropped out of sight for some years, the punches and matrices finally came into the possession of the distinguished Paris type-founders Deberny & Peignot, who, in singularly generous fashion, returned them to the Cambridge University Press in 1953.

Composed, printed, and bound by
The Haddon Craftsmen, Inc., Scranton, Pa.
Typography and binding design by

WARREN CHAPPELL